Framing a Life,

Building a House

Eileen Sypher

Goose River Press
Waldoboro, Maine

Copyright © 2010 Eileen Sypher

All rights reserved. No part of this book may be reproduced or transmitted in any form or by any means, electronic or mechanical, including photocopying or recording, or by information storage and retrieval systems, without the written permission of the author.

ISBN 978-1-59713-094-3

Library of Congress Control Number: 2010923475

First printing 2010

Cover: Graphics by Sandra Cassineri
        Photo of Hennin Post & Beam Frame by Eileen Sypher

Goose River Press
3400 Friendship Road
Waldoboro, Maine 04572
Email: gooseriverpress@roadrunner.com
www.gooseriverpress.com

Credits:

Excerpt from MRS. DALLOWAY by Virginia Woolf, copyright 1925 by Houghton Mifflin Harcourt Publishing Company and renewed 1953 by Leonard Woolf, reprinted by permission of the publisher. Excerpt from A WRITER'S DIARY by Virginia Woolf, copyright 1954 by Leonard Woolf and renewed 1982 by Quentin Bell and Angelica Garnett, reprinted by permission of Houghton Mifflin Harcourt Publishing Company. Excerpt from Emily Dickinson reprinted by permission of the publishers and the Trustees of Amherst College from THE POEMS OF EMILY DICKINSON: VARIORUM EDITION, edited by Ralph W. Franklin, Cambridge, Mass.: The Belknap Press of Harvard University Press, Copyright 1998 by the President and Fellows of Harvard College. Copyright 1951, 1955, 1979, 1983 by the President and Fellows of Harvard College. Excerpt from Maurice Merleau-Ponty reprinted by permission of Northwestern University Press, from THE VISIBLE AND THE INVISIBLE, translated by Alphonso Lingis, English translation copyright 1968. Originally published in French under the title LE VISIBLE ET L'INVISIBLE. Copyright 1964 by Editions Gallimard, Paris. Excerpt from "The Nine Houses of Milarepa" from DRIFT ICE by Jennifer Atkinson, published by Etruscan Press, 2008, copyright 2008 by Jennifer Atkinson, reprinted by permission of Etruscan Press. Excerpt from Louise Gluck's THE WILD IRIS, copyright 1992 by Louise Gluck, reprinted by permission of Harper Collins publishers. "Anecdote of the Jar", copyright 1954 by Wallace Stevens and renewed 1982 by Holly Stevens, from THE COLLECTED POEMS OF WALLACE STEVENS by Wallace Stevens. Used by permission of Alfred A. Knopf, a division of Random House, Inc. Excerpts from THE SACRED AND THE PROFANE, THE NATURE OF RELIGION by Mircea Eliade, copyright 1957 by Rowohlt Taschenbuch Verlag GmbH, English translation copyright 1959 and renewed 1987 by Harcourt, Inc., reprinted by permission of Houghton Mifflin Harcourt publishing Company. Three quotes from pp. 54, 156-7, 227 (189 words) from POETRY, LANGUAGE, THOUGHT by Martin Heidegger, trans. and intro. By Albert Hofstadter, copyright 1971 by Martin Heidegger, reprinted by permission of Harper Collins Publishers. Excerpt from "Choruses from 'The Rock'" part III in COLLECTED POEMS 1909-1962 by T.S. Eliot, copyright 1936 by Harcourt, Inc. and renewed 1964 by T.S. Eliot, reprinted by permission of Houghton Mifflin Harcourt Publishing Company. Excerpt from "On a Tree Fallen Across the Road" and "Mending Wall" from THE POETRY OF ROBERT FORST edited by Edward Connery Lathem. Copyright 1923, 1979 by Henry Holt and company. Copyright 1951 by Robert Frost. Reprinted by permission of Henry Holt and company, LLC. By H.D. (Hilda Doolittle), from TRILOGY, copyright 1945 by Oxford University Press; Copyright renewed 1973 by Norman Holmes Pearson. Reprinted by permission of New Directions Publishing Corp. By Dylan Thomas, from THE POEMS OF DYLAN THOMAS, copyright 1945 by The Trustees for the Copyrights of Dylan Thomas. Reprinted by permission of New Directions Publishing Corp. Reprinted with the permission of Scribner, A Division of Simon & Schuster, Inc., from I AND THOU by Martin Buber, translated by Walter Kaufman. Copyright 1970 by Charles Scribner's Sons. Introduction copyright 1970 by Walter Kaufman. All rights reserved.

For John

The ninth, unstruck ever, is built of a sigh—a pavilion of salt and spider-silk...

--Jennifer Atkinson, "The Nine Houses of Milarepa"[1]

This hut...was built in some remote and primal scene, which we call paradise, whose location cannot be found on any map.[2]

--Joseph Rykwert, *On Adam's House in Paradise*

Contents

I	To Build It Around One	7
II	What is A House?	20
III	I Will Build a House	34
IV	Coming to Tools	63
V	Prime Moves: Writing a House for the Body	92
VI	The House's Place	127
VII	Building the First Time	164
VIII	Leaving	205
IX	Building Again	226
X	A House of More Than My Own	267
Notes		295
Bibliography		301
Acknowledgements		315

I

To Build It Around One

I offer you three "building" scenes. The first, whose words are echoed in this chapter's title, is from Virginia Woolf's 1925 novel, *Mrs. Dalloway.*

> ...*Big Ben strikes. There! Out it boomed. First a warning, musical; then the hour, irrevocable. The leaden circles dissolved in the air. Such fools we are, she thought, crossing Victoria Street. For Heaven only knows why one loves it so, how one sees it so, making it up, building it round one, tumbling it, creating it every moment afresh...* (5)

Clarissa Dalloway, hearing Big Ben's peal mark the minutes as she goes to buy flowers for her, equally ephemeral, party that evening, asks why, why love to do anything? She answers: we just do, do continue again and again to "build it round" us. The "it" is unspecified, the "building" continual.

The second scene is my retelling of a story told to Evans-Wenz and inspiring Jennifer Atkinson's poem. It is about twelfth century Tibet's most important saint after the Buddha, Milarepa.

> Milarepa, wishing to repent for his black magic, goes to the Lama Marpa for help. The lama asks Milarepa to build a house, a round tower, for his son, promising him that when he's finished it, Marpa will instruct him. Milarepa begins the first house. Halfway through the construction, Marpa tells Milarepa to stop, tear it down, and carry the earth and stones back to their places. Milarepa does. Marpa tells him to begin again, but this time the house should be a semi-circular tower. Halfway through Marpa again tells him to tear it down. The third house will be a triangular one. Again, Milarepa is asked in the middle to tear the house down. This goes on for several more houses. Milarepa is anguished, suicidal. He says he'll never learn, never be cleansed, never achieve liberation. He leaves the lama and wanders, only to return later to Marpa who at long last initiates him.

The last scene in this triptych of building scenes comes from a fourth century monastery. It is a story told by the little known monk, John Cassian, about Abba Paul, who wove baskets while he prayed.

> [Paul] could not do any other work to support himself because his dwelling was separated from towns and from habitable land by a seven days' journey through the desert...and transportation cost more than he could get for the work that he did. He used to collect palm fronds and always exact a day's labor from himself just as if this were his means of support. And when his cave was filled with a whole year's work, he would burn up what he had so carefully toiled over each year. (Norris 2008, 1)

All of these are scenes of building, of human making, a party, houses, a full barn, building in the face of time. Though separated by centuries, though the "builders" react differently, these scenes speak the same thing: we create, we build, we accumulate, yet *what* is built, the noun, means little. We may even destroy it. It may, after all, be built but of "salt" and "spider-silk." It may be found on no map. Instead, it is *building* as a verb, *our* building, and not the *thing* that we build that is the cosmic point of it all.

And yet, when the thing one builds around one is a house, we often expect the angle of the story to fall not on the building but on the house itself. This is why Milarepa's story of destroying his houses is so startling. It upsets us. When we are talking about building houses, we expect to celebrate the completed, solid house— not the completed builder. In some sense, then, a memoir about framing a life by building a house, a story about the builder, which is what this book is, runs against the grain. Why this is so has everything to do with what "house" has become in the public, as well as private, imagination. The house has become bigger and more important than the builder. Marker of social identity, assumed solid investment, place of refuge and seeming promise of stability in a world that seems increasingly unanchored, the house has become our obsession.

I well know this pull of the house and the ways in which it can pull a life off keel. For years of my life I was increasingly obsessed with having a house, four walls around me on what I deemed a big enough piece of land. In my teenage years, I would travel up and down the river in a small boat, looking longingly at the houses on the shore. One of my boyfriends was a carpenter, and we'd make plans, house plans, together. My obsession flourished when I was in my thirties, an impoverished academic, my husband a graduate student, and nary a house in sight for us in the crowded and expensive Washington, D.C. area. We rented an apartment for several years. I could not recognize my self there. Our furniture, our books, even our relationship, did not suffice. I felt cramped and claustrophobic. I became painfully sound sensitive. Strangers were much too close. I began to wait to hear the faint noise of my adjacent neighbors. A rental house provided some relief, but it was not enough. I believed I needed to own a house, our own house, and that time was running out. I believed I would have to speak to this obsession, answer its call, before I could get my life back on keel. I would, it turns out, have to build that house to get myself back to center, to frame my life. I would have to build a house to begin to get to the "me" that I was building it around.

Indeed the only way for us to own any house in Washington D.C., and a house on land we could love to boot, was to build it ourselves. The idea was preposterous to many of our friends (and our parents) at the time—both my husband John and I were inexperienced with tools. But my house obsession trumped our lack of experience. All I needed was finding a beautiful five acre meadow in Maryland and then attending a three week course at an owner builder school in Maine and I was off and running. In 1987-8 I built our first house. And, because we chose to move, ten years later, in 1997-8, I built another, this one in the Connecticut woods in back of my birth house. The building was very different each time, as I became different through it. There will be no more houses. "Building" has become for me, at last, a verb, something I do every day. But I needed to build houses in order to know my own power of building a life. This is that story.

I say "I" built the houses, but I had a lot of help, a lot of it. The consequence of building, perhaps the most important and surprising personal consequence, was that I came to feel less and less that *I* in fact was the builder--or even one of the owners. One would think just the opposite would happen when one is building a house. One would think all that time, all that work spent in building, would deepen one's sense of singular possession. But in fact I came to know at every step along the way what I couldn't or did not do myself. And I came to feel that what others did would always be their work, and not mine. Then, when I chose to leave the first house, like a beloved it was, to leave it, sell it, in order to build another in a place I loved even more, in Connecticut, I fully knew dispossession. I would have to learn to take all of this first house I had built into me.

    I hatched the idea for this memoir sometime in the course of building the first house. In all the books I'd read to prepare me for house building, no one ever gave voice to the kinds of thoughts I was having about building, and then about leaving to build another. Perhaps some of this had to do with the two house story being unusual. Perhaps some of this silence had to do with my being a woman, coming into what is still largely a man's world. Perhaps some of this had to do with my being at the time a professor of English, so that I was pulling together all sorts of images from books as I was building. Perhaps some of this had to do with a growing spiritual dimension to my life, at the time eastern meditation, that I felt resonated with the slow strokes of building. Whatever the reason, I felt a book was waiting out there which would speak of all these things. It has now been ten years since I finished the second house. I am no longer a professor, I am now a Christian minister, but I am still a woman with a memory of a journey that I want to tell, a journey about beginning to get the "it" in Woolf's phrase, that the "it" is our lives and not our things.

In so much of my story to come the past looms large, for I was at so many turns aware of how much I was bringing with me as I learned to navigate building a house, some of it helpful, some of it an obstacle, some of it personal, some of it cultural. But underneath it all, I was bringing with me our cultural malaise. I was bringing with me our increasing homelessness as a people. We are nomads without a tribe. I do believe some sense of homelessness is our fundamental condition on earth. But, along with Edward Casey, I agree that we as a people have made ourselves more homeless than we need to be. We live in a time, Casey says, in which *place* does not matter much, does not matter enough. And we need a sense of place. We are a people who have forgotten what the Greeks once knew, forgotten in our preoccupation with time, and that is the power of place, of knowing oneself emplaced (1993, 6-7). Casey calls for us to "appreciate once more the intrinsic ingredience of place in our time-bound and spaced-out lives" (8). "Place," Casey says, "belongs to the very concept of existence" (15). Casey reminds us that the Hebrew word, *Makom,* the name of God, means Place (17). The Hebrew Bible reminds us always of God's being in place, however blind we are to God's presence. Jacob falls asleep in "a certain place" and dreams of a ladder going up to heaven. When he awakes he says "YHWH is in this place, and I, I did not know it!" (Genesis 28: 10, 16; Fox). Christian ascetics knew the power of staying in place for nourishing spiritual insight. *Stabilitas* St. Benedict calls it. I needed place. I needed stability.

One of the titles of Casey's books is *Getting Back Into Place*. The implication of his title is that we need to work to get back. And it is not enough to "find" a place. It doesn't work like that. Rather, Casey says, "we must build places in which to reside" (111), places in which we can *dwell*. Casey stops short of saying we each need to "build" our own dwelling places, as in building a house. There are many ways that we work to dwell in a place, many ways our bodies transform a site into a meaning-filled place, daily habits being among them. As Casey puts it, "The body has everything to do with the transformation of a mere *site* into a dwelling *place*. Indeed, *bodies build places*. Such building is not just a matter of literal fabrication but occurs through inhabiting…"(116; emphasis his). Not everyone needs to build a house in order to dwell in it. I did.

I am hard pressed to find a Biblical story which underlines the importance of building houses. But there is one story highlighting the importance of *craft-in-place*. It is a story from the prophet Jeremiah, one of his most powerful stories. It is a kind of Milarepa story. God says to Jeremiah (18:2): "'Come, go down to the potter's house, and there I will let you hear my words.'" God uses the scene of ordinary domestic craft in a house, the making of a pot, perhaps for the potter's family, perhaps for sale, we do not know, as a teaching site for Jeremiah. God uses the visual image before Jeremiah of the potter spoiling one vessel and then going on to refashion the clay into another as a visual metaphor to show Jeremiah how God is with human beings, God's clay. God, however, says God will *intentionally* "spoil" his creation if they err—and God will build them back up according to God's design.

Is the potter just any old teaching tool God chooses, or does the vehicle of the metaphor, the potter, a craftsman, carry some particular and unique weight in this illustration? I do believe the potter does. I do believe that the vehicles of metaphor matter. God chooses to bring Jeremiah to an ordinary scene of a craftsperson at work, building it around him if you will. Biblically we need not roam far to discover why: God has said that humans, made of clay, have been fashioned in God's image. We are pots, earthen vessels. So when God says that God will refashion our human clay as the potter does, the act of crafting clay is honored. The work of God must go on. And yet so must the work of the potter. There's a mirroring in this scene: as God molds human pots, the potter molds earthen ones. As God crafts, so God calls us to craft. Craft, building pots—and I would add, building houses-- is our eager response, our mirroring response, to the ever creating God.

There's a particular emphasis in *Jeremiah* on the insistent, ineluctable power of "thing-ness," on the material, and on *our* making it with our bodies. "Thing-ness," in our time, is the province of phenomenology. Such philosophers and theologians are working to restore the body in place to a philosophy and a theology too long neglectful of it, as it favored mind and soul. From Descartes' "I think, therefore I am," to Paul's injunctions to the church to "let the same mind be in you that was in Christ Jesus" (Philippians 2:5) (and so, implicitly, less in the "body"), the body has taken a back seat. And, as Casey says, these ideas infect our daily lives. We cease to attend to what our bodies are doing—and we cease to attend to the power of other bodies working beside us.

To use a simple illustration of the power of the living, embodied being, the power I felt on the building site when working next to another: take this passage from E.B. White's 1938 essay, "Removal." White is talking about the potential of the then new medium of television to alter our body's intimacy with another. White says, "Together with the tabs [tabloids], the mags [magazines], and the movies, it [television] will insist that we forget the primary and the near in favor of the secondary and the remote. More hours in every twenty-four will be spent digesting ideas, sounds, images— distant and concocted. In sufficient accumulation, radio sounds and television sights may become more familiar to us than their originals. A door closing, heard over the air; a face contorted, seen in a panel of light—these will emerge as the real and the true; and when we bang the door of our own cell or look into another's face the impression will be of mere artifice. I like to dwell on this quaint time, when the solid world becomes make-believe, McCarthy corporeal and Bergen stuffed, when all is reversed and we shall be like the insane, to whom the antics of the sane seem the crazy twisting of a grig." White ends this prescient analysis of the fate of our senses in our time with a comment on its emotional impact on us. "When I was a child people simply looked about them and were moderately happy; today they peer beyond the seven seas, bury themselves deep in tidings, and by and large what they see and hear makes them unutterably sad." (3)

To look around one at the near, and to be looked at in the near: again, the story from *Jeremiah* brings us the spiritual power of bodily reality. God brings Jeremiah to the potter's place, to *look at him* in order to get the story not only in his mind and in his heart (because there is a real potter) but also *in his body*. There is that evidence of the spoiled pot which the potter has made which speaks as no image alone of it can. And there is the image of the potter, seemingly uncomplaining at his failure—he just carries on until he makes a good pot. God knows this. And God understands Jeremiah will hear God here, in the midst of this place of craft, of another's bodily making, as Jeremiah could not otherwise hear. *Jeremiah*'s story calls us to the schoolroom of the senses, of human making together, as the root place of spiritual hearing.

Or, to take another example, this one from my own experience, this one of bodily contact with the other gone awry. Recently I spent part of a year as a chaplain intern working in an inpatient psychiatric unit at a hospital. I daily talked with people who had tried to kill or mutilate themselves through cutting or eating disorders or through refusing to take medications which they often saw as poisonous. At one point I heard a talk by the head of the psychiatric admissions unit. She said that lack of self-esteem is our most pressing national psychological disease. I began to connect the dots: these who abuse themselves, having usually been abused, and who sometimes have abused others too, have not before themselves the safe presence of another, a real other, because their sensory experience has been abusive rather than connective. In pain, they have tried to retreat to an absolute darkness, void of any body. Often in the locked unit, in the company of others like themselves, these patients came face to face with an other in whom they could begin to trust because they recognize that the other has suffered similarly. Face to face: Susan Stewart in her book *Poetry and the Fate of the Senses* says that our senses are absolutely fundamental in our encounter with and recognition of others (3).

For Emmanuel Levinas, such face-to-face meeting, as White speaks of, as the patients lack, is the crucial place in which our otherwise appropriating, self-aggrandizing consciousness of the other is transformed. The other, experienced face to face, empties my own consciousness, sets in motion a self emptying, a kenosis, in me and so *increases my responsibility* to that other. What is phenomenologically fundamental to this building memoir is that as an owner-builder, *I* built in the *face-to-face* with *others*. Though they are now locked out by habit and key, they are still now in this house years later. A little like Yeats in his poem "The Tower," I witness in my dreams and my daydreaming a procession of them. Their faces I see, now in memory, calling me again and again to a sense of responsibility for them—changing what this house is to me. I did not begin to build a house for this reason, for the reason of the other. But in the building, side by side, face to face, "house" changed. My pot-making abilities, and theirs, became my focus—not the pot itself.

In the story that follows, the story of my building two houses, I claim that building a house oneself, or at least as much of it as one can, with one's mind and one's hands, can root one in the ground and restore one's body, and mind, to some health. I cannot claim this is Edenic health. At every turn in this story, as I built, I confronted my own trespass upon the land, my utter dependence upon others' skill and materials that few in the world could afford (and the ones who labored left), and, perhaps more seriously, the ever seductive pride of craft and pride of ownership. Perhaps if I had chosen to build a bird house I'd be in less danger. But by choosing to build a house there is no way my practice, or my conscience, can ever be pure. I can laugh at the couple who appeared in one of the newspapers years ago, a couple standing in front of their 9' high double entry doors and smiling as they said, "we wanted to make an impression." But when people enter my house and look up at the massive beams and sigh in awe, aren't I taking pleasure in the impression I've made? I'm just not tactless enough to announce this in words.

This book is a building story of living in a fallen world, doing the best one can as a spiritual seeker, in my case a Christian, but the best can never be quite enough. As far as I know, no one has yet claimed that house-building can be a spiritually important, however flawed, activity. But that is what I am going to try to do here.

Those of us for whom *building* the house comes to be an obsession each have a different reason for this, a different personal history. Mine was rooted in childhood anguish. I will tell this story only here at the beginning, for it is the beginning of all my house longing. Looking back, it seems inevitable now that I would have to build a house. I needed myself to make a new house, a house apart from my childhood house. I needed both the separateness of myself, and also the solidity that I would know by building.

This is my story, my memory. I was a little over five years old. I was in another part of the house that now sits five hundred feet from this one in which I write, my second house. It was a hot summer's day. A car pulled into the driveway. It was my uncle and my mother. I already knew something was wrong. My mother opened the outside door into the kitchen. My grandparents were both there. My grandmother had just made strawberry shortcake. How delicious it looked on the table.

I cannot ever hear my mother's words. But I know now that she told her parents that she had walked into my father's hospital room and found him dead. The sweet peas she had brought with her were still in her hands.

What I remember, instead, is that I immediately insulated myself from that room, that kitchen. I built a kind of bubble around me. I felt sometimes, in my imagination of this moment, that I was peeping around a door, or I was looking at the scene as if I were on the ceiling.

I was, in Casey's words, being "situated," placed, in that kitchen that summer's day in 1952, placed by the strength of our overwhelming grief. The door would always, after that, open with a risk, the strawberry shortcakes always hold a threat. Even as I would learn to bake many strawberry shortcakes later, so I would learn to build sturdy doors, different doors, doors I would hang, doors I could control. I had to build a house. I had to carry my bubble with me. But I had to become the one who was placing myself through my own will, and I needed walls and a thick door and lots of land to do that.

II

What Is A House?

I imagine the title of a book of our time, "My House, My Self." As our houses became more than mere transitory sheltering caves, as we settled in place and cultivated this thing we call individual identity, our houses became more and more extensions, even mirrors, of our separate and distinctive bodies. Casey says the house to us is become a kind of "mega-body" (1993, 119). But whose body? Casey quotes Michelangelo, "'there is no question but that architectural members reflect the members of Man'" (118). Our commonplace, the home is a man's "castle," is but a variant on this. Women living alone, commissioning houses for themselves, never mind building them, is recent in human history. Women have not, until recently, been able to see the structure of the house itself as a mirror of *their* bodies. Women were decorators, but not architects— nor builders. The bones of the house were for much of human history those of the man's body, paid for by him and owned solely by him.

The next chapter explores my steps as a woman, inexperienced in building, in awe of the house's bones, in coming to be able to declare one day in a Maryland meadow the inaugurating words: "I will build a house." But here, I pause to dismantle this idea of the house as the masculine body and his secure self. "House" has not always been what it is now. Understanding this demystified the house and so made room for me, as a woman, to take possession of it.

The single family house, imagined mirror of the male self, is not really that old—only some four hundred years so. Before that there is something startlingly different, something more amenable to women, about people's relationship to houses. Mircea Eliade (1957, 172) identifies two broad historical perspectives on the cosmos—which reveal themselves in two very different perspectives on the house. He suggests we are now on one side of a great divide, which is why we can't understand Milarepa's story. Eliade says that earlier, "religious man" lived in an "open cosmos." This person traveled on the spiritual and always surprising road of pilgrims as a nomad. Caves and tents and what we now would call shoddily made dwellings were our homes. We now, on the other hand, says Eliade, live in a "closed" cosmos. The sign of this is that we feel we need to live in an enclosed, permanent house.

Milarepa, then, is not so odd in his time. In his epoch the house was seen as porous, easily dismantled, to begin with. It was, in conception as well as in fact, regularly broken open. Eliade illustrates: in parts of Europe and Asia, when a person within was dying a prolonged death, family and neighbors would remove one or more of the roof boards. This was so the soul could quit the body more easily, the roof symbolizing the head through which the soul was thought to exit. Landscape architect J. B. Jackson, himself mapping two house epochs similar to Eliade's, compares the early dwellings of the Pueblo Indians (often built by women) with the kinds of houses that began to be built in Europe in the eleventh century. The early Pueblos did not, says Jackson (1994, 36-7), appear to build with any concern about how nature might destroy the building. They did not care. They did not improve the site, attend to strong foundations, or consider any of the other natural strains on a structure. He concludes that they chose to ignore the forces of nature, and instead focused on "celestial, ahistorical" time. They would build and rebuild without complaint, without expectation that the house itself would survive long.

It is in medieval Europe, says Jackson, in the beginnings of our modern house epoch, that the house begins to become a "counter-environment," a place that can (we hope) withstand the assaults of historical time. The closed, private house, the material thing, begins to circumscribe the eternal. And, in a secular culture such as ours, one concerned more with what is here, material, than with what is elsewhere, in the spiritually immaterial, the house is also our most valued possession. It is our monument to ourselves in life, to a self we can't imagine ever quits it. Shelley's king, Ozymandias, may have built himself a statue; we build us a house. And most of us don't imagine future onlookers viewing its decay as he did not. But even if we do, the house seems all the better a grave marker than a plain stone in a cemetery no one visits. People can drive by the aging house years later and say, "oh, so and so once lived there," and we imagine we will be better remembered. And, of course, the house is all the better a grave marker than a stone because it is convertible into cash for our heirs.

Neither Eliade nor Jackson considers the history of gender relations in his account of the way "house" has changed. Though I prize a solid house, there is also something more open to me as a woman about history's earlier house, social as they were, porous, mutable, something less formidable than the later house. Surely this has something to do with the long history of the transformation of the house as shared family and community workplace to house as a sign of the ascendant male property owner's ability to sequester and control his wife and children? Reading Eliade and Jackson I cannot but help put two and two together—and begin to free up the house's "bones," its perimeter, its visibility, its accessibility for myself.

In contemporary America the single family house has become our collective dream and our national nightmare. The house, sign of our individuality, marker of our economic status, promise of our immortality, protection of our increasingly private family life (who now wants a front parlor for guests or a front porch?), has been stretched to the breaking point, mortgaged beyond possibility, football in divorce settlements, and place of inestimable grief when the walls fall down. Nothing so unsettles us in contemporary America as multiplying stories of foreclosure. Nothing so sickens us as people buying others' foreclosed homes. Nothing terrifies us so much as the fear of our own potential homelessness in a society in which few doors would open to let us in.

Knowing something of the malleability of "house" I could begin to imagine myself as a builder of one. Yet it was coming upon a particular image of "house" that smoothed my way. The image of house that first pulled me in those beginning times was one from the woman poet H.D.'s long poem *Trilogy* (1998, 8-9). It is the image of the house as a shell with each of us like a busy mollusk spinning one out of our bodies in order to protect ourselves from the otherwise incursive sea. H.D.'s image of a house is that it is *both* porous and enduring. H.D. calls the mollusk a "master-mason planning/the stone marvel." Though it at moments needs to let in the sea, it wants of this not "too much." She praises the mollusk: "Be firm in your own small, static, limited/Orbit and the shark-jaws/Of outer circumstance/Will spit you forth…"

I loved this image of the endlessly busy, vigilant mollusk. I felt at home with her (couldn't it be a "her," imagined by H.D.?) I loved the idea of her very own body spinning the shell by which she can keep the ocean out, a shell which grows as her own body grows. I did not dwell on what philosopher Gaston Bachelard says is our initial, and terrifying, amazement at such a creature: that it can remain alive inside stone (1958, 107). Rather, I focused on her snugness and her control. She is like any attentive home body fixing the roof, mowing the lawn and trimming the boundary hedges, checking the locks at night, choosing whom to open the door to—and adding on a wing as need be for the growing family. However tiny the house, the plot of land, the psychological resonance of this home shell was symphonic, like a conch shell held near the ear that safely opens the sound of the far-off ocean. Far from cutting us off, this kind of shell, this house, seemed to offer me, a woman, a safe and distant vantage point from which to hear a vast and overwhelming world.

H.D.'s image of the shell contained its own warnings, only some of which I sensed in the early days. For shells do cast spells. I could not dream house apart from history. Marjorie Garber in her tour de force *Sex and Real Estate* catalogs a number of these spells of the historical house: house as beloved, mother, body, dream, trophy, history. And books such as *House as a Mirror of Self* offer several stories of people who are caught up in different house spells—as mirror of the self, as a memory of a childhood space, as a partner space. For it is impossible to build any house without recognizing what walls have come to mean. However we project them, as mother's womb, as palace walls, as safe haven, we do use the wall beyond that of our own physical bodies. We project some need of ourselves onto their screen. In psychological terms, we try to make the walls the constant object. But because the walls are a projection of our own fantasy, a fantasy fed by an entire economy around the house, we are potentially caught in a dangerous, narcissistic trap. The house, after all, never talks back to us. It never shows us where it came from, in us, in the world. And, perhaps worse than these, the house, we feel, is never good enough, and so we are not. The house never does quite satisfy. I did not bank on any of this at the beginning.

One of the particular spells the modern house shell cast on me early on was that I would be grown up only when I had a house of my own. Since World War II in particular, as private housing became more affordable in the United States with the availability of low interest mortgages with low down payments, the dominant script for the young has been to move out of the parental home into homes of their own. It is private walls, rather than a community or an extended family, which now, it is promised, will support the growing self. Never mind that many young people can't afford to leave their parents' homes. Never mind the pain of leaving this childhood home. Nancy Mairs harrowingly puts this last this way in her memoir, *Remembering the Bone House,* "If we want to retain our own recognizable selves [as children], we mustn't move elsewhere. Our feet must retrace their steps through the house, out the door, to school, back, weaving a pattern of undisrupted order: no change, no death. As long as we stay where we are, we're safe" (1990, 54). The Hansel and Gretel story, the leaving behind the scraps of bread to get back, the scraps the birds eat, looms ahead for all young people. It means losing one's way. It means feeling as if one is being kicked out by one's parents. It means a terrifying separateness. Coming to our first house, looking up at walls and roof, down at floors, there is a grief here, in this new separateness—as well as the promise of a new self. Well I remember the day I greeted my mother at the threshold of the first house. I felt as if I were now fully an adult, at 40. But when my mother first stepped over the threshold, as I watched her timidly enter my house, look up at my walls, and over at my kitchen, I wanted to hold her, both for herself and for me. It was another act of cutting the cord between us. I wanted to say, these walls mean nothing, they will not separate us. Nothing has changed. But they do mean, and there is change. But we do it anyway, move out to our own walls. It's our social script, the next step after gaining a room of our own in our birth houses. And I was going to take it at whatever cost.

I was under other historical house spells in my house obsession. The house had to be a certain size, the land of a certain acreage. And only my husband and I should live in it, no boarders, no relations. Though I'd grown up with my grandparents, by the time I built I was under the national spell of the nuclear house. When we moved into our second house and my dying mother-in-law moved in with us, I confess I was distressed, even angry at moments. This was, I felt then, "my house," mine and my husband's alone.

I was lucky enough to be able to act on my house obsession. I was lucky to be able to bypass the obstacles in the way of a woman building and even luckier to be able to navigate around the dangers of my house obsession. I had the ability to learn and the money, albeit scraped together. But even more than these things I was lucky enough to have a partner who would stay with me through all the difficult navigation of building, through the deep water, the storms and the shoals. And I was fortunate enough to be able, with his continuing help, to be able to do it all over again, build another house, another shell for my changing self.

Carl Jung tells a story in his memoirs that is now mentioned in almost every building memoir. It is a story which validates the central role ongoing house building plays in organizing a single life. It is a prototypical twentieth century equation: house and life. It is his narration of his building his house at Bollingen, a house that keeps growing as he does. He adds wing after wing following the changes within him. The new wing often appears in a dream. By the time he builds the last part, the tower, the tower, he feels it as a "place of maturation…It gave me a feeling as if I were being reborn in stone. It is thus a concretization of the individuation process....At Bollingen I am in the midst of my true life, I am most deeply myself" (1989, 225). I did not add on to the first. I went on to build an entirely new house. But the principle is the same: building did help me grow in self knowledge as the houses gave me a mirror. My walls were like a tree's rings, strengthening the trunk. Jung knew this.

Yet Jung experienced earlier than I did the erosion of his fantasy of the possibility of an armored house shell. His account of what happened to him after he inhabited the tower suggests that the walls were never just an echo chamber. They were porous. Not only does *he* grow, but his consciousness of others grows. It is the archetype for my story here. As he builds he first exudes the confidence of a found self: it was, he says, as "as if I am spread out over the landscape and inside things, and am myself living in every tree...." In the silence around him, his thoughts then "reach back into the centuries, and accordingly anticipate a remote future." He picks up a stone the builders would reject and, as he looks into it, words come to him from the stone, announcing that "I am found everywhere. I am one, but opposed to myself. I am youth and old man at one and the same time" (227). But then, high on his self-expression, other voices erupt. He remembers an earlier moment, when he was inside his first tower, in which he heard what seemed to be a concert outside. The next day he asks the herdsman the meaning of this. He says it must be the voices of the departed. Jung explains this as a "synchronistic" phenomenon—his experiencing time long ago with previous inhabitants, because they shared this place. For Jung, living in a place he built *connects him with other psyches*,--and generates his theory of the collective unconscious. Odd it is that building a house for oneself, the single most important material investment most people make, sign of one's social identity, vessel of one's privacy, could also be, at the same time, a route to expanding awareness and sympathy. It is not the saints' road of divestiture; it is far humbler, a less likely road mired in the world of property. But it is a pathway all the same.

I started out thinking it was the *having* of a house shell that I wanted. I did not know that I would have to do some work to inhabit the house, and that "in-habiting" would mean not settling into the shell's impermeability, but rather knowing more and more its porousness, if not to the weather or to the physical presence of others, then to their memory. More gradually did I begin to hear what Jung did: the voices of others, the past, the hauntedness if you will, of my house. I had thought I understood what Pascal meant when he says "I have often said that the sole cause of man's unhappiness is that he does not know how to stay quietly in his room" (37). I emphasized the fact of a room. But I had misplaced staying quiet and focused on the room. I had understood "dwelling" to be noun, and not a verb.

Dwelling as a verb reminds me of the word it shelters, *well*. To dwell is to be well-like. And a well has no seeming boundaries. It does not mirror *me*. I think here of the old-fashioned "dug" wells, the wide ones with lids that one can pry off and peer within, that have no discernible bottom, only some identifiable markings along the side and perhaps a glint of the water beneath. Like this well, so the condition of dwelling cannot be circumscribed, cannot be defined, can only be "peered into"--for glints. I think that I can say, however, what *dwelling* is not. It is *not*, for example, the same thing as *inhabiting* in the traditional way we use that word. Habits can kill dwelling. Bachelard says that "the successive houses in which we have lived have no doubt made our gestures commonplace" (1958, 15). These houses then cease to remind us of the history of our bodies living there. Perhaps this seems restful, but it is also passive, entropic. Can we not live in our houses, with our objects, and keep alive some consciousness of them as both living museums, signs of life before, and as possible places for future meetings? Such a conscious way of dwelling, for it must be conscious, engages all of our nerves and connects us viscerally with others—and nurtures in us a different relationship to things, to the house in particular. Dwelling is a way to take the roof boards off and open the windows and doors. It's a way to live where we are now, in this time of the private house, with all of its spells, and yet live in a once-again open cosmos. If we can learn to dwell, we can make a bridge to that lovelier, freer, spirit-filled place. If we can learn to dwell, we can "create it every moment afresh."

But how to do this? How to keep the nerves alive? The philosopher Heidegger says we must dwell "poetically." Poetically means "to make." To dwell we must open the channels. There are two routes that this book offers: one is building a house and then building again, the other is writing to others (so inviting others' reading words) about it.

Heidegger does not say that building a house is a necessary step toward dwelling. Building can, in fact, for him be a detriment, because it can urge undue attachment to one structure. We might then attend to only what we've cultivated, get lost in the "ours-ness" of it. But on the other hand, building, as an extended form of "residing," one abounding in all the minutiae of the house structure, reminds us that we "are," that we persist in time and a place. Building gets us fully into our bodies—and connects us with other bodies in the house site. If we build in the right way, open, receiving, if we build with the door open to dwelling, building can deepen our dwelling. Buying a house, by itself, doesn't help us—although we are encouraged to think it will. When we turn our dollar over to another, we hardly have a relationship with that other. We may know pride in being able to buy such houses, but we don't necessarily dwell in them. Because I could not purchase a house, because I had to struggle to build one, struggle over a long period of time, I began to learn more about dwelling. By building I was cultivating a deep relation to place. The plow was so slow, the furrows so deep, that I learned how to stay with, to spare, preserve things, my own body, others' bodies—and so also, Heidegger says, the divinity. I felt like Jung at his new house hearing voices, except I was always, too, touching and smelling and seeing and hearing others around me in real time, tools, my body, without which the houses would never be.

But as important to building, and more practical—who of us can continue to build houses?-- we need to speak, especially *write*, of these things. This is where the "poetry" part comes in. "Measure-taking," re-minding us all of our larger horizons, requires poets. "Authentic building occurs so far as there are poets, such poets as take the measure for architecture, the structure of dwelling" (1971, 227). Poetry is memory and language, our voices which remain as long as we do, wherever we live, and even beyond us. Like turtles have, it's our movable shell. And, more: language translates one to another across century and culture, as silent houses do not. Sharing a language connects us as humans. Language breaks open walls. Writing a building story, we restore attention to the process of building, to the way a thing is made, both by ourselves, each of whose life is already a web of relations, and by others. And from then on that "house" will be the "book" on the house. Such a house, remembered through writing, can never be lived in habitually and will always be rebuilt.

To illustrate this: my first house is, I am certain, not showing any wallpaper tears where the paper wraps around a corner in the master bath. I know this, and I know why. One day, one hot, humid summer day, a day in the full 90 degree sun, my husband and I spent nine hours tying "rebar," ¾" diameter, ribbed pieces of steel, into the footing trenches before the concrete we'd ordered for the next morning would cover them forever. This steel, called "rebar," short for "reinforcing bar," would exponentially strengthen the concrete that would soon be poured into the trenches, or "footings," on which the basement wall would eventually sit. The heavy house to sit on these walls would not, then, settle in uneven ways into the soft earth beneath. We were giving the house impenetrable shoes to stand on. The wallpaper will not tear. The people living in the house now do not know why, they do not see our bodies tying the rebar that summer day, and yet they benefit every morning as they enter that bathroom from its apparent solidity (even seeing wallpaper tears, one can become anxious). They need words, such as these, to open the house up, to see the solidity they sense—and to recognize our part in creating this not only for ourselves, while we lived there, but for them and those after them. They need to look under the footings. Because I built that house, because I know every square inch of it, traced it with fingers and knees and leaned against it with shoulders, I think of them now moving within the house in ways I did not, before, similarly imagine others now in the other houses I've passed through. But because I imagine them (and continue to dream about them in that house), I now begin to imagine others I know in their houses when I'm not there—sitting with coffee cups, reading in the waning day, writing by the fireplace remembering their own heartbreaks, crawling between their sheets at night. I am becoming more gently aware of the unspoken, invisible parts of their lives—and loving them more because I share now this intimacy, safely in imagination, with them.[3]

These words, here, are my ever growing shell.

III

I Will Build a House

At a certain season of our life we are accustomed to consider every spot as the possible site of a house.
--Thoreau[4]

A year or so after we'd moved into our second house, we volunteered our house for the church's biannual Tour of Homes. That day a woman, whose name I never learned, stood at the foot of the stairs and looked up at the massive Douglas Fir timbers supporting the house. Many of the others touring the house that day, men and women, focused on one thing or another, the furniture, the birch flooring, the geo-thermal heating and cooling system. But this woman seemed to take in the whole. In a thin and timid voice she asked me a question: "however did you do all this?" She wasn't asking me to tell her how to put in a window or nail down a subfloor so it wouldn't squeak. She wanted something else. She wanted to know *how,* how I as a woman, could come to *imagine* building at all.

I find it hard to answer her. I don't have templates I can use from other books written by people who have decided to build. The full-length stories are all written by men, and men don't worry her fundamental question, how could you dare to do this? It's as if building is still expected of men, whether they are skilled or not, but not yet for women—this despite a growing number of women carpenters and contractors. Though two women framers worked on my second house, women from whom I learned how to use a nail gun, the story of such women has only been told in vignettes, and then by others.[5]

Perhaps one scene alone from the most famous "building memoir" in American literature[6] tells the difference. In *Walden*, Henry David Thoreau begins the story of his house building with the following words: *Near the end of March, 1845, I borrowed an axe and went down to the woods by Walden Pond, nearest to where I intended to build my house, and began to cut down some tall, arrowy white pines, still in their youth, for timber* (36). Hardly any woman reading this sentence would assume it had been written by another woman. First there is the borrowing of the axe. I could, were I Virginia Woolf, make up a story about "Thoreau's sister" to parallel her imagination of Shakespeare's doomed imagined one in *A Room of One's Own*. If I went to a neighbor's house and asked "him" for an axe, since probably the axe would be in "his" tool shed, what would the conversation be like in 1845? Although the women were hardier in these pioneer times, I'm not certain I'd get off without any questions—what are you going to do with this? Can I help you?

You're going to cut large trees? Or even, perhaps, where is your husband? In fact, I'm not certain I'd get off with the axe at all.

So the borrowing of the necessary tool: that might be obstacle enough in itself. But even if I were to get an axe, could I then speak as Thoreau does—in his matter-of-fact tone: "I borrowed an axe and went down to the woods...and began to cut down some...pines...for timber." I'd not be calmly walking down to the lot (I can see his gait now as he swings his axe). I'd be worried if I could cut a tree to begin with—and then not have it fall on me.

What seems utterly odd to me is that Thoreau feels no presumption at all in undertaking building nor any need to account for how he might have learned some skills. These connected questions, *how did you dare dream you could build* and *how did you learn*, do not structure a man's building story.[7]

Thoreau's story, the American Ur building story (Pollan 1987, 97), did invite me as a child to love his woodsy solitude and his rich philosophical reflections. But *Walden* did not invite *me* to imagine I could similarly build my own hut. It's not that I couldn't imagine a woman living alone in a house. I'd known many women who had, some widows, some who had never married. And some of these houses were in remote places. No, it was not this about Thoreau. Rather it was his *claim* to *establish* a house, his sense of a right to stake it out, that seemed stunningly foreign to me. "At a certain season of our life we are accustomed to consider every spot as the possible site of a house." Really, I thought?

Thoreau's presumption does not stop at building his hut. Thoreau implies that his efforts contribute to the human portion of the heavenly built mansion. Thoreau says, "I sometimes dream of a larger and more populous house, standing in a golden age, of enduring materials...which shall still consist of only one room, a vast, rude, substantial, primitive hall, without ceiling or plastering, with bare rafters and purlins supporting a sort of lower heaven over one's head..." (218).

Now this part of Thoreau's ambition thoroughly stuns me. I'd like to say this is because my theology is better than Thoreau's, that we don't participate in the building of the heavenly mansion. But there's more to it than this I suspect. Were I a man, I might more readily imagine myself working on my house in Paradise. Joseph Rykwert claims that the primordial hut dream, which underlies all our shelter dreams, is our dream of Adam's shadowy house in Paradise.[8] Is it because a house isn't claimed for Eve (is she always outside at the tree?), that women still have trouble claiming a potential idyllic space that they have created? A number of years ago I taught Woolf's *A Room of One's Own* to retired adults. I asked the women if any of them had rooms of their own (I didn't even ask them if they had an idyllic room of their own!) Several of them actually became testy with me (since doing so might involve their claiming a waiting room for a child long gone).

Though it takes a lot for women to imagine building their own houses, I've found that in talking with women about building it takes very little to arouse their energy. While I was a student in the Shelter Institute, I heard a story. A woman, a woman like me, inexperienced, timid with tools, had come to the school to try to prepare to become a builder. Someone, maybe one of the instructors, invited her to sit on a bulldozer. Someone showed her how to operate the levers. No one could get her to come down. She stayed there for eight hours. Once when I told this story to a group of women considering whether to join in a Habitat for Humanity Women's Build, a woman approached me to tell me that in hearing this story something leapt inside of her. She would sign on. Remembering this story even got me on a bulldozer. When we were grading the hilly terrain of our second house lot, I asked our excavator (and neighbor), Pete, if I too could climb up onto his bulldozer, if I too could try to operate its levers. Although I'd imagined this woman's feelings for years, I wanted to know them in my body, for myself. Together Pete and I climbed up onto "the big dozer," "Smokey" he calls it. Laughter tumbling out of him that someone else could share with him this daily joy he feels in his "dozers," he sat beside me in the cab, patiently showing me how to work the levers. He then said, "you've got to feel it in your ass," the back and forth movement of the loosening boulders. You've got to feel when to push forward, when to back off. I remember I was afraid as I pushed over my first boulder, afraid and elated. I can still now, years later, remember that moment when I moved the lever that moved the dozer's mouth that pushed aside a rock it would take many people to lift. And I can remember exactly where I buried that boulder. Later I posed for my husband in the seat of the dozer. John likes to tell others I've never smiled like that. After that day, Pete began to refer to me as his "sister."

Such vignettes, however, may not be enough to account for the underground rivers at work in me so that I could one afternoon, in a Maryland meadow, say the, to me, strange words, "I will build a house."

I tell the story of our coming upon that land as if it were like any love story of two people meeting. I say, if we had not gone to my husband's colleague's brunch in an old farmhouse in Maryland on a certain day in February of 1984, for example, it would not have happened at all (how I loved the word "farmhouse" when my husband first uttered it as he walked in the door one winter evening as I sat in the living room of our rented suburban 1930s bungalow). Or, I say, it would not have happened if we'd gone, and not looked about us as we passed on the way in, at the red barn and acres of open fields on the crest of a hill, a look that prompted us to say, together, as if in one breath, "this place reminds me of Connecticut," our shared birthplace. We could have been talking at that moment. We could have been lost in a song. We were, instead, looking out the window and that changed everything. All these moments, I say, if they were otherwise in just one slight way—the whole history could have been different.

Three weeks later we were walking with the real estate agent over a five acre meadow, still not certain of what we were doing there. The field was still sodden with the thaw of early spring, the stubble of last fall's mown grass rough even through our shod feet. One hundred year old oaks and sweet gums ringed the property, except to the south where, some five hundred feet away from the center of this meadow, stood an immaculately kept brown stained house surrounded by orchards not yet in bloom and a large dormant vegetable garden. I heard the real estate agent's words: "garden," "orchard," "river walks" (the Potomac River was over the crest of the hill). And I saw above me a dome of ebulliently clouded sky, the first glimpse I'd had of anything resembling an eastern "big sky" since I'd moved to the Washington D.C. area some five years earlier. This was it. The place "chose" us, I say.

Stories of returning exiles tell us that we are not entirely clay on the wheel of place. When the exile returns home, even though he or she does not at first recognize the place, something happens. Czeslaw Milosz at eighty goes back to his childhood place, his home in Lithuania. The place has been utterly transformed, so that Milosz, at first, does not recognize anything. It was long ago, he says, remembering his grandparents' farm, "an experience of enchantment with earth as a Paradise." Now all has changed, the orchards decimated, the house destroyed, the lawn a forest. Only a random oak or elm has survived. His will to find home fails to help him.

And yet Milosz does find his home place. He begins to walk, and in his walking, seemingly aimlessly, he finds his feet remember the contours of the land. As John O'Donohue puts it, "left to itself, the curvature of the landscape invites presence" (1997, 86). Milosz at last sees. "Suddenly the realization came that during my years of wandering I had searched in vain for such a combination of leaves and flowers that it was here that I have been always yearning to return" (1998).

I was not standing in a meadow I'd ever stood on before in Maryland, not like the forested hill of the second house in Connecticut, my birthright hill. Yet something about it was familiar, or at least the right land. And it was in wandering in this meadow that I, like Milosz, knew I had been yearning for it for a long time.

Milosz's story suggests that more happens in such perambulations than merely setting our bodies into some "right" location. We would be but detached visitors on a tour but for undercurrents, but for our own *place-making* activities at work within us. As Milosz walks over the once familiar landscape of his childhood, he can't discern the early, now invisible landscape of his memory until he has done some daydreaming about that past, a daydreaming provoked by his very walking; both acts, dreaming *and* walking, are necessary to turn the "site" into a "place." The "site," in Casey's observation, is comprised of things, the "place" by reveries, those daydreams that occur between our unconscious and fully conscious thoughts. Milosz has found, yes, but also made a "site" his place.

I was, that early spring day in Maryland, bringing my own yet unwritten guidebooks with me, familiar stories, childhood memories, scattered images and already magical words, "garden," "sky," "farm,"—as well as habits of thought I may have even brought along with me into the world. And I brought along a desire for a house fully my own, born of my body, a desire that had, at this point in my life at least, become nearly an obsession. I was prepared, in short, to lay tracks here. I was the one that day who said, with a bold and untutored confidence that has often misled my husband, "we'll build a house." He assumed and I implied by my voicing this with certainty that I would and could take charge of this project. It would be as simple, I thought, as moving a household, which I'd by then become used to many times over, as solitary as writing a doctoral dissertation, which I'd also done. It was neither—neither simple nor solitary.

Peering into the past before this moment in the meadow, I look for a narrative, for connecting, causative threads. Yet I find myself able to begin in several places. I marvel at books like *Women Builders & Designers* because in searching for origins, Goldfrank sticks with the obvious: how did you, girl, learn to call yourself a carpenter? How did you learn to think that you, knowing nothing, could build a house yourself, or almost by yourself? Yes, I do have to get to these more practical questions. But first I've other, more fundamental questions as well. How could I presume to make room through architecture, plant my feet on uncultivated land and build up to the sky? There is a boldness in this physical gesture that stuns me yet. How could I think "I'll build a house?" And why should this landscape attract me because it reminded me of Connecticut (in the case of the first house) or actually was Connecticut (for the second)? These are glimpses of some of the pieces of the before, the guideposts illuminated by later light on this landscape of the past.

Perhaps to love houses, to love them so much that one will do anything, even take to building them without any knowledge, one has, above all, to have a powerful dream or memory of some paradisal place, some absolute, essential home that must be remade—and remade by one's own body at work. Not everyone perhaps has this dream, this memory, this intensity of the need to remake or to dwell in a particular place—and certainly not the need to create it oneself. I'm not even certain the men in the contemporary building memoirs needed to live in a house as much as I did (they don't talk about this at any rate). And the woman in the hallway? I don't know about her need. But without this *need, for house, for making house,* without some extraordinary prompting, she'd be hard pressed to fuel her otherwise uncertain confidence.

My memory on this point, the point of my house need, is rooted deep in me, the stories I tell about early "house" in my life unassailable, like fortresses. And the peculiarities of these houses, how they came to be, their placement, their character, would influence all that came after. I grew among images and stories of houses built by relatives and houses given as unexpected gifts that changed whole lives. I grew under the spell of "house." I did not hear the words, "real estate," "builders," "mortgages." Houses were very personal. People I know built them or were active in their building. People saved money for them and changed life directions because of them. People stayed in them for years. In my childish imagination, I extended paradise well beyond these simple truths: people neither sweated to build them nor suffered money anxieties over them. These houses were surrounded by abundant gardens, with pear trees so laden that the canning jars filled a wall of the cellar; with potatoes so plentiful that they filled bins, their musty fragrance opening the earth again; with lilac bushes so high over my head in the door yard that their perfume enveloped my small body, linking in me always the scent of "lilac" and that spot of ground on which none now stands. I grew in a narrated version of paradise, of which the house was the centerpiece. Like many before me, I saw in these houses of my childhood dreaming the very "shadow" or "outline" of the first house, the unrecounted, unremembered, lost house of our first parents. And so I tried to get it back.

The house, unlike other things, movable things, carries with it a spell, a spell of being anchored to land. The house promises an end to wandering, an end to exile. This spell of the immovable house took deep root in me because my grandparents were Swedish immigrants. As their second generation heir, I knew that they had experienced a fundamental and wrenching displacement. We never talked about it. But I knew it. As house became their antidote, so it would become mine.

My grandparents moved twice in their lives. I tell a different story about them from that I tell of my own moves, partly because their story is, I think, different, and partly because I need a different story, a story of stillness at a beginning. And I track my beginning with them, with this maternal set of grandparents and with this generation. Having moved some twelve times, I can't afford anything but a still and simple beginning. I often wonder at people who are fascinated with tracing their genealogy, who can grasp the endlessly receding line of ancestry and live content with never being able to place these named people geographically, in some house, some town. I have often suspected that the accomplishment of a fully drawn chart is compensation for the essential anxiety of this enterprise.

My grandparents' first move, from their small farming village in Western Sweden, was, I suspect now, so wrenching to each of them that in all the years they lived with us they could not tell my mother nor me more than four stories combined or offer more than a few scattered images of their early lives. And these stories were recounted with a brevity that, inviting no response, spoke its pain: my grandfather's only description of his father, "he was rough." Or, "I crossed the ice one morning, against my father's wishes, on my way to school. My ankle took the full blow of a hockey puck. Unable to walk, I said nothing for two days." Twenty years of ulcers that eventually led to osteomyelitis, he had to have that leg amputated below the knee. Then I did not ask questions. Did I want us, their lineage, and me, to be their singular desire in coming here? Did I want to shut out that mysterious time before in a shadowy landscape? They were, I know, from the same farming village, living just three miles apart, but had not known each other. I see my grandfather crossing, surreptitiously, over my grandmother's fields. I see each of them finding the same small town in Connecticut—hearing words, "there is work," or "there is a Swedish community there." I've only one story about the desire to cross itself and this is of my grandmother. I see her, a lovely tall girl with long brown hair and a small waist, standing on the pier with her parents. They were having a final negotiation. Her father had promised her money to go to school to become a teacher, but had spent it on other things one too many times. He was now promising again. She shakes her head (too timid to speak). She will go, with her sister, to join a brother who'd already gone over. It was too late to make a change in plans. Some decisions are like that. Now, knowing more of history than I did then, I expect she knew somewhere that it was always to have been that way—in 1900, her father uneducated, the lot of local girls to marry, how could it easily have been otherwise? She never saw them again, the expense of travel and the arduousness of her pregnancies making it difficult.

One day that early life and any hope of a return closed forever for her. My mother often told me this story in the years after my grandmother's death. For my mother too it was a story that marked the essential rupture of the immigrant. My grandfather had received in the mail a black-bordered envelope, the kind custom of those years to prepare the recipient for bad news. The letter announced my grandmother's mother's death, the last of her parents. My grandfather hid the black-bordered letter in the inside pocket of his coat, thinking to spare my grandmother until their third child, nearly at term, was born. But in the invariable press and drama of daily domestic life, my grandmother hung the coat on the clothesline to air. It was early spring, sunny. The yard was filled with the scent of lilacs. As she moved along the clothesline, pinning that coat and other garments of that day, taking out her brush as she walked, she invariably smelled those lilacs. She did that day what she often did, but this time it was to be different. As she pulled back the coat's lapel, to brush and smooth, there, poking out of a pocket, was the warning, the black-fringed letter. She would know, of course, what it meant, know that it was for her. She would not have upbraided my grandfather. Rather she would have looked up at the watery light, across the sodden lawn, and say to herself, weeping with the quiet invisible tears she had practiced, "it has come, at last, my mother." I would always remember this story. Years later when my own mother was in the hospital and I was walking in the garden, I thought to myself, "has it come at last?" It hadn't. Not just then.

This story was a warning to me, the establishment of a boundary I would not cross. Of all my moves, none has been so final, no rupture as complete with my birth family as theirs. I could carry these images with me, the pier, the envelope addressed from some desk at some relative's house in that village, but I needed to keep my grandparents here. I would become that teacher. The envelope would always be at that particular clothesline, the suit freshly aired, the hand that reached for it the next moment consoling my aunt then in her belly.

The more I heard and embellished these few images as I grew, images of leaving and loss, the more dislocated I felt in my beginning. What was there before? Who were they? How could I know who I was when the first twenty years of their beginning remained so far away, such an incomplete portrait? They could not tell the stories that would fill in that gap.

I was not alone. My mother shared this fragile sense of our place in this new world. And so when my grandfather had to be placed in a nursing home, my mother and I traveled back to Sweden. We wanted to walk their roads, to look at their houses, to see their views, to eat and talk with those still "left" (an odd locution, implying always some kind of failure of nerve, some lesser choice on their part). In my mother's halting Swedish which she'd learned as a child, in my willing ears, we tried to piece it all together, their past. But we were not exiles in return. We had never been there before. We couldn't retrace steps. And our stories? They didn't match others', nor could we quite comprehend the ones they told. We found a place that did not look like home. The roads were dusty, the fields vast, the houses settled among a few trees. I saw one man hoeing his garden, and his stoop reminded me of my grandfather's. That is all. Even the story my mother came with, that of my grandmother's young brother drowning in quicksand behind the house we ate a feast in was a surprise, the quicksand gone, the brother never even heard of. We heard that my grandmother's father went back and forth to America seven times before she left for good. He could not decide where to live. He did not take them with. We felt a family of silences. That day she stood at the pier: it was nothing new, really, for her, this being alone on the shore. And I learned that my origin story of the still, solid place across the Atlantic was a persistent fiction, one that I needed, but a fiction nonetheless. From the beginning of my second generation life, I was—and still am--an immigrant's descendent, restless, homing. The yearning for home, suggests Edward Levinas, is proportionate to one's feeling of being a wanderer.[9] Wandering fuels the urge to dwell. Adam and Eve were, in the garden, not conscious of the home of Eden until they had been cast out. Their longing, their descendants' longing, for home comes later, in other words, is the rest of the Bible story. Our "home-world," says Husserl, is connected with the "alien" one at the door (Casey 1993, 229).

Once my grandparents arrived in America, stunned irrevocably by that one unimaginable move and so dreaming of some "home" again (how could the dream of "America" really compensate for lost hills and familiar trees?), they traveled little and changed dwellings only once in their sixty some years here. This is the part of their story I liked. And they liked it too. The family hovered about this first house in America of theirs, in fact or in imagination. They lived for some forty years in a house my grandfather had built for him (with a mortgage my mother knew little of for years). I spent my first year there and though I've no distinct memories of that time, my mother told many stories of her own childhood there and so I always see the house through her. I see her walking the cow to pasture in the 1920s and cringing from her friends' taunts. I see her in the cellar helping my grandfather cap beer. Or she is out in the field collecting dandelions for his wine. At Christmas she bundles up her five cent gifts in the sled they would tow up the road two miles away to an aunt's house. I witness my mother tumbling as an infant out of a high chair too near the combination gas/wood stove. By the time my grandmother ran back to the kitchen from the dining room where she had followed her toddler, my mother had fallen head first onto that stove, severely burning her forehand and mangling her right thumb. Through my mother's tales I see my grandmother standing before her ironing board in that kitchen, all day standing, ironing others' sheets, tablecloths, clothing, so she could help pay for one daughter (not my mother, who would refuse such help) to go to Normal School (a college for teachers) to become the teacher my grandmother never could become. I see the day my grandparents sat at the card table and the mail arrived, with a check from my mother who was then, in the '30s, working with a group that traveled around the country and who made decent money, enough to help her sister through college, enough to buy her baby clothes later and enough for food. My grandmother threw all the cards up in the air that day and announced, "I'm going grocery shopping." I see the boarder my grandfather threw out of the house because he'd been drinking and the foster children they took in, all to help them financially and whom they would help. And I see the Polish Catholic boyfriend of my aunt's that my grandfather, appearing at the foot of the stairs late one evening in his long johns, ordered out of the house because of his religion. And, off on the porch, out of time, for memory knows only place, I see my infant self sleeping in the carriage through all sorts of weather.

These stories wove for me a thick, protective shield around this first house in America, a shield more impermeable because during most of my lifetime my grandparents did not in fact live there. The house was kept for years (my grandmother needed to think she would return), opened only for their fiftieth anniversary celebration. For they moved from this house they'd had built to live with my mother three miles away, to help her with her two young children when my father entered a tuberculosis sanitarium in 1950. When he died two years later, they never left her. Thirteen years later my grandmother would die in what had been my parents' bedroom, after an illness of two years. My grandfather would live for another twelve years with us.

Perhaps the mat of stories was so thick about this first house of theirs because moving in with my mother was their second dislocation. That first house was the Ur-house, the Abrahamic house, the oneiric house for the "new" life in America, the house of their fledgling family, sign of their settledness, tenaciously recreated for us because there could be no going back to Sweden, to their real first houses. And, too, once they'd moved to America and begun to lay new tracks, how could one learn to lay them again, even if only three miles away? In moving again my grandmother in particular had to give up the new tracks she'd already laid in America: her daily walks to neighbors' for coffee and cards, her trips out to the street to purchase doughnuts and meat from the delivery carts, her walks to that clothesline near her daffodil bed and her trips from her kitchen to her dining room where she would put away her china and cut glass in the sideboard. Moving in with my mother, farther out in the country, no near neighbors, no Swedish neighbors, her walks were to a different clothesline and her interior movements circumscribed in a smaller house, no china closet, one over which she would no longer have full domain. My grandfather's tracks may have felt less strange to him when he moved. He kept his same job at the piano factory. He had to walk out the back door to a different garden, but a larger one for all that. And his barn was bigger at the second house.

Whatever the loss of place for both the second time, the second move could have been nothing like the first. After a first like their first, perhaps there really is no other. This second time, they knew the roads, the trees, the date of the first frost for their vegetables and flowers. And the stories they told and the ones they knew of their friends, who still came to visit them in the second house, were the same, told, retold, emended in the Swedish that reminded them always of that childhood they'd left for good.

Were my mother and father any more in place than these grandparents? Again, I partly know, partly make a story, in which they too are much more "in place" than I. They too were born three miles away from each other. They met in the late 1920s when he offered her a ride in his Model T as they were both returning from the fairgrounds in their small town. I pass over that road yet, though I do not know the exact spot at which their eyes first locked. Their marriage was delayed for years as my mother traveled about the country working. She always knew she would return, although not, I'm sure, to him. When she did, they resumed their courtship and married. They moved then, temporarily to New Mexico, for his ailing health. They stayed sixteen months, living in a low, flat-roofed concrete apartment building, one that was still standing some forty five years later when I found it on a trip to Albuquerque. My parents moved back to Connecticut to a small farmhouse given to my father by an aging German immigrant bachelor who had come to look upon my father, a neighbor and at that time a young man, as his "son." My father helped him for years, getting him food, picking him up in his car. As our story went, one day as my father was standing with him in the yard. Mr. Lampe, Charles, handed my father the deed to the house. I imagine my father's utter surprise. When Mr. Lampe died in 1945, leaving the house, his beer steins, his musical instruments, his peonies and weeping mulberry behind, my parents, my mother five months pregnant with me, began their cross country return. My father supervised the renovations, paying cash he'd saved, and he and my mother lived there together with me for three years until, in 1950, he had to enter a different "house," a tuberculosis sanitarium, in order to protect the rest of us. He came back to the gift house maybe twice, weekend visits of unbearable brevity and of always uncertain timing to my young sensibility. My mother would live on another forty four years in that house, annually, like the monks of old, walking the boundary lines of the sixteen acres on which it sat, so reminding her body of the stability of her unstable domain, and dying, suddenly, in the night, in the same room in which her mother had died thirty three years before.

But this, my childhood house, was never narrated as that first one of my grandparents was. I know little of those three brief years of a "typical" life with mother and father and, late in this period, my infant brother. I have photographs. I have a couple of memories. I've one story of my father yelling at his drunken brother. I, a toddler, was playing in the dusty driveway. Harry drove in so fast he almost ran me over. Or another story: one night fifty chickens smothered to death in the corner of the hen house for fear of the weasel.

But the stories around the house itself were always stories of danger. Only the extensive land, the surrounding nineteen acres, was intact. The only "good" story about the house was that at the start: of the German immigrant giving the house and land to us. It was the other house, my grandparents' house, that was safe. I grew up in a house that could not be narrated. The structure itself, with its gambrel roof sloping toward the ground and its welcoming porch, gave promise of stability, perhaps of refuge. But there was that summer's day in 1952. Later in my life I both wanted to move back in there for good, to make the house more impregnable to death, and I never wanted to live there again. I would eventually find a compromise, a vantage point five hundred feet behind that house. It was the vantage point from the second house I built over thirty years after moving out of my birth house. This was *my* house, from which I could safely watch from a distance my birth house's seemingly serene stability—without hearing an echo of a door opening.

And so I carry about deep within me these stories and images of these two houses, different kinds of stories, different densities of story. But the two, my grandparents' house, my birth house, "placed" me as a child in the dyad, in the space between them. There was a third, more shadowed, position: my father's house, the house he'd grown up in, sat at the top of the hill not more than a half mile from my parents' farmhouse. It was the destination of all my mother's walks with us. It, too, was a site of stories, but few stories, about the grandparents I never knew, my father's father my mother never knew, about dairy farming and pitch black nights and a hundred acres of loneliness. It was the third part of a stabilizing triangle, weaker in my imagination, but there all the same as a story of successful, fruitful generation, both of progeny and milk. Theirs was an older house, an 1832 house, but it reassured me to know that, like my parents living in the house Lampe built, my father's family was only its second occupant. When we told its story, as we told the stories of many of the houses around us as I was growing up, it was always as far back as "we" remembered; any house would always (and to this day still does) bear the name of the first person we knew who lived there. Our local invisible maps, my brother's and mine alone now, have always been circa 1950.

I did not think of "place" while I lived in my childhood house. Place was present and so unnamed. I was content moving between all of these three houses in my imagination of "house." The triangle of these family houses stabilized me somewhere in its middle. The triangle defined me. It was only after I found myself three nights after leaving for college waking in a strange dormitory room and hearing the bell toll four times that "place," "home," began to appear fragile and illusory and so began to become a concept, an idea—and a thing longed-for, at all. I remember sitting in a philosophy class one afternoon and the professor, Mr. Holmes, saying something that riveted me: he said, when you come within twenty minutes of your childhood home, the very molecules of the air seem to shift. In acknowledging my loss, he helped me feel more at home on this campus one and a half hours away from the world I'd known. For over twenty years after this remark, particularly the farther away I moved, I'd remember his words every time I passed a particular stretch of granite boulders and pine trees within ten minutes of my childhood home. I became still, alert. The landscape around me began to fill out, to become softer, protective. I often wept at the sight of the worn clapboards of the eighteenth century houses I would pass, sitting there so modestly and rightly on their rises, the tall oaks shielding them, the laurel softening the edges of the trunks, filling in the under story yet not in the cloying way that other flora I'd since come to know did. My birth house was not an eighteenth century artifact, it was but a simpler 1930s farmhouse, but it took its own rightful place within this Yankee landscape, modestly yet privately situated on its own substantial acreage of field and woods, approached by highways that hadn't been important roads since the 1940s. And as I came upon this place at last I would feel, for a moment, as I always did. Like Eliot's "broken king" coming to the holy shrine at Little Gidding, I would find it always the same, "the hedges/white again, in May, with voluptuary sweetness."[10]

With this landscape engraved within and sporadically revisited, with readings of novelists who love place and house, George Eliot, Virginia Woolf, Marcel Proust, to remind me that my desires were not foolish, my longings, so powerful, not insignificant (for whoever spoke of these things?), I yet suffered my moves for years. I'd weep driving away. I'd walk home to a new apartment in a strange neighborhood, looking down at the sidewalk which I can yet see, summoning up memories of people I'd once known to help me finish my walk, or spending hours with my mother on the telephone, waiting for her to name people and roads I knew, or holding my books in my hands, with their known stories, characters, places, so that I could get used to strange windows. After trying these strategies to relocate myself again and again, other, more disturbing eruptions, fear of strangers' sounds filtering through to my living space, let me know I was not fully managing this dislocation. I remember one "I Love Lucy" episode in which Lucy holds a glass to the wall to hear what others next door are saying. These shows, often dramatizing the struggles newly close neighbors have with each other, provided a critical role as they mirrored for me and many in the 1950s our own living tensions as we began to move about more. I didn't hold the glass up but I might as well. I thought then that I wanted to be alone. I now think that maybe what I wanted was to feel connected. Hearing sounds from people I did not know only reminded me of how isolated I was in a dislocated place. I do know that once I'd met my numerous neighbors (a meeting which the sounds would often provoke me to initiate), I would not mind their noise nearly as much—especially if I liked them.

I struggled on for years trying to place myself through my imagination. I'd inhabited literary space for years as compensation because these spaces seemed so expansive. But once I had a "real job" these imaginary houses no longer provided enough solace. It was some fundamental failure of imagination, some primitive need for the thing itself. I know now I was not so strange. Edward Casey argues that the place world is not imaginary, but material, fundamental. Georges Poulet, writing on Proust, remarks,

> *But most often anguish, the anguish of seeing the mobility of places, aggravates still more the mobility, already so frightening in itself, of our being. For how is one not to lose his faith in life, when he perceives that the only fixity he believed he found there—a fixity of places, a fixity of objects that are situated there—is illusory? The mobility of places takes away our last shelter. It raises the anchor. To what are we able to cling, if, like times and like beings, places are also swept on in this course that can lead only to death (1997, 12-13).*

Knowing these thoughts, I can look with more assurance now at Milosz, saying more boldly, how could you survive all those years without being physically in the very place at your root? I can take some issue with Bachelard, for whom the daydreaming of house, the occupation of psychic space, memory space, reverie space, can suffice. I see that they seem to have some other kind of "self," one which they can carry around with them without needing to be in the material place to which they feel most deeply connected, but I also see that I am not wrong because I need the thing itself, nor foolish for taking so many years of my life to bring that thing, the house, into being.

I was, in all of these years, as I now see them, longing for some still, settled place. I was longing to know again something of those childhood houses, repeatable stories, people whose histories I knew, a memory of my own walks and windows in a place. But settled in such a place, I knew also that I would have to live in a free-standing house, a "single-family house" as this is now called. It was the singularity of this desire, for a free-standing house, that would propel me to build one. I'd no choice in the matter.

I was, of course, in desiring a single-family house, under our national spell. I was also under a familial spell. Given my history in houses, how could I be an adult if I didn't have my own? It's not only that I might not "know" myself as my mother's daughter did I not live in the same kind of dwelling as she. It's more than that. The strategies I'd used as a child to solidify my "I" I couldn't deploy if I didn't live in a house. I needed walls on all four sides separated by air from another's dwelling place. I needed light on two sides of a room. I needed to see a field out the bedroom window. I needed to be able to hang my laundry outside on a warm day. I needed to enter the house not by a series of steps through a common hall, but up the stoop through a comfortable and worn, welcoming door. I needed to hear an oil burner in a basement humming during the winter and an attic and cellar that I could explore if I wished. I needed my own separate, free-standing house to safely reenter the vortex of that early childhood triangle.

My friends have a habit now of saying that I have good house karma. They say this partly because they love the houses I've built. They also say this because my family was given not one, but two houses. While the first of these I grew in, the second was given to my family when I was out of graduate school. It was the summer cottage in Maine that we had visited off and on for years of my childhood. It belonged to a friend of my mother's, who one day also handed her the deed. My mother put my name on this deed the next day. I could live there in the summers. It was a place where I could plant perennials, a place where I could know the post office, learn the back roads. It was a place of stillness for two months a year for all the years of itinerancy.

There was more to this house, however, that has a bearing on my coming to be able to one day say the words, "I will build a house." The gift of this house had more influence than any other single childhood event in making me into a dreamer of a new, solace house, if not quite yet a builder of one. Sometime in the late 1920s, early 1930s, a young woman named Fannie Smith, sister of the woman who later gave my mother the cottage, suffered excruciating personal loss. First she gave birth to a child who died after a year, having never "been right," as was the customary phrase at the time. Then she gave birth to a still-born child. As if this were not enough personal loss for one lifetime, shortly after the death of her two children, her husband was killed while crossing a railroad trestle. By this point physical escape from Connecticut, at least for the summer months when she wasn't teaching school, was her only refuge. She came to Maine with another one of her woman friends, also a teacher.

Together they decided to hire the friend's father, a sometime (and not very skilled) carpenter, to build them each nearly identical summer cottages on a remote portion of an island on a glacial river. They must, the women, have had some say in the design. Even if they didn't, the *idea* of having a cottage built belonged to each of them. Perhaps they bolstered each other. The houses, some 800 square feet each, one green, one red, stood on concrete piers on ledge, with open rafters and studs, and large four paned windows that could be hooked open to the outside. The houses stood some 50' apart and the trees were then small, so they were in view of each other. They used outhouses, had no electricity until 1951, and drew water from a spring. Fanny lived in the cabin all alone in the summer months, waitressing in town to make up her then minimal teacher's pay. After two years another single woman friend, another teacher, visited the two women and purchased an adjoining parcel where her father built her a similar sized, though better constructed, cottage. This woman would later marry; the other two never did again. It was, however, always a "woman's colony," houses commissioned, lived in, and maintained by women who thought nothing of meeting porcupines on late night trips to the outhouse or chopping firewood for their fireplaces and woodstoves. The one I knew as a child, Fanny, had a house built to mark a "getting on" with her single life, to create a solitude for healing in a place of still extraordinary beauty, a "room of her own" writ large. How did she do it? What were her thoughts? Was she afraid? All this is mute, all soaked into the 2x4s, some of which we've now covered over with sheet rock. As I feel the studs, I know I am her spiritual, as well as literal, heir.

But in my life for the rest of many of these years of summers in Maine, there was always impermanence. First the "living" in a "house" and not "owning" one was more critical. After years of apartment living, we finally rented a house. Anxiety ebbed from my body, registering in the last episode of a bad back that I've had in almost thirty years now. I still recall the bliss with which I got down on my hands and knees and scrubbed someone else's dirt from the white and black tiled bathroom floor of that rental house. These tiles I did not know; we'd not tiles like these at home (we'd no tiles). But I did recognize that these were not "generic," the same in every apartment. These had been laid there in the 1930s, when the bungalow was built, by some tile man whose name I would never know and whose skill was so advanced that there was nary a trace of a tile laid slightly off center (we, not experts, would always leave traces behind on the tile floors we'd later lay). I hung up a small lace curtain after the bathroom was disinfected and took a long hot bath in the now gleaming white cast iron tub. I wasn't "home," not yet, but I was making progress. For the first time in almost twenty years I was more "in place" than I'd ever been since leaving my childhood home. It was only temporary. It was in the wrong place (the suburbs felt too crowded to me) and the house wasn't "ours." But something was very right, for a time.

As often happens in every life, I could not look ahead (even when we think we can, we're of course surprised). My husband got a job he came shortly to hate, and I began to face job insecurities myself. But before we let these pressures become very visible, we let that Maryland field "find" us. It perhaps was an inner wisdom guiding us, because if we had not responded we might not have persevered through our different job crises. We might have left town altogether. We "knew," however, in some corner of the being we shared, some unillumined corner, that we needed to "stay" put. I certainly was not, at this moment, planning, as Thoreau says every person does, to "build" a house. I wasn't even dreaming houses, as Bachelard says we all do. I couldn't "think" that big, either way. I'd just bought the first matching pair of shoes and handbag I'd owned in my whole life when my husband got his first job. How could I dream of making a whole house, never mind living in any house other than this fairly inexpensive rental? I mark this moment; millions of people are at this very moment not dreaming of houses because the idea is too foreign, too large, an imagination requiring courage seemingly unthinkable for those whose lives are constrained by severe necessity. But one small step onto that meadow, coupled with the possibility that we could make land payments, cracked open the egg at last. A few steps, a job to pay the mortgage, and I blurted out those first words without which nothing else would have happened. They were not Thoreau's words, not quite. But they would do. "I *will* build a house." It was time I did so.

IV

Coming to Tools

Without tools, there is no building. And yet when we see a made thing, we rarely imagine the tool or the hands that made it. And so we have forgotten about tools, about what they can do, and so also what our own hands can do.

If we have not forgotten, we are afraid of tools. We don't know their names. Or we have segregated tools by profession and gender. Circular saws and Cuisinarts: we rarely speak of kitchen tools as tools. More often, they are "gadgets."

How often do we find ourselves in the middle of a small household project without the right tool, or even knowing what that right tool might be? Even if we know the tool, it is apt to be lost in some box which we hope to sort out someday. Caring for tools, sorting them, sharpening them, has been relegated to the retired putterer. How often are we in the kitchen with a dull knife? How many of us would choose to take a child, as God does, to a pottery studio just to look at the craft of it?

Janice Goldfrank's interviews with women builders reveal that most of them learned about wood-working tools from fathers who taught them or through shop classes in high school. But what about those many of us who had no fathers to teach us? Or who never took shop because it was unavailable to us?

Gary Snyder's poem "Axe Handles" (1983) is inspired by a 5th c. B.C.E. Chinese poem from *Book of Songs*. The Chinese folk song opens, "How do you shape an axe handle? /Without an axe it can't be done." Snyder illustrates with a story. A father is teaching his son, Kai, how to throw a hatchet. Kai decides he wants one of his own. He remembers there's a hatchet head in the shop and there's material for a handle also there. Together the two men, father and son, use the working hatchet as the pattern from which to cut the new handle. The speaker remembers Ezra Pound's phrase, "When making an axe handle/the pattern is not far off." And the father then remembers his teachers, and that he is teaching his son who will go on to teach his.

I did not have an axe for a pattern. I had no one to teach me how to throw a hatchet. I did not take shop. I was a most unpromising case.

Yet I can track a history with tools. In tracing it, I can try to answer the woman on the stairs who asked me how I could "do all this." And, by tracking, I can also remember that I can build again. And I can encourage others, especially women, that they too can build.

I grew knowing that there was a world of shop tools. That world was physically bounded off from me in one particular space. It was a space about which I was always curious. In that protected space was waiting for me a world of carpentry tools.

We had a red barn next to the house. Two wings of that barn had once housed five hundred chickens. When my grandparents moved in to live with us when I was four, my grandfather turned one wing into his shop. In that shop he had, among other things, his case of beer, delivered every Friday by the "beer man" whom my grandmother and mother would never name, a case hidden and protected under burlap (the only cooling he had for it); he even had his own outhouse out back. The barn was his acknowledged space, the main house ours. He need only come in to the main house for meals.

I often went into the barn in the early evening to sit with him just inside the barn's open double doors. We would look patiently over his growing garden. But I rarely went into the adjacent shop. I wasn't prohibited from entering it, but I didn't go in unless invited. The shop was filled with imponderables: old wooden chests whose sticky drawers contained black files and wrenches I could never imagine using, dented brass oil cans, fifty year old hammers, some of their heads wobbly in their handles, saws with different size teeth blotched with rust. The only object I could understand the purpose of was his sharpening stone. He'd invite me in then to watch him sit on its bicycle-like seat and then begin to pump the pedal with his foot. The large stone would slowly turn, releasing at the same time tiny drops of water from some old soup can perched above it. My grandfather would hold one of our old kitchen knives against the stone. The contact of knife with stone sounded painful. But when he was done there it was, a gleaming sharp blade.

Though the room of tools strangely encouraged me, led me to think one might be able to do things for oneself, like turn a dull knife into a sharp one, easing the paring of vegetables, the tools remained as in a mass. I remember once in those years scoring a 30% in mechanical reasoning. I remember fearing I'd failed some intelligence test because I didn't even know what a gear was, never mind being able readily to sort my left from my right hand. This is because my grandfather did not teach me, or my brother, about the tools or their use, short of how to get a hand saw to bite into the wood. I suspect now, looking back years later, that he himself did not feel up to the task. He really was not a carpenter. In his job at the nearby piano factory he kept the tool bin, checking out tools to the other craftsmen. At home he tinkered. He would throw nothing out. He would try to repair old toasters and gather pieces of string. Once he told me, "the depression can come again, at any time." My grandfather's shop was a museum, a bulwark, a place in which to make repairs. It was not a place for building.

And yet these off-limit, mysterious spaces waited there, as an invitation. I think the turn down the tool road really began for me when my aunt taught me to sew while I was in high school. I was motivated to learn because I wanted to imitate some of the clothes the richer girls wore. And I knew some of the students would make fun of me if they knew I sewed so I kept it a secret. I did not understand the gift of this industry at the time: I was learning I could make things that I wanted. Shopping was not an activity in my family. We always shopped with one specific object in mind, such as shoes or a winter coat. I was learning to choose carefully what I wanted to work on, because it took time. I was learning through sewing to tolerate my stitching errors. I was learning through sewing that the clothes I made were peculiarly mine. The little labels I sewed into the back of the neck, "Handmade by Eileen," reminded me of this every morning that I got dressed.

Sewing, born of a kind of necessity (even as our first house was to be in many ways), also taught me critical skills, although I did not *know* for a long time that these *were* what some of Goldfrank's interviewees refer to as skills that translate. (Sewing also taught me to prefer working with fine fabrics, a habit which turned out to be expensive when I later became a crafter of houses.) A carpenter boyfriend, quick with his tongue and often incisive, once said as he watched me clean and oil my machine: "if you can maintain a sewing machine, you can learn to use any tool." Goldfrank's interviewees liken the use of a sewing machine to the use of a jig saw. But I learned a lot more from sewing than attentive machine use and maintenance. I learned to plan my course of action in detail. I learned how to lay out a pattern on fabric and how to measure my body so I could make adjustments on the pattern before cutting. I learned to "measure twice and cut once," every carpenter's mantra. When I started to use the machine on a project, I learned to pay attention to details—to sewing straight lines, to letting the machine guide the material rather my pulling it through. I learned that a tool must be respected, as well as cared for, so that it can do what it is best at doing. There's no sense yelling at the tool or trying to do something with the wrong tool. Patience, respect: I recall one of the instructors in the owner-builder school I attended giving a talk on tools and reiterating this point. He held up in front of us a Japanese saw which pulls the other way from the saws we're used to in the United States. One has to have the right tool for the job, but equally important is the attitude with which one uses it. One has to learn to move with it, without strain, without effort.

Sewing can prepare one for even more: it can prepare one for *designing houses*. One on the women Goldfrank interviews draws a connection between her home economics and architecture degrees. She speaks of how designing her own clothing helped her think about what she wanted the clothing for, the most suitable materials for its use, and the design which best met her needs. These habits of thought she says she carried into house design (163). I was never very bold at designing my own clothes, which is perhaps why when I turned to designing our houses I was drawn to timber frames. Just as I used a store-bought pattern for sewing, I gravitated toward the simple template timber framing invites. (Although one can design any shape house using large timbers, there's an economy and simplicity in imitating the old and simple rectangular shapes with angular roofs, capes, saltboxes.) I found these simple shapes reassuring. My friends lived in capes and saltboxes. I understood some deep, familiar grammar at play here.

Sewing is not the only kind of work women have traditionally done which can prepare both their minds and their bodies for learning how to build a house. Sewing may be the most obvious household task through which women show themselves that they can also make a house shell for their bodies. But women are, in fact, Goldfrank reminds us, also quite skilled at mastering many other domestic tasks, tasks that require both planning and patience and that effect powerful if subtle transformations: cooking, gardening, child rearing: all of these are like house-building—if only we are urged to name them in the same breath—and if only women overcome fear about making something lasting. We garden and the plants die in the winter. The newly cleaned floor is dirty tomorrow. The wall you raise, on the other hand, will be there perhaps for centuries. A house can be so frightening for many women: it's a visibility, a permanence, many of us are not trained in. Contemporary feminists are in the process of re-naming domestic labor. If we think of keeping house as a kind of building, we can all get on bulldozers. Another woman Goldfrank interviews likens making window trim to gourmet cooking. She urges women to be patient and attentive, totally focused on the work at hand (186-7). Thoreau says: "every man is tasked to make his life, even in its details, worthy of the contemplation of his most elevated…hour" (81). Women are surely "tasked" to do the same.

Reading and writing also helped me become a builder of houses. As I taught and wrote about English literature, I studied not only the power of place in novels, the power of windows and doors and garden views. I also studied how often building is used as a metaphor for writing and how much the structure of a novel or poem is like architecture. In her Diary, when Woolf says that she's working with a new kind of novel structure, "no scaffolding; scarcely a brick to be seen," she goes on in the next entry to remark that she has some "bricks for a fine one" (22-3). As a student and teacher of literature, I was already an architect-in-training. I just needed someone to tell me this, the same way Goldfrank shows women telling other women, yes, sewing, baking: you are a carpenter in training.

The skills many women already have: these are bridges. But people are also bridges. Like sewing, baking, writing, it's often a question of recognizing that support for what it is. Julia Cameron suggests that at the beginning of every new project we undertake we need to identify the people whom we know will support us. She urges us to draw a circle and inside the circle name the people who could help. I spoke with a young woman once who was building her own house. She was inexperienced like me and had been to an owner-builder school as I had. She'd hired a carpenter to help her. We got to talking about the rest of her family. She told me that her father and brothers were both in the construction business, but that her brothers didn't believe she could build her own house. She recognized that her father would have supported her had he lived. It was only her mother now whom she knew she could call on to support her throughout, even though her mother knew nothing about construction. Her mother even accompanied her to the building school. The woman has now finished the house.

My mother also helped me cross the divide. I instinctively knew when this idea of building erupted in me, that she would be the one to support me even though she too knew nothing about house building. Like the other woman's mother, she accompanied me to Maine so I could go to building school. Every morning she'd pack my lunch as I headed out in my pickup truck. She'd be waiting for me when I returned in the evening, eager to hear about what I'd learned. As I years later drew my inner circle, I saw that my mother had always been in it. I saw that she had in fact prepared me for building all along. My mother, as I came to understand her, was a cross-over person. She had her foot in both the domestic, the inside house, and what, in my childhood, was called a "man's world," the world of outside work. A hundred years earlier, she would have been a pioneer woman.

The signposts of memory are worn. I see a woman teaching me by example how to stretch outside the well-kept house I was already perched on the edges of. Though so tightly, fearfully indrawn after my father's early death (in all the formal photos her posture, her face, is unmoving, she's dressed in waist-cinching shirtwaists, and hats master every stray wisp of hair), there was a wild side to her when she was at home, in her housedresses, workpants, and garden shoes. I loved this mother. I'd follow her into the chicken yard to watch her flail the feed bucket around to scatter the last of the scratch feed. I loved hearing her tell (perhaps I saw?) of heaving one hundred twenty five pound bags of chicken feed into the bins in the barn while she was pregnant with my brother (not wise she confessed afterwards). And she'd cut brush, her therapeutic activity, after my father died. Every evening after she came home from her office work, leaving us in the care of her parents, she'd go out for a couple of hours and clean out all the brush, as many uninvestigated, tangled parts of her past and present as she could, extending as far into our sixteen acres as was possible. This took her a whole year. She'd even turn down the commiserating potential suitors who showed up early in her grieving, but rarely later, in favor of underbrush. For me though, her most impressive move was the way she handled snakes. Wincing, she nevertheless dealt with them, hoe or spade in hand. Though sometimes she was I think, afraid, her fear never stopped her. She knew she needed to protect her children and she knew she needed to reassure herself that she could learn to run the household alone, without a mate. Her own childhood training as the second of three girls and my grandfather's "boy" (collecting the million dandelions he wanted for wine, the beer capping, the walking the cow to pasture) had prepared her for this. Now she was a clearer of land, an outside woman, and I was her outside girl, both of us returning to home periodically with gratitude for its comfort and safety, if also some sense of nameless loss at its ordinariness and confinement. No wonder she never doubted my ability to build a house, though I'd never seen her lift a hammer or saw a board. Although she loved to "keep" her own house in later years, it was always the outside projects, the ones that required large physical movements, that thrilled her. Even at eighty she was rolling logs downhill and picking up the cut pieces to go into the pickup. It was quite natural for her, when she first walked into our first house while it was still under construction, to step assuredly over the piles of debris and look around her, approvingly, at the structure--as any builder would have.

But how, supported by translatable skills and "safety" people, does one really get from the sewing machine in one's bedroom out to that shop that was off-limits to me? Here is a spatial divide that I cannot easily cross. I can only point to the fissure points in the boundary between these worlds, for they felt like two worlds to me nurtured in the 1950s, the inside woman and the outside man.

Although my mother drew me outside, the shop still stood apart, forbidding. And there were other locked tool spaces. Chief among these were my father's tool chests in the attic. They'd been largely unopened since his death. Some twenty years after he died my carpenter boyfriend had the temerity we all lacked to open them. I felt as if it were the opening of the ark. The tools were neatly arranged and seemed unused: a complete set of finely sharp metal files, a complete set of gleaming drill bits wrapped in flannel. I now suspect my father had never used these tools much. He'd rather acquired them during the years he worked in the factory that made them. The males in my line were collectors, not users, of tools. The boyfriend picked up each tool, lovingly fingering it, smiling as he looked down at it in his hands, turning it over and over. It was a silent form of communication, man to man, the dead to the living. Later, in some ritual act of possession, I would insist on bringing these bits down to the first house site. I learned to use a bit and brace to drill large holes in our porch sills for the oversize carriage bolts that would connect them. I didn't have a large enough electric drill nor a long enough drill bit for it anyway. Both would be expensive to purchase—and besides, these brand new gleaming bits in flannel, handed down through my family, begged me. Many owner builders tell of using the tools at hand. Looking at professional carpenters, I am still overwhelmed at their complex array of tools. It does take longer to use hand tools, but there is a safety, a quiet, a meditative rhythm in getting the bit and brace to work just right so that it bites into the wood. Because there was no noise from the bit and brace, I could watch and smell and shavings from the new hole slowly spiraling out. The same sensual pleasure prompts me still to prefer the scythe over the weed whacker. The quiet of the scythe allows me to hear the swoosh of the blade. I can feel my body bend at the knees at the moment of cutting. I can often smell the newly cut grass. Gerard Manley Hopkins, speaking of the new furrow, says: "plough down makes sillion shine." You can only see the momentary shine where the blade has compacted the earth if you are moving slowly enough and it is quiet enough to look. Using the bit and brace and the scythe binds me to my ancestors and to wood and field. With no one to teach me their proper use, I try to recall from dim memory hand positions and the proper stoop of my grandfather's body. Their patterns seem not near, not inside the shop, but so very far away.

Here were the waiting tools, forbidden, unused, inviting. But other parts of my past waited for me as well. I grew in the early years just after the Second World War among people who built their own houses. Somebody in the family scattered all around us always seemed to be building a house, which sometimes meant doing some of the carpentry but which always meant supervising the construction to some degree or other, painting, cleaning up, finishing off a part later on their own. Dotted among the houses I visited as a child were always houses under construction, houses whose plywood subfloors and open studded walls I walked among with ease. These builders were middle-aged parents with young families, families building often on family property, or nearby, families who needed housing after the war. Take the case of my father's family: eight children grew up in a two story, 1500 sq. foot farmhouse that sat on one hundred acres. All of the eight children settled within ten miles of the homestead, most all in houses of 1,000 sq. feet or less on smaller tracts of land. One (my father) had his house and sixteen acres given to him (although he had supervised a major renovation before we moved in), one gained his through marriage, one settled on a piece of land separated from the original homestead. All the new houses were simple cape designs. The carpenters who started these houses were local. There was no such thing as a construction company or even a builder in the rural part of the state where I lived. It was always a "carpenter." Even to this day, my family refers to those carpenters by name. The dwellings were always single family houses (there were few apartments around, and these were in town, old houses that had been divided up).

Some of the houses that I knew in the 1950s were in the increasingly ubiquitous ranch style— one floor, five room affairs, low sloping roof. The members of my family who chose to build in this style partly did so because it was new, but also because this is the style of architecture that the banks lending them money preferred. The banks wanted to ensure that any house could be easily resold. This meant that carpenters no longer could exercise as much of their own creativity as they did before the Civil War, when the idea of template houses and pre-manufactured house kits (such as the Sears houses) began to take hold.

My mother-in-law and my maternal aunt, both born in 1918, each chose the ranch design for their houses. My mother-in-law started marriage in a second story apartment in a two family house that was built in the early part of the twentieth century to accommodate the housing needs of the nearby factory workers, factories that made candy, metals, rubber, brass, and chemicals. This house she, her brother and widowed mother had bought together in 1943; now she and her husband and two children shared it with her brother and his family, each living on a different floor. She chose the plan for her new ranch from a catalog, ordered the plans, and then, with their carpenter, modified them to suit their needs. In her case, she wanted room for her beauty shop in the back, which allowed her to work and supervise the children playing in the back yard. They could be seen through its windows as well as through the large picture window in the adjacent living room, a window which she'd arranged for. This rear facing living room was to become the architectural script of the new suburban house, although she did not know it. The house was built on cleared woodland that would soon become one of the first of the new subdivisions. From here people would have to drive to work at the factory. Although my in-laws hired a builder, my father-in-law acted as the partial contractor, hiring out the plumbing, electrical, and heating jobs himself, and taking care of the painting and landscaping. My mother-in-law, meanwhile, altered the house design in other ways. She proudly told of her changes to the builder's plans, ones that he later incorporated into the other houses he subsequently built on their new suburban street: stairs directly from the garage to the adjoining kitchen and a small picture window instead of double hung windows in the kitchen (no one who works at the sink likes double-hung windows which cannot be opened easily).

What we find beautiful in a house shape is influenced by our own associations. I always found my in-laws' subdivision deeply uninteresting, too grid-like, too predictable. I'd not grown up with this housing pattern. In my older, Yankee town, a town laid out initially around the needs of small farmers and ship captains rather than factory workers, new building was more scattered. The property had been carved up much earlier and so there were no large farms nearby in danger of being developed on the new suburban plan. Nor were there large industries expanding rapidly, requiring a larger work force—and housing for them. My Yankee geographical housing map, my relation to a carpenter, rather than a builder, my wariness of modern cookie-cutter design was all to play out in my own building process.

In the way that members of my extended family built, whatever the style of the house, either doing much themselves or supervising numerous small details, they were building what architect Christopher Alexander calls "a good house." In such a house "each detail has meaning. Each detail is understood. Each detail is based on some person's experience, and gets shaped right, because it is slowly thought out, and deeply felt."[11] Such a house is good for the ones who build it and good for the ones who live in it. And, Alexander goes farther, such a way of building a house is good for a town, a community, because the lives of the owners and the other craftspeople become bound together, by act and by story.

One of the reasons people I knew did so much work themselves on their houses during the 1950s was that the rules for procuring a mortgage were still rather stringent and my family, like many at the time, was still culturally unaccustomed to the idea of carrying any mortgage at all. My father, a saver who'd married in his thirties and who'd had our house given to him, lent his cousin the money to dig his well on a sliver of property next door which he had sold to him; if my father hadn't lent him the money for the well, he wouldn't have been able to get a mortgage from the bank so that he could build. When my father renovated the house he'd been given, he paid cash for it all, so that the house never carried a mortgage. Mortgage money was, I now know, around then. Under pressure from a developing building industry and the banks, The National Housing Act of 1934 established the Federal Housing Administration, or FHA, which made available for the first time low interest, long-term mortgages. Mortgage money had been around since after the Civil War but the terms were, by today's standards, onerous: a typical first mortgage in the 1920s covered only 50-60% of the price, and the term of the loan was 5-7 years; a typical second mortgage was a three year term at 18% (Wright 1981, 199). The FHA, in contrast, would lend up to 80% of the house's value with a twenty year maturity date, at 5-6% interest. But in return for lending money (as indeed they had all along, but now the numbers multiplied exponentially) the banks wanted to assure the house's "resale" value and that the house would be constructed according to typical building practices that could be regulated. From this point on in American architectural and building history we were never the same.

    I did not go through a bank in any traditional way when we built. I couldn't. Not only was I an inexperienced owner-builder (what kind of a risk was that?), but our house designs were quirky by their standards. By the time I built our first house in 1987, I could barely get a building permit with myself named as the General

Contractor. I had to take out a special license and swear that I would not resell the house within five years. And since I was building a timber frame house in a part of the country that had never seen one before, I had to work my way through the office that would eventually issue me a permit only after an engineer (which the head of our timber framing company fortunately was) would stamp his approval. The head of one of the inspection units was so stunned by this kind of construction he personally came out to the site to take pictures.

During the fifty year period since the establishment of the FHA had sprung up a vast building industry basking in the security of this government money and a complex infrastructure of permits and codes, all designed to ensure the harmonious transfer of mortgage money between owner and bank. The FHA enabled a generation, including a generation of many members of my family, to live in single family houses with sanitary conditions, minimum room sizes, a minimum number of bedrooms, and minimum window and door openings. For those, like my in-laws, it and the competitive savings bank mortgages they spawned (my in-laws didn't borrow through the FHA) enabled them to live a little away from the noise of the factory on a quiet, safe street, a cul-de-sac, a safe place for their children to ride their bicycles after school and back yard lawns for them to play in under the mother's supervision. The new mortgages helped solve the housing crisis of the post-war baby boom.

But the price of this institution was to be dear in other ways. Housing became a pre-packaged commodity, like an item of clothing one buys at the mall. One can now choose from among an array of floor plans in a glossy portfolio, select the color for the carpet and the siding, and add more expensive lighting fixtures and the like. Since the payments are spread out over twenty or thirty years and since, many think, we'll probably sell the house anyway (for, we hope, a profit), all we care about is our ability to make the payments for a while. Furthermore, our mobility means often that we care that the building hold up well only during our tenure. Michael Pollan comments on this in his book, *Second Nature*, as he meditates on people no longer planting slowly maturing and stronger shade trees in their yards. If you're going to move on, if your children won't live in your house, why not go for the more rapidly growing, shorter lived pin oak and silver maple? It's tempting to spend money on visible light fixtures rather than on reinforcement for the concrete footings, which will keep the wallpaper from tearing years later as the house settles after you've moved.

Our collective attitude toward building it ourselves was to change with all of these changes. Our building roles became redefined as selecting fixtures and sweeping up at day's end. But we've also forgotten in this process what the pleasing building patterns are. We've forgotten, as Christopher Alexander says, the "pattern," the deep grammar of what a beautiful building is, the pattern that lies within all of us and that we all somewhere long to "bring…to life." "In some form, every person has some version of this dream [of building one building that is 'wonderful, beautiful, breathtaking, a place where people can walk and dream for centuries']."[12] And building piece by piece helps us approach and open up this dream. When we lost control over our dwellings, we lost control over the work of our own hands and the beautiful house in us shrank.

What I take from my early years walking around the subfloors of relatives' houses under construction was that one could be alone with one's own house while it was being built and change it oneself. But these were largely men doing the building. I did not see women using carpentry tools. My aunts cleaned up, they painted, but they didn't use circular saws, table saws, nail guns, drill presses, even hammers and drills. They used the broom and the paintbrush. But the image was there before me all the same: families built their own houses.

And so I'd all these images, secret places, evidence around me of building, all lying fallow for years. I knew that day that I stood in the Maryland meadow and announced that I'd build the house that I'd need more help than this. I knew I'd need to do what I'd always done in such situations: go to school. Six weeks later, after signing the papers on that five acre meadow, I was seated in a Maine schoolroom at one of a number of long tables, facing double blackboards. The windows and ceilings were tall, the building a gambrel roofed, rambling three story turn-of-the-century structure visible from Route 1 and in sight of the Bath Iron Works and several navy destroyers under construction or repair. These are parallel structures, each nourishing large building schemes. Thirty three of us, eleven of us women, people in their twenties and their fifties, carpenters, people who, like me, had never held a circular saw and didn't know which end of a "joist" was up, wives of ambassadors, college professors, young women wanting to do for themselves, people I would never see again but whose futures I would always wonder about, from Canada to North Carolina to Indiana, were scattered around, notebooks open, pens poised. We were faced by members of the Hennin family and others associated with their owner-builder school. I had come to the "Shelter Institute" of Bath, Maine. Founded in 1974, it is the oldest continuously operated owner builder school in the country, offering courses spread out over the year. The building shelters a bookstore, a "general store" consisting of sample faucets, pieces of marble, and eco-flush toilets (all of which Shelter students can order at a discount when they build), and a tool store. Spread around on tables are albums and scrapbooks with pictures students have sent in of the houses they've built. Models are strewn around on the tables. In addition to this in-place help, students have always had access to free round-the-year practical advice over the phone and, since I left, over email. I was a regular caller.

By 2009, this concentrated building powerhouse had turned out 23,000+ home builders. The Hennins, Pat and Patsy (Patsy has since passed away), started the school in response to the back-to-the-land, self sufficiency movement that flourished in the early '70s, a movement that drew large numbers of people especially to Maine. Over the years, as the owner-builder movement subsided, the nature of the students' motivation in coming shifted from those looking to build their own houses, to those expecting to have some involvement in overseeing others' construction or those looking more for diversion. Some even come thinking they know more than they really do, having watched "This Old House" or visited Home Depot, not realizing that there is a veil between watching and shopping and "the real thing." Some of them come having already contracted with the Hennins to put up their post-and-beam frames (they started their own post-and-beam company, *Hennin Post&Beam*, in 1980). They want to help in the process, and the Hennins encourage this. Fewer people come into the course now, however, believing they can build their own houses themselves. Students today, observe the Hennins, are more fearful of increasing regulations, both building and monetary, are fearful of legal constraints, and fearful of the process itself. This, for the Hennins, who do this work as much because of their passionate philosophical and social vision as because of business, is a great loss. If people keep losing the confidence to build, then they become ever more fatally dependent on others, not only on other, sometimes fraudulent and shoddy builders, but more generally on others to do everything. Building, understanding how things work and being able to fix them, is, for the Hennins, the route to a critical self sufficiency. What gives the Hennins hope is that although few students come in now with such commitment or belief in their own powers, many do change after a few days of taking the course. Their perspective shifts, at least for a time. Many still return years later to say how much this single course changed their lives in profound ways. There have always been numbers of women in their courses, stimulated in part by Patsy's knowledge and active role as one of the instructors (and house builder herself). Now, there is less of a sense of gender division among students in the class, however, than there was in the 1970s. The course has more to buck now in the way of social obstacles to owner-builders, yet, on the other hand, has gained more in gender equity as it has become more acceptable for women to wield tools.

On a recent trip back to the present location of the Institute, several miles north on Route 1 in Woolwich, Maine, this side of Wiscasset heading north, I stepped into the new, large framing shed. Twelve men, under the supervision of Pat and his son Gaius, were learning to cut hemlock timbers. This was Monday. By Friday they would be raising a 24x24 one and a half story cape timber frame. Groups of men (not by the course's design) were learning to use lovely long curved Japanese saws, learning to saw with the wood, learning to exert no excess energy. Some of them walk about with visible confidence in what they are doing, at home in a wood shop, some with that barely perceptible hesitation that says "I know I should feel at home here but I don't." Pat, his eyes glittering, his voice supportive, encouraging, yet directing, like the wonderful teacher that he is, says to one, "you're working the saw too hard, work with the wood." I think of myself as a teacher of words, and how I could learn from this. The student backs off, and begins to let the saw bite in, to let the wood receive it as it will, like the sewing machine pulling the fabric along, like the essay flowing from the neglected corners of one's brain where the new thoughts come if we are receptive. I watch them shave the wood to get the end of the timber squared off. One takes his framing square and holds it both ways alongside the wood. It is clearly square, but they wish Pat to reassure them as he does. They are becoming slowly and inevitably energized by his and Gaius' love of the process (Gaius says he loves all the joinery and the frame raising the best; this is the next step for this frame.)

As I watch, as I feel again the old buoyancy that building, of few things in this world short of love, springs in me, I realize with a start: I know more at this point than these men do now. I've never hand cut timbers. I don't know this. By Wednesday, when I stop back, they will already have learned other things, things I don't know, like how to sharpen a chisel or mortise out a beam. But I know about the relation to the wood. I know about square. I know why they are doing this. I know what's got to come next. And, most important of all perhaps, I know that I could do this. In fact I want to take this course next year. I see in this moment that here, sixteen years later, I am now connected to the timber, to the tool, and to the process. My feet are planted firmly on home ground. And it all happened here.

Every morning during three weeks in June of 1984, I would sit at one of those tables taking copious notes or asking questions either of the instructor of the day or of my neighbor, who was handier than I ("which way does a joist go," I remember asking one day, proud that I now knew the difference between a "joist" (which is a horizontal framing member) and a "stud" (which is vertical), but stymied by which end of the piece of wood was up (the narrow end, so the depth of the wood can take the load of the floor that will sit atop it). The syllabus of the course, as I reread my full notebook sixteen years later (a syllabus that has changed very little, except in the introduction of new materials and technologies), is stunning in its complexity. I took as good notes as I did in my philosophy classes in college. Like a good lecture, each is organized both for content and level of difficulty. Trained as a lawyer, Pat Hennin knows how to make a case, how to order the evidence. Each member of their team knows how to give a lecture, how to answer questions, how to assess how much the students can take in, how to mix the theoretic with the practical. In the early days of the course we were warned: we will begin each day in the classroom. And we will begin with "the big picture." The opening went something like this: "Some of you want this course to be an entirely hands-on course. But that's not all this is about. To learn to use the tool, you have to shift your understanding of what you are doing and you must believe that you can do what you are about to do." This is what separates this kind of course from one offered at a trade school. This is a course for someone like me, someone who needs my mental mapping rerouted before I can even approach those tools. This is a course, as one of the graduates once told me, that "demystifies" building. And demystification is a complex process.

  The course stresses owner control over the building process, over every part of the building process. One of the graduates I met while I was building the second house (the discovery of a fellow graduate forges a bond as profound as finding a fellow alumna) jokes that when he attended they learned to make nails. It was not quite this extreme, but I did take notes on such things as how to install a submersible pump in an artesian well and I watched as Pat completely disassembled a chain saw and then reassembled it. (Legend has it that on his honeymoon with Patsy their car broke down. In the middle of a deserted road he completely took the engine apart. Patsy could read the tea leaves.) We had lectures on road grades, the importance of culverts, and on how to mill our own beams from our woodlots, if we had them, and then to select which ones went where in a timber frame, or post and beam house (a house made with several large as opposed to numerous smaller framing members). To learn which size beams were needed, we had to learn all about loads, or the amount of weight a building will carry, with furniture, with people, with people concentrated as on a deck, with heavy snow loads on the roof. Since these tables are not in building code books, anyone who is making a timber frame or even ordering one made by another needs to know how large each framing member needs to be. I now can do this. For our first house, I calculated that each basement post (we used a timber instead of a concrete, or "lally," column) was holding up 35,000 pounds. Then I could look at another table to determine how large the concrete footing needed to be under that post, and determine how much reinforcing bar (or "rebar") I needed to add to strengthen that footing. It was the course that led to the rebar that led to the wallpaper not tugging around the corner in the bathroom now used daily by the new owners.

Even if all this information weren't directly useful for me, and some of it wasn't, I discovered that it was mentally critical. First, I learned not to fear any part of the building process. Any part of it could be dismantled and understood, and, if I chose to learn, I could do it myself. These lectures and workshops shattered some wall that had previously existed between me and my domestic environment: I could look through the walls. Although I was trained as an academic, a researcher, it somehow never occurred to me that the place where I lived was a rational system that I could understand. Suddenly I realized that behind walls were conduits carrying electricity between the panel and the individual circuits. There were plumbing pipes, sometimes expensively running the entire circumference of houses where bathrooms had been badly planned (to this day all my plumbing is consolidated and the hot water tank underneath so I don't have to wait for hot water). Leaks in ceilings became ominous for me. I realized that water, the great enemy of every house (I can still hear Pat saying this), was slowly rotting something somewhere. I would ignore it only to spend more money later. In short, my physical environment became infinitely more interesting and changing and I was becoming much more able to control it since I was beginning to understand that it worked according to rules.

  Second, I learned a shift in emphasis and attention, a kind of frugality in a way, a pleasure in things working well behind the scenes, as opposed to a pleasure in their finished, visible state alone. This kind of shift is more subtle, but it encourages a builder to concentrate on doing the things that are in the long run most important and doing them well. And these often are the things hidden from others' sight, such as a well-soldered pipe, or the right size nails used to secure a subfloor. But if the pipe leaks or the floor buckles, these things will provoke a daily, subliminal tension as one lives in the house-- and they can be fixed later only at great cost.

  Equally important I think to the mental shifting that went on in those brief weeks was the physical exposure I got to building. Of course I'd been to house sites before. But I'd never been expected or wanted to participate. After each morning class period, we could visit a variety of houses under construction in the area, some of them being built by Shelter students, others by carpenters connected with it. When we built our first house, because our friends knew we were doing a lot of it and we were in charge, they'd come out to help us. To this day, some fourteen years later, they still refer to "their wall," or speak of how the experience gave them a sense of accomplishment and understanding of the sometimes arduous conditions in which builders have to work (that summer it seemed to be 95 degrees and humid every day). As Shelter students, we had access to a number of willing strangers' house sites. I watched my first concrete pour, a fearful experience I never quite got over. Concrete is so unforgiving. When the truck comes, you'd better be ready for it or else you'll lose it. You must know when to work it, how to remove air pockets, and later to smooth it, because you can't go back and fix it without the great labor and expense of jack-hammering. Watching this one pour, however, would encourage me to think we could do our own concrete footing pour for the first house. I stood in the Maryland trenches, shovel in hand, because of those Shelter moments.

But the Shelter course also worked in another way on me, a way I was more familiar with. When it couldn't give me direct physical experience, for we hadn't time for all of this, it gave me stories and images. It gave me the story of the woman on the bulldozer. It gave me visits to Shelter houses where I could meet the men and women who had built them. It gave me more photographs. It said to me, you are not alone. You are part of a building culture.

After the Shelter course, we didn't build for almost two years. But it was a fruitful fallow time. I've learned to respect this waiting time—waiting then for job solidifications, waiting, before the second house, for the first to sell. During the first waiting period it was time to read and to prepare myself internally to do something I'd never done before. I needed to lay tracks in my mind, both learn what a house was made of and, as important (though nowhere could I find this written), what order to proceed in. Student as I was, I read probably a hundred books on building—trade books on concrete, on carpentry techniques, books of house designs. Every night I would pull out a book I'd bought, or a magazine, or a library book and lie on the sofa reading and taking notes.

    This fallow time, this reading time, I've always felt is in some ways the best part. It's dreaming time really. The house is always perfect. It can be changed in a minute. One isn't locked in. One isn't anxious. One isn't sweaty. One isn't fatigued beyond all expectation. This is "virtual" house time. But in addition to the considerable pleasure it affords, which I think is a necessary prelude to bolster one in the turmoil that is to come, this time also, on deeper levels, beyond the practical, allows one to assess and reassess what kind of house one really wants. Once you are underway, changes can't be easily or cheaply made. And there's the cost: each decision you make can exponentially increase the cost: a gable, a bump out, a width that wastes dimension lumber, extensive plumbing, all of these things add up, slowly but forcefully at the end. One owner builder I interviewed, another professor, likened house building to book writing with this difference: "when you are building you can't go back and change the introduction. You have to anticipate everything at the beginning." Although I didn't appreciate all of this while preparing to build the first house, I had a strong sense that this was so. I knew I'd never before been involved in a project in which so much depended on the planning stages. My patience as a seamstress was coming into play.

There were deeper layers to this time. I was, without even quite knowing it, becoming the architect for the house. I wasn't just dreaming. I was beginning to think "house," in specific terms. I was drawing thousands of plans, on paper for the first house, on the computer for the second. I was making many models with little people and little furniture so that I could inhabit the new space long before I walked in it. I was playing with space. I was in the moment of conception. For the woman standing in my hallway, this, designing, is also barely to be comprehended. It is another one of her large, unformed questions.

V

Prime Moves: Writing a House for the Body

What of architectural beauty I now see, I know has gradually grown from within outward, out of the necessities and character of the indweller, who is the only builder,--out of some unconscious truthfulness. --
Thoreau[13]

*A truly transcendental phenomenology needs to return to the life-world, and thus to the lived-living body that animates it. It also needs to return to place.... it has to pass through the **exacting gates** of space and time before its own right of way is recognized.*

—Edward Casey[14]

Early one morning in the mid 1980s, wearing jeans and a chamois shirt, I climbed the narrow stairs of the three storied, 1890s gambrel-roofed building in Bath, Maine that then housed The Shelter Institute. I entered a wide and high, light-spilling room filled with rows of worn, dark-colored, long wooden tables facing a blackboard.

A wood stove sat in the corner. The June air was cool and salty, the light clear and slanted in the especial way of Maine northern light. The gate of this place felt propitious. It was old. It was quiet. It was humble. It invited me to cross its threshold. It was a footfall that would change my life.

Perhaps the image of the solitary writer in the tower is an archetype—the writer replacing the soldier once watching there; the writer sitting at the high desk; the writer looking down and not out the chinked wall; the writer penning letter by letter documents that will preserve, spare, and reveal the world, copying sacred scripture, imagining visionary poems; the writer drawing lines as a spiritual practice, attending to the stillness and depth in the word and so what its fixedness opens; the scratch of pen, the smell and stain of ink, the touch of the quill focusing all the senses just here. At the moment I slowly climbed, I remembered these monks, and Keats and Yeats who also loved towers. I remembered too Mrs. Dalloway climbing to her high solitary room, the quiet and safe room of her own. I felt myself walking humbly in line. I was about to enter a new solitude, as I would pick up what was for me a new writing instrument. I was not, in "writing" a house, out to save civilization. I was, however, without fully knowing it then, trying to persist in place, exist in stillness, and so trying to spare, preserve my own soul.

On the tables waited all sorts of strange writing materials: sheets of tracing paper; pieces of masking tape (which I later learned would secure the corners of the paper to the tables); a "T" square (with which we could draw lines perpendicular to the table's edge); a white three-sided architectural ruler with four scales in each valley (so we could draw precise lines); a special gum eraser and brush to sweep away the small filings; and, most important of all of the drawing tools, the odd-looking, slender metal tubes into which we would place thin shafts of graphite, leads of different hardness: our drawing pencils. The laden tables commanded attention. These were architects' tools. Some of them, I later learned, had been used for centuries.[15] The door of the tool shed had been opened. The instructor would soon invite all of us then gathering to sit and so cross its threshold: "today you are going to draw on paper the house you as yet only dream."

    The three-dimensional house that will take root in the land must first be imagined and then scripted exactly to scale on paper. The law now requires this paper. The local agency issuing the building permit needs to study this paper and then sign off on it. It needs to ensure that the house is up to code. It will study every window drawn in every bedroom to be certain it is of a minimum size to permit human egress in case of fire. The builder of today needs the paper.[16] If someone other than you is building, the paper you design or approve ensures the builder will follow your desires about exactly where that window is to be placed in a room. And if you are the builder, the paper serves as a mnemonic device, reminding you exactly where you imagined that window in the room and in relation to other windows in the house. The paper, and the eventual collection of drawings, which will eventually be reproduced in what are called blue-prints (because the print is blue), is, in short, consequential. This is why when we see someone on a building site carrying a roll of papers under the arm, we say, "Here is the one in charge."

But drawing one's own house on paper also does far more. Rybczynski observes that the very length of time it takes to draw brings the house inside of one (2002, 38). Drawing's gentle tediousness (and I speak here of hand drawing, still preferred by many architects and much preferred by me!) focuses and slows the mind to see and feel the dense "this-ness" of the house to come. The skeleton that drawing produces shows the house's bones, almost each bone of the house, bones that need to be assembled as drawn, line by line, bone by bone, nail by nail. The slow process of drawing prepares for the slow process of building.

I was not afraid of desks, of writing materials, even new ones, facing me on the tables. I liked the idea of sitting at these desks. They reminded me oddly of my elementary classroom, although here I was pleased that long tables would connect all of us. I could also see that the waiting materials on the tables bore some resemblance to other materials I used every day: the tracing paper replacing vellum, leaded pencils replacing my fountain pen, fine lines replacing letters. And the idea, of building a thing on paper, was something I also knew. I was used to spending hour upon hour searching for and then rearranging words in order to try to build my own thoughts into a structure others could mentally walk in. All my writing and teaching had centered on constructing arguments that I hoped would have some architectural elegance to them. And, perhaps above all, I knew that whatever I "wrote" I could rip up. I'd done so many times before. There was nothing final about putting pencil to paper—no, not yet.

What I *was* afraid of was *what* I was being asked to draw. I knew how to ponder fissures, gaps, in literary texts. But a window? A real fissure in the house boundary? What were the consequences of this? What window? What size window? Where to put the window? What was the symbol for writing a window into a perimeter line of the house? What would a window just here look like from inside? From outside? I felt overwhelmed.

What I didn't know, in other words, as I faced the desk that June morning was how to *think* and then *write* a *house* on paper. What I had been building on paper with pen up to that point in my life had been abstract structures, idea buildings. And what "house" had been for me up to that point in my life was oddly similarly abstract. House was just an idea. What I was being asked to draw with the pencil that morning was a highly concrete house, a house with details, with bones. I was being asked to write a structure that could be built with nails and wood. I was being asked to write a structure in which every bone of my body, and not just my mind, could enter. And there was more: others would walk in this structure, enter its gates—I could pretend they never entered the gate of my book. In short, I was being asked to *place* my body among other bodies—place it on the ground. It seemed a new kind of visibility. It felt like a new nakedness.

The possibility of my *placing myself* was not something I'd ever really thought about before. I'd *been* placed, but I'd not decided to *make* place, at least at such a fundamental level as to build a house. As Heidegger puts it, I'd been "thrown," at birth, into a particular house and family, I'd felt thrown into schools and jobs and into whatever apartment or rental house was ready-to-hand. Oh, I "chose" the school, the job, where to rent, but it hardly seemed this much of a choice. In not placing myself, I had been dis-placed.

I am not atypical. Edward Casey identifies place-lack as our central disease. He asks, "Where have all the places gone?" (1997, 197). Time, and not the solidity of place, had regulated me. That bell I heard once at four in the morning as I lay in my dormitory bed at Mt. Holyoke continued to chime for me almost every quarter hour thereafter. It was my form of the ubiquitous watch or the digital clock on a computer screen. And at moments when I wasn't hearing the bell, I thought of space as vast and empty. As I sat in my astronomy class I shrank in my chair as I imagined the mapped, calculated heavens. Where was I? Where could I be? Where in this vast calculus of time and space? In short, not "just" here, not fully here. I had not passed through "*exacting* gates of space and time"— I'd been passing through only vast, inchoate ones. What kind of "I" was that? I was dis-placed, lost in time and in the "empty theater" of infinite space (1997, 197).

Philosophy had, Casey tells us, by the middle of the twentieth century, begun to re-theorize place. Husserl, Heidegger, Merleau-Ponty, and Bachelard went back to the exacting gates abandoned with the fall of ancient Greece. Phenomenology reclaimed our attention to the expansive minutiae of our movements in a specific location. Phenomenology claims that it is this specificity, this concreteness, which is the source of real knowledge.

I, as yet, was, in my little life, still behind the philosophical eight ball. Here I was, about to sit at this table and pick up a pencil that would help get me into place. The lines, the pencil would be like casting an anchor off a boat, my hands holding this pencil would be like *Jeremiah*'s potter sitting at the wheel about to start a jar, a thing in place, a container for all the healing ointments and life-giving water; anchor lines, jars: how had I missed these lessons before now?

Class had not quite begun. Before I sat with the gathering others at the table, I walked over to a side table. What happened at that moment was not part of The Shelter Institute's formal curriculum, although certainly every object in that schoolroom, as in the room below, the "store" of house parts (faucets, slabs of marble, hot water heaters, tools, books), operated like a Montessori classroom, there to feed an adult starved for this sort of play. What I did at that moment was to pick up at random a particular "toy" in this learning laboratory and it did for me what fingering other toys might do for others. One touches a seemingly non-descript thing, like a chisel, without expecting anything to come of it, only to discover that it, after all, clefts memory open wide. The feel of the wood-handled, steel-headed sharp chisel reminds one of a father bent over a workbench notching out a piece of wood. It is a madeleine[17] of the building world. Tasting a thing, touching a thing, a tiny physical thing, a body memory, opens another, otherwise lost.

That's what happened to me at that moment, in a way. But unlike Proust's taste of the madeleine or Jung's fingers feeling the stones, unlike Milosz's footfalls reminding him of the home slopes, what I touched with my fingers didn't summon up an acute personal memory. Rather, "house" itself began to shift meaning for me. The touch of the model changed "house" for me. I began in that ever so slight internal turning occasioned by touch to move from being what I had been: a *consumer,* a voyeur, a potential purchaser, a decorator of an inert thing, a house, to what I never before imagined I could be: a potential *producer* of one. The house was about to be born from *me.* I was about to become its prime mover, not with a dollar in my hand, but a hammer—but first a pencil.

No one around me knew what was going on in me, nor perhaps did they even see what I was doing. It was that unremarkable, especially in the context of that Montessori-like teaching room. What I had done in wandering over to one of the side tables was touch several of the three-dimensional house models strewn about. These were odd-looking things, crude boxes made out of ordinary cardboard. I picked some of them up; they invited that kind of handling. I idly fingered the boxes, lifting off their rooftops, which had been pinned to the side walls with ordinary common pins, the kind I regularly used in sewing. I peered into the window holes that had, sometimes roughly, been cut out with a knife. Save for occasional interior walls similarly pinned or glued to the floor, these models were bare inside as well as out. Their blankness, their emptiness, their crudity, challenged me. I knew that these models signified "house" but I did not know this kind of model. I could not "place" it. Therein lay the critical difference, the difference that would tip some internal balance, provoke some utterly new possibility. Here was an object, made of very ordinary materials, yet one I could not read in my ordinary way.

I had seen house models before. In museums or in the foyers of large buildings under major renovation I had seen richly detailed models built by architects, constructed out of balsa wood or plaster of Paris. When my in-laws purchased their house plans from a catalog in the 1950s, they were mailed a model of their new ranch house. This one, being mass-produced, was much less detailed than the architects' hand-crafted models, but all of these house models I'd seen were finished, complete with siding, windows, roofs, perhaps even a shrub or two around the foundation, or even a tiny replica of a person in the kitchen. They implied a building that was already fully conceptualized (by someone), promising in their detail that they would become real buildings. Their detail said to the viewer: the one who gives you this knows what is going on; be confident in this person. These models were designed to be set on a table; they invited viewing (rather than touching) from above and from around each side. The viewer circled the model, as if it were a museum piece. Yet this particular art object, unlike a sculpture, stimulated the viewer's desire: this would be "my" house or our "company's" new house, it said. This iconic-model similarly reminded the owner/viewer that the architect of this was a kind of god-in-charge, while simultaneously flattering the owner/viewer whose power lay in holding the purse that would enable the model to become life-sized.

These kinds of house models I'd seen before. I'd never touched them. They weren't mine. I didn't have the cash to commission an architect or have someone else build me a pre-packaged house.

I had as a child also touched another kind of miniature house, one a little closer to me as a girl child than architectural models: the dollhouse. The dollhouse isn't a model; it doesn't promise enlargement, or eventual replication. The dollhouse, while a concrete thing, is also an imaginary space. As I approached this table, however, I couldn't help but think of a dollhouse. Since these crude cardboard models didn't invite attention to their exterior but seemed rather to invite me to peer in the windows, I found myself similarly focusing intently on the interior as I would in the dollhouse. But here the similarity stopped. The dollhouse's interior was rich, elaborate with embossed wallpaper, miniaturized furniture, tiny crockery. These cardboard rooms were bare. They did not even seem to ask to be furnished. Also, it was difficult to see the interior of these models—one wall had not been cut away, as in a dollhouse, to invite viewing of multiple rooms at the same time. The dollhouse view makes available the sight of fine furnishings. It's a kind of street-side view into a house, a dreamer's view, a consumer's view. [18] This view, here, of these models, was a bird's-eye view of the almost abstract *form* of a whole house.

No, the cardboard models in front of me were about something entirely different. I could not read them in any of these more familiar ways. Their bare outsides, their careless grouping together on the table, did not point me to a professional in charge or remind me of my own responsibility to provide capital. They engaged no pride of potential possession. When I looked inside the models, their bare interiors did not cajole me into furnishing them according to some invisible standard of taste. These models didn't provoke my desire to own or position myself in some hierarchy with other owners.

Rather, these models opened another way. In their sparseness and amateur quality, they pointed me to other students, to the ones who had constructed them, students only slightly more advanced than myself (in that they had some whole design for a house whereas I had yet none). Like a dress in the making, only pinned together as yet, these models were a work-in-progress. They opened a window into their makers' struggle for form—for a flow of rooms, a feel of roof, an angle of light from a window. I knew from them that I'd also be expected to construct my own three-dimensional model to set beside these others on the table. And I knew I could do it. I was part of a democracy of models here. No one would laugh at my model. Each person would read mine in the same way I was reading others'—as a promise, a potentiality.

It was the power of a miniature one has made, the dollhouse, the tinker toy building, and the drawing that was at work in me in my few moments at the side table. These miniatures provoked and emboldened my dreaming (Bachelard 1958, 152). In entering imaginatively into these models, and then tentatively into the minds of their makers, I began to shed my old ways of viewing the house as something bought (or given). I began to see it as a thing in process. And, I began to see it as a thing I too could make alongside them. I began to imagine my *own* box, a material jar for *me,* a shell spun out of my own body.

I was, however, also *outside* these models as I stood at the side table, even while I entered them imaginatively. I'd chosen to come here, to this building class. I needed to be looking *at* and *in* to these abstract, crude models as well as inhabiting them. The "outside," the "wholeness," the limits of these models were critical for me to grasp. In seeing, looking *at* them, in being able to touch them, a whole, though miniaturized, "house," I could just begin to imagine myself as big enough to make this, after all, small thing. It reminded me of the way I felt when I was in a small plane one afternoon flying over some of the mansions in Newport, Rhode Island: I remember saying, these aren't much. I am bigger. I later built similarly bare models of both of our houses to scale, using foam core, an Exacto knife, glue to adhere the walls to the floor, and pins to hold the roof on temporarily so people could peer inside when they wished. It was the presence of these models that many of our friends found the most reassuring part of a project utterly foreign to them. It reminded them that a specific object, a unified "house," was going to emerge at the end of interminable small steps. The miniaturized models made the project seem manageable. The models were also reassuring to me. I would continually move them (no museum for them) to different locations in the house I was renting. There they would silently coax me and reassure me by their relative size that I could build an entire freestanding house. They said to me, "you are big enough to finish this."

Seeing, touching the models pricked some long dormant kinesthetic energy. It was like the feeling that rushes through the legs as one walks toward the gym. I'd not before been to the "gym" the models promised, but nonetheless they promised that expenditure of energy that would paradoxically re-energize.

My lingering moment with the models was too soon over. Class was beginning. It was time to sit at the table and pick up a new thing: the drawing pencil. I was now ready to draw a two-dimensional floor plan of my house so that I could make my own model to set beside the others. It felt a little like that moment when a parent gives your new two-wheeler bicycle (on which you are barely balanced) a sudden push.

Was the terror of that moment the same for me as for others sitting next to me at the long tables? None of us were architects. None of us had that degree. All of us faced at least that anxiety, the anxiety of being "unprofessional" attempting something "best left to the experts." But did the men feel differently from the other women nearby? The carpenters from the unskilled? The aged from the young? These are our secrets.

I felt an unaccustomed embarrassment at the limp helplessness I felt as I first picked up the pencil in my right hand. I was the only one in my family to be given a room of my own. I believed in, taught others, Woolf's *Room of One's Own*. Yet though I'd had that room of my own, I'd never, even as a child, *made* one, made a tree house or a play hut for myself as I imagined some of my fellow students had. My outdoor houses as a child were always impermanent, porous--glades, the walls tree trunks, the roof a canopy of leaves. Indoors, I didn't even rearrange my furniture when I played dolls; rather I'd crawl under my bed and bring them all with me. All my houses were but temporary refuges, imaginary refuges. It was one thing to buy a dress pattern and cut out fabric (both the pattern and the fabric were often difficult enough for me to choose), and then, after sewing the dress, tentatively wear it, hoping that people would compliment me on my choices. This, here, these lines, what they portended, was far more risky. It went much further. I was being asked to extend the boundaries of my body out, maybe as much as forty feet or so. No one was giving me a pattern book or an array of fabrics for this task, not yet. I was being asked to come at this whole thing from a more primary place that didn't yet exist, that of some fundamental will to "big house space" for myself. I knew, as well, that I wasn't alone any more, playing in glades or sewing in my room by myself, able to walk away or throw the whole project away, which I'd sometimes done. In undertaking to build, even in undertaking to sit in this class, known to my teachers, the Hennins, in front of whom I, good student that I was, didn't want to fail, I was making a more public kind of commitment to write my body onto the earth more largely, more boldly and more permanently, mistakes and all, than I had ever yet done. I knew that I couldn't hide or retire this house to the attic.

That moment of picking up the drawing pencil opened the door to many such anxious moments as I continued to draw alone in the year to come. The thoughts would crowd in: "I can't do this." "What do I think I'm doing?" Colleagues would wonder at the amount of time I spent away from reading and my academic writing in order to draw houses. I wondered. For months tracing paper would be taped to my dining room table. My back and neck would ache from long hours of sitting hunched over in the chair as I sketched page after page. For the second house, it was little better. I'd climb to the study in another rented house and tuck my knees under the computer chair. The cursor became my pencil—and taught me more about computers.

Eventually, with seemingly endless practice, I would reach some point in drawing both houses at which I knew instinctively that I had to stop. Then I would develop one "final" set of plans for each house: bird's-eye view floor plans, one for each floor; "elevations" (or sketches of the exterior of the house drawn frontally, one taken from each side); a couple of "section" drawings (which provided a glimpse of how rooms would look if one stood on a single imaginary line cut through the floor plans stacked on top of each other, much like the perspective one has looking into a dollhouse, but these from an odd, atypical angle, such as a cut-through a bathroom); "framing plans," or drawings which showed the size of lumber to be used for floor joists and walls. To all these would be added expanded drawings of detail areas, such as how one corner of the house frame would be connected with the foundation and what the foundation would look like at that corner as it goes to ground. And then there would be several "schedules," lists of window and door sizes. After I had blueprints made of these drawings, I would roll them up, tuck them under my arm and walk into the permit office, handing them over. After the building inspector approved them, I'd pick up the rolled plans along with the permit (they'd keep a copy). This permit, this small 8 ½ x 11" sheet of paper, would "permit" me to pound those laborious few stakes in the earth marking the house corners and then make the phone call summoning the bulldozer I'd hired to cut a swath through the first house's meadow for the driveway. It would raise its iron mouth and begin to eat away at the clay earth until we'd a gaping hole five feet deep and some forty feet wide. That hole that early summer's day in Maryland was the startling, ineluctable, consequence of my first drawn lines that June morning in Maine.

The first, really tiny, act of my picking up the drawing pencil was like rooting an insignificant leaf in a fertile growing mixture, out of which a whole plant, root, branch and all, would slowly grow. The house flowered out of me. I was incising lines onto paper that would deeply root not only a house in earth, but also my body itself as a living building. Scrubbing the bathroom tiles in that newly rented house, "sweeping it" to make it "mine" (as the Shakers say) was nothing compared to this. *I* was myself *placing* my body, intending to plant it afresh deep into the earth, underground. I was rooting the particular branch and flower that is me. I was only one among the others, other drawings, other models, but I was fully that, one.

The root and branch had special characteristics. I would have to think, as I never had before, on my body's own choreography, the way I liked to move in a house. And I would have to learn to ask my husband to think about these same questions. How had I moved? How could I? In trying to think about these most mundane of places, "kitchen," "library," "living area," "bedroom," "bathroom," and arranging these places, I was making conscious my heretofore unconscious choreography, that ritual of movements so familiar that were I to wake in the dark I would know where to turn a corner and where a bathroom was. Now I had to plan this. But also I was, by attending to this drawing, saying, in print, then with bulldozers and hammers: I am a body that needs to cook, that needs to sit to read, that needs sleep, that needs to bathe. I was declaring that I legitimately took up some room and should make room. I was no longer being moved willy-nilly into place. I was claiming it. I began to understand the significance of Woolf's arriving at her own room at the end of *A Room of One's Own* and feeling finally safely and contentedly "there," ready to write.

What, however, exactly was this body that I was placing, rooting, by drawing? This was a new question. I knew it to be more vulnerable than I had before imagined. I began to see this needing part of my body as I drew its place. And others looking over my shoulder did too. This was a "book" of mine that others would open—not a fixture on a library shelf. This wasn't like the medieval practice of drawing symbols on one's own hand to help jog one's memory, a memory one could keep to oneself.[19] This drawing on a paper spread out on the table said to me and to others: I am this way in my private space, the space inside the public space of the road outside, inside the buffer space of lawns and fields that bridge house and road.

I was losing some essential privacy. It's not that I would be completely naked in the drawing; it was, after all, only in code, a code of fine lines. But it was in a shared, easily decipherable code. Others that would read those plans, others who might not know me, or who, if they did and were asked to visit the house, would not otherwise be admitted into some of the finished spaces of the house. But they could now see the drawings, almost like moviegoers who read the two-dimensional vertical version of others' private rooms. They would know as they looked where I chose to stand to brush my teeth in the morning and whether I wanted to be at the kitchen sink in private, invisible to others seated at the dining table. I'd already a repertoire of those motions inscribed deeply within my body's memory, of teeth brushing and sink standing, memories accumulated over years of bathing and washing dishes in different rooms. But now, here, I was *intentionally* making a place for these activities *and* revealing this part of my body to myself and others who might look at the drawing. And, of course, I dimly knew even when I was drawing the plans for the first house what I most certainly knew for the second: there would be months in which many people would be at work on constructing those private spaces and many months in which neighbors would be welcomed to visit all parts of the house under construction. There are many people out there who know what my intimate spaces look like: this building class where we were learning to draw together our own plans, the permit office that would later study the finished plans, the strangers hired to complete work on intimate spaces. Thoreau partly rebelled against this visibility. He chose to hide in the woods. I couldn't. The "private" house is now, in the land of building codes, banks and even owner builder schools, a misnomer. And drawing it for oneself and for others begins to make it public.

Begin I must, despite these erupting vulnerabilities. Before I could draw the first line, I needed to make a critical decision: I needed to decide what the house's "footprint" would be. The footprint is what the drawing of the outlines of the house's exterior circumference, looked at from above, is called. Literally, I needed to choose the prints my feet would make everyday should I walk the house's perimeter. I needed to "take a walk" around the outside of the house, a little like birds circling, dogs or cats nesting, or monks walking the boundary to learn the inside and outside and so stabilize their place world. Husserl, in attempting to explain this mystery of circling, in the human case by walking, says walking "unifies" the self, draws the body together in kinesthetic energy (Casey 1997, 2004). Our encircling seems to draw the cloak around the body, sheltering it. I needed to decide exactly how long I would walk before my feet would stop, turn a corner, walk again, come to an exterior door, then a window. The house's footprint would of course change over time as I considered its aesthetic, psychological and financial implications. Would a window just here look best, from inside the room, from outside the house? Did I want to create a cave-like feeling, with small steps? Or an expansive-feeling room, with many steps? And how much would the window I imagined or the many footsteps cost? But, for now, just now, I needed to commit myself to drawing even one footprint.

After beginning that morning in class with the footprint, I then had to begin to draw all the other room lines inside of it. I had to decide how many rooms I needed, how many walls. Where should the doors be? Where should I eat? Where read? What rooms should be next to which others? As a novice designer I had as yet nothing to guide me but my own unconscious experiences of walking in such rooms. I would have to summon this. Then I'd have to think about where or whether I wanted to follow whatever I sensed of rules. For example, did I want, as chief cook, to be isolated from guests in a separated kitchen—what did such space partitioning do? From this morning at class on, every room I entered I'd now begin to pay attention to. I watched how rooms helped people move about. I considered their height and breadth (I learned the dimensions of my gait and the width of my hand, in case I couldn't pull out a tape measure). I was becoming an amateur social scientist, psychologist, and architect all at the same time.

Christopher Alexander speaks of the terror those of us face who try to design a whole house: "to give birth to such a whole seems like a *monumental* task: it requires that the creator think, from nothing, and give birth to something whole: it is a vast task, forbidding, huge; it commands respect; we understand how hard it is; we shrink from it, perhaps, unless we are very certain of our power; we are afraid of it."[20] Alexander's aim is to coax us out of this terror of conceiving of our own "house wholes." He attributes this collective terror to a misperception of the house, as of any work of art, as a mysterious "creation," when in fact a well-working house is a "system" of "simple rules." If we are patient in following them, the house will form. His project is to break down these rules, rules, which he argues, are archetypal features of good houses. Alexander's archetypes, once I began to learn them, helped me *see* the rooms I visited as if for the first time.[21] Why was I drawn to one room and not another? Because the first had light coming in from two and not just one side—and light helps us see others more clearly (Pollan 1997, 77). Why was a window seat in a bay window so inviting? Because it meets our human needs for a balance between sociability and some privacy. Each detail of a room began to interest me— ceiling height? A casement as opposed to a double-hung window? A pair of casements that opened out onto a garden?

Thinking about rooms I changed how I saw not only them but also my own body's response to them. I felt less isolated. I felt myself more of a public body—and an historical one as well.[22] As I thought more about "bathroom," where it should go, how many, I saw that my "I" was part of a specific culture and an economic class that had already pre-choreographed some of my design "choices." Although I knew abstractly that some of my *thinking* patterns were historical and cultural, this is what I'd studied and taught, I did not think until then about the ways in which my *body* was similarly so. In putting a bathroom *inside* the house, for example, I was saying I belong in this time and place. My Swedish-farmer great-uncle's outhouse, his only plumbing on his New York state farm, would not do. And in putting *three* bathrooms in my house, one accessible only through a "master" bedroom, I was saying to myself as well as to others: this house belongs to people of a certain class. Similarly, when I had to decide on the house's siding (wood shingles for the first house) as I drew the elevations, I had to decide how far apart these exterior wood shingles should be spaced. I chose to have what is called a "6" exposure." Since each shingle is 18" long, the smaller the exposed portion, the more shingles one needs to use and so the more expensive the siding. Because I chose a smaller "reveal" of the shingles, 6" rather than 7" or 8", because I'd chosen thus more shingles, I was subtly communicating to myself and others driving by that this was an "expensive" house. A colleague building his own house in New England reminded me of the importance of 6". What has always astonished me is how even people who don't know anything about a 6" exposure can still interpret the wealth of a house from its shingle spacing. Wearing siding is like wearing clothes. We are all expert, if often unconscious, interpreters.

Adding such expensive details even to my drawing newly focused for me that I chose to accede to this spell of culture. But not only the spacing of the shingle lines of the drawing showed me this. So did the empty white space on the paper all around the outside of the perimeter walls. I was designing a thickly clad house whose boundary would be breached only at the doors—and then only at my invitation. I knew that all those doors should be visible only from the road so as to discourage thieves breaking them down. I knew I would have to fasten locks to them. I knew that the white space outside the perimeter walls of the drawing could be hostile and that the house would need the protection of laws against illicit boundary crossing, against transgressing, the original meaning of trespassing: "to step across" (Mitchell 1998,10).

But at the same time, that white space on the paper outside the perimeter walls of my floor plan also signified to me an order *beyond* that of my culture and class: an order of nature. This drawn house would come to sit on ground. That blank white space signified that ground, that wider territory, of garden, of woods, of street. And only some of that land was owned by me, and then only temporarily, in my lifetime. There was an odd solace in that thought. I believed, hoped, that my later acts of landscaping would be ones of incorporating my house, of rectifying its presumption, of smoothing over, beautifying the iron mouth's gouges. I even at that design moment knew that landscaping for me would be a kind of sacrificial act, an act of appeasement, of placation, of celebration for the green things that survive the dozer's mouth, thieves' desires, my desires.

Perhaps it was constantly seeing the white space outside the footprint of the house that encouraged me to approach every detail on the floor plan with a kind of reverence, as if this plan, this project were in trust to me. If I were graced to be able to own land and be in this class, I'd need to take this all very seriously. Each design decision became important. I began to think about hallways as more than mere passageways, but as also lingering places, places in which I could slow the transition from one kind of room to another, and so become more conscious of what I did in each space as well as the space between them. I began to think about what I would see outside of windows—were they low enough to the floor so that, sitting, I could see the flowers on the ground? Were the windows large enough to bring in light and a calming view? Would the plants inside receive enough nourishing light? Did the windows fall in the right direction I was even then planning for the house—south or east or west places—so that I would use less of the world's available energy to heat and cool the house and so that, an early riser, I could wake to the streaking sunrise? Was the window in the right place in the room for the library chair I imagined, so that it could give my book light and others with me a sometimes needed sighting of a far-off horizon during pauses in conversation?

The shape of the whole house could, I also hoped, be a reassuring "materialization of spirit," my spirit, the spirit of all who worked there (Hale 1994, 76). I wanted to signal harmony, proportion, and so peace in the geometric lines of the house. I did not want to signal undue protection, and so encourage fear, with high walls, fences, and dense high shrubs. I wanted, rather the house to feel "open" to any outsider's gaze, with bay windows, porches. Inside, I wanted others to experience balance and the kind of open space and height that now, for many of us in America, cultivates serenity—as our lots shrink, our impulse is to open to the sky. I wanted to show visitors that each of us, man and woman, had private space, so helping others feel that our marriage and our social ideal valued this kind of balance and solitude. I wanted others to know we had a small, dark room that we dedicated only to meditation and prayer.

In drawing a house, in short, I was scripting a self that I knew to be even more connected with the material world on many levels, the socially visible world and the world of aesthetic form. Before I had believed that the "world" and even my own "body" were in some box out there that "I," as the mind that saw, contained.[23] I'd been raised, after all, in an unconsciously-held Cartesian view of the world, one in which matter, things, seem out there, and everything mindful and soulful seems somewhere else, disembodied, in the mind. And the second, mind, is far more important. In designing-to-build I began to shift my way of seeing. I began to escape a little from Cartesianism. I saw gradually, first in my mind, then on paper, then in a model, then in the real thing, that my body *was inescapably in place*. Focusing all the time on the body as I thought about the house, vision and matter, mind and body, became more and more a seamless fabric, their borders opening, their differences beginning to evaporate.

At the same time as "I" became placed, since I focused in drawing on the body moving, the body engaged in different rooms and activities, I also understood that I could never see the *whole* of the house at once. I would never see all the drawings at once, even as I would never occupy the whole house at any one moment. Rather I always experienced only a shifting array of parts. Similarly then, I could not know my own body as whole, but rather as an only partially visible assortment of parts. I presumed there was a unity, even as I presumed that "house" was discrete and unified. But I had to take this now on trust. Bachelard so astutely observes "the house furnishes us dispersed images and a body of images at the same time" (1958, 3). The house challenges the notion of a *knowable* unified body. And, as I gradually gave up this notion, I could see instead different activities of my body coming ceaselessly into view. The body, my "self," became defined more as a series of activities than as a single fixed thing. Like one who navigates a winding path, I was learning to register both "equilibrium" and "momentum" at the same time (Hiss 1990, 34).

When I drew my first house on that dining room table in the rented house, I took a year. And then I threw it out. We didn't know if we could afford to build, after all, given job uncertainties. By the time we knew that we could, we had changed our house minds. Our architect friend used to counsel me, "take a couple years to design, for you will change your mind." I never felt I wasted those hours in designing the first version. I became used to imagining. I became used to precision. By the time I built that first house, since I had come to know every turning of a wall in my careful fingertips, it was as if the pencil and the saw were the same. The pencil gave me confidence to use the saw. By the time I designed a second house, I could throw out many designs more readily. I had a software program that made it almost too easy to change dimension lines. But by then I did not need the patient teachings of the pencil.

The houses I would come to design are deeply implicated in the world around me. Their outside, as well as their inside, is not utterly unique. My body does not move within a space that it alone structures. It, rather, moves within space that is partly pre-arranged. Even though I designed the spaces, my designs took their place within some recognizable grammar of design current to my time and place. Some designers, professionals, especially gifted people, stretch this envelope. My houses did not. My houses are within the bounds of conventionality and they reveal both aesthetic and practical mistakes. I could not say, with the assuredness of Jung, that the houses I built reflected my soul's progression. For me the forms were always out there, shapes to be played with, adapted, but not *my* creations. I felt really as if I were a gatherer. I knew that I didn't want one of those ready-made house designs in the house plan books that have been widely available ever since the turn of the nineteenth century when a building boom followed the Civil War. Once mortgage money began to be available, once the banks became partners in home ownership, the era of standardized taste began; predictable, "saleable" houses became the norm (Wright 1981, 202). Once I'd looked into the empty cardboard model on the table, I turned away from the glossy photos and news-printed designs in these contemporary "pattern" books. I would study some of these floor plans for ideas. But I had to be the one to gather my house design.

To gather my design, I turned to the grammar I knew the most consciously, one which I came to know through my apprenticeship at the Shelter Institute. This grammar favored energy efficiency, cost savings, and ease for the builder, who was also supposed to be the homeowner and the one expected to repair the house. So, for example, I tried to stack the plumbing all in one interior, so-called "wet" wall. That way a pipe would be less apt to freeze and, if a pipe leaked, the leak would be contained. I also tried to minimize corridors and maximize solar gain in the winter months. Rooms could be any shape or size, as could windows—in fact this was desirable, but the whole design should be energy-efficient and friendly with the earth.

While Shelter's concerns consciously influenced my design, a number of unconscious patterns also erupted in me. Some of these were as idiosyncratic and as small as the love of a certain window style. I continue with surprise to discover the roots of my preferences in my past. In attending a college reunion recently, as I approached from a wooded path my old 1930s brick residence hall, one I particularly loved, I saw before me across the expanse of lawn the glassed-in first floor study protruding slightly from the rest of the four story structure. A row of Palladian, sometimes called "round-top," windows topped each French door or floor-to-ceiling window. I suddenly realized, "ah, yes, this is why I wanted Palladian windows upstairs." I don't even remember noticing those windows while I lived in those dormitories. But the architectural detail lived an underground life in me, the study, a sign of some collective student attention to contemplation, its fronting a sweep of lawn, promising solitary walks across it or a serene distance as one gazes across it looking up from a book. Now I awake to look out of a large Palladian window which fronts the tree tops and the sky beyond, my bedroom a promised refuge for journal writing, dreams, night visions, the moonlit or sun-flooded sky, a promise of an endless serene space. Then, as now, I must have been stunned by the effect, when seated within, of an arc framing a tree line, the arc a kind of dome of the sky within the house paralleling the arc of sky beyond the tree line, and the effect, when approaching from without, of an arc framing what the inward eye knows are necessarily higher than the code-mandated ceilings within.

Once I'd gathered a few design rules and preferences, I needed to consider with my husband the kinds of areas we'd like in the house and which of them needed to be enclosed and which needed which exposure. I'd also need to think about which rooms should be next to which others. Where did my study belong? How near the common rooms? Which exposure?

Then I needed some overall container for all these ideas. I needed a defining shape for the house. This isn't how Jung built his house. It's not what Wright recommended. But I needed a shape, simple, serene, *whole*. Two of them immediately seemed right to me given our past. One container was a New England house form. This was the architecture in which we had grown. Over the years the capes and saltboxes became beautiful to me in their stability and pure simplicity. Many of our development houses, of whatever price, have no distinguishing shape, no clean lines, no shape of which one can say, that is Tudor, or that is a mid-west farmhouse, or that is a bungalow. Architect Jonathan Hale claims that these development houses lack a pattern, a harmonious design, proportion; in the disconnectedness of their patterns, they mirror for us a disconnectedness in our own life form (1994, 2).

I wanted a house that had a nameable shape and one that, furthermore, was not just like one nearby. I also wanted a shape that evoked memory, and the plain New England styles among which I'd grown up did this. Living my first thirty years in old New England towns, visiting museums like Sturbridge Village, reading books like Sarah Orne Jewett's *Country of the Pointed Firs* had etched these simple shapes deeply within. In searching for the design for our first house, it was in driving around Jamestown Island in Rhode Island one summer afternoon that my husband and I both realized that it was the utter simplicity and quiet of the cape style that pulled us toward it. We'd already designed a more modern house after one in a book about homebuilders. In an afternoon we threw it out.

At the same time, another kind of container emerged as we opened ourselves to what the whole of this house might look like. By accident, we'd heard of "house kits" which used timber frame construction. We'd been told they were inexpensive and good for do-it-yourselfers. A timber frame, or post and beam, is one of the oldest forms of a house. In this construction style, a few large timbers do what many small sticks of wood now more commonly do in the houses built since the 1830s (Wright 1981, 15). In the 1630s in the United States, large trees were plentiful and communities were close-knit so there was always labor available to help lift the heavy timbers hewn from it into place. Gradually, however, post and beam fell out of favor. It was less amenable to mass production, easy transport, and ease of erection by a small crew without the benefit of a crane. Then, too, once fiberglass insulation replaced the older, less efficient forms of blocking cold air from entering the house (lath and plaster), if one wanted to build a timber frame that used this thicker insulation, one would have to build, in effect, "two" frames to form the house's envelope: one, the timber frame, the other a "stick-built frame," or one that uses 2x4 or 2x6 studs between the vertical timbers, so that the factory-produced insulation could be stapled between these studs. Timber frame houses became, thus, very expensive to build. With the advent of new systems of insulation for refrigeration buildings, however, all of this changed. Large sheets of rigid insulation were glued between exterior sheathing and the interior finish material, often drywall. Someone had the innovative idea of adapting this insulation system to the timber frame structure in the 1970s and almost overnight small timber-frame kit companies emerged. What appealed to us was not only the cost of these kits, but also what they promised the owner-builder in the way of a completed shell. The company would come in and erect the frame of the house, spline the panels together and screw them around the outside of the frame, cut out holes for doors and windows and then install those, and even apply siding and roofing if one wished (many companies contract whatever parts the owner wishes). Now enclosed against the weather, the house is ready for an owner-builder to tackle the interior.

These timber frame kits attracted me immediately. They were practical, yes, from my point of view. But there was more to their appeal. I sensed that if I had to wait too long for the shell to be enclosed, which I would have had I used conventional framing, I might lose momentum—or try to tackle more of this part of the project than was wise given the house's height and the steep pitch of the roof. The kit idea gave me, working often alone on the first house, unskilled, scared, a jump start. It promised me some instant, visible, vertical whole by which I could know that a house was indeed forthcoming.

There were other things about the timber frame kit idea that appealed to me. The timbers acted as a horizon, a boundary, for the design. They provided necessary constraints. The timber framers I know say that they can frame any design with timbers. But I also learned from them that if I designed the house within certain parameters, the cost would be significantly less. Cost was absolutely an issue, but I think almost as compelling was the idea that I would be given design parameters. So I learned what the framers found ideal. I learned that the dimensions of the house should be divisible by four, since plywood came in 4x8 sheets and plywood formed the exterior sheathing of the stress-skin panels. I learned, for the first house (since at that time the timber framers had to make their own panels; now there are factories that do this and they can efficiently produce a wider range of panel shapes and heights) that it was cheapest in terms of labor and materials if my ceilings were 8' high and the widths of the house's sides were divisible by four, since 4x8' panels would need to be screwed in to the frame.. I learned that the fewer the odd angles and bump-outs, the easier (and cheaper) for the framers. I learned that a 12/12 roof pitch (or a 45 angle) was preferable because of the ease of cutting this angle. And I learned that the framing members themselves had structural limits. Our first house was framed in a hard wood, red and white oak, and it used traditional joinery, meaning that pockets were "mortised" out, ready to receive the chiseled protrusions of "tenons" of adjoining members. Then angle braces and collar ties, attached not by nails or steel, but rather by oak pegs, would work to keep the frame from "racking" or twisting. The maximum unsupported span in any room could be 16'. Our second house was framed in a soft wood, Douglas Fir. The Hennins, who built this frame, had developed a system of modifying (and strengthening) this traditional frame (a modification in fact introduced into timber framing by the nineteenth century). They used steel angle braces to attach the joists to the carrying beams. With this modification, steel being exponentially stronger, the joists, even using a softer wood such as Doug Fir, could span twenty feet unsupported by any post. Furthermore, I learned that 10 or 12' "units" perpendicular to these 16 and 20' spans were, again, the most economical to frame. These parameters, of height, of size of units, of uninterrupted walls and a steep roof, gave me, for the first house, my cape, and, for the second, my saltbox, which is essentially a cape with a lean-to off of one side. I'd never played with tinker toys as a child, but playing with these "pieces" in my mind was something I could get. It was like geometry. I was comforted by its angular simplicity.

    Yet the timber frame system offered me more than a kind of manageability, a geometrical simplicity of design, more than safety.

One snowy January day, my mother and I visited the first timber frame house I'd seen in Vermont, a house strangers opened to us at the request of their local framing company that we were considering using. I recognized a new, looked-for stillness within, a new sense of rootedness, of being at rest. Perhaps it was partly Vermont, the acres of snow-filled fields outside the window, the birdfeeders near the window I can yet see years later, the books lying familiarly about on the tables. Or maybe it was only the frame itself. I do not know. But after that moment, I needed the reassurance of such a frame, one entirely visible from the inside of the house. I needed to see the mortised joints, the pegs, the steel hangers, the bolts that secured the frame together so vigorously. I loved the irregularity in the wood, the knots, the checks. Though our frames were planed, I still could feel, and feel yet the energy of those trees in the house. It is a strong energy, like tree energy. I calculated that a single post in our first house was holding up 32,000 pounds. In our second house, four valley rafters meet, unbolted, at a single point in the middle of the cathedral ceiling, their angles planed so they can neatly greet each other in the center, forty feet off the ground. Pat Hennin, to get the four corners to meet, delivered three strong taps on one downstairs supporting post with his sledge hammer and it slid into place, where it rests still, unmoving. But, paradoxically, despite all this visible tension in any timber frame, because it is still, because it won't move, because it is perfectly balanced, it is restful in its rest. Wrapped in a blanket of thick insulation, it is profoundly quiet as well.

        This timber frame gave me one other gift as I was beginning building. It gave me the promise that, since all the interior partitions I would later build were non-load bearing, they could be moved. If I made a mistake with my floor plans, I could change them. Of course, after each house was up, I realized this would take a little work (new drywall, rerouting electrical wires), but I liked the possibility of being able to change them. Then too, when the timber framers left me alone in a protected shell, I could also redo the floor plan that I'd already worked so many hours at. Once I was in the space, once I could see the light coming in the windows, once I absorbed the particular energy of this space created by this light and the heights of the ceilings and the peaked roof, I made changes. I would take out a door to the den in the first house, and also rearrange a closet to take advantage of a balcony for the bedrooms. In the second I would add a small wall to make the dining room area's sitting space more private, more contained. It was like being given endless second chances. It was the promise of revision.

One lives in the house one designs long before one's feet touch the floor. The real house always surprises, but it is already familiar. I knew it better than I knew my own body. The thing I did not know about the real house, however, was that as the house left my imagination, as the drawings got sent off to the permits office and then the timber framers, electrician, plumber, my house was going to be placed on the land, in a neighborhood, become that thing built by other hands along with my own. This was a hurdle unlike the others, ones of dreaming of building, of tools, of designing. I could have done all of that and not been concerned about the place of the house. But knowing its place, thinking about its consequence in that place, would deepen the burden of house for me. The sense of burden grew after the second house was done. Only then could I think one day, "how many birds' lives did I disturb?" I couldn't think it at first when I built. Now that I have, the house is a heavier thing.

VI

The House's Place

*There is no place that is not haunted by many different spirits hidden there in silence, spirits one can 'invoke' or not...These 'spirits' do not **speak** any more than they **see**. This is the sort of knowledge that remains silent.*
                                        --de Certeau[24]

    It is
not modern enough, the sound the wind makes
stirring a meadow of daisies....
    think twice
before you tell anyone what was said in this field
and by whom.

Your memory is not
powerful enough, it will not
reach back far enough.
                                        --Louise Gluck, *The Wild Iris*[25]

I already live in the landscape.
                        --Merleau-Ponty[26]

The cardboard model sitting on the table, the one I crafted from the drawings of the house, the one I carried around with me for months from room to room, now becomes small. The earth is being prepared for the real house. Yet the earth cannot be moved around. And it comes with its own history.

I already knew the houses' landscapes before I built. I walked the Maryland meadow for two years, in sodden spring, in Sweet Gum-reddened fall. As a child I had played on the hill on which our second house now sits, and I knew stories of my father's venturing there from time to time. I knew myself differently in these places before I built the houses. I knew myself then only as only a visitor. I am certain I stepped on worms and bugs as I walked. But I am more certain that when the building began, silent havoc was wreaked on nature. I have a friend who is a Jain. The house she built has boardwalks over the grass so that no one will trample on any living thing. But I wonder always how she reconciled herself to excavation, to trucks, tramping people, or the inevitable desecration of deer pathways and birds' nests.

The new house, whose growing history the owner builder does know, comes with an unfathomable land history that she doesn't. And yet as I heard the conventional language of place and often repeated it as I built, it was as if that land had no history. The county called the land a "lot" and a "parcel." On paper the land was an empty box, marked off by dimensioned boundary lines. It is easy to begin to think the land is "virgin," and we its masculine claimers. With surprise and perhaps distaste we find some trash in the grass, or an arrowhead in the leaves. With surprise we awake in our new house to find it haunted with what people in the eighteenth century called the *genius loci,* the spirit native to the place.

Perhaps some rudimentary attentiveness to these already presiding spirits of place comes more readily to anxious owner-builders who, moving ahead line by line, step by careful step, are often looking for reassuring, welcoming signs in the landscape. Perhaps actions that require patience, such as drawing, slow the step. If you think you're going to cut the tree down, perhaps guessing its rings, its seasons of innocent growth, you might be reluctant. In his book, *House-Dreams,* Hugh Howard talks about how he and his wife found the land for their house. They'd been thinking about building a house for years. One day they walked a piece of land and she sighted a wildflower, a mayflower—a flower which Howard's mother used to point out to him on walks in his New England childhood. The flower, rare now because it resists being disturbed, became for them a symbol of what they wanted their house to be: a house that belonged to this particular place—and one that, as well, wouldn't disturb the mayflower. They found when they opened to the silent presence, the mayflower, a memory. Here was a spirit, of mother, not anchored in this particular place but in a flower in that place. Howard builds their house there.

Flowers are, admittedly, easier to welcome than previous owners of a house one buys. Many people don't even care to know much about their houses' (or lands') past. I've only come across one book devoted to tracing the stories of the writer's house's prior inhabitants: *If These Walls Had Ears.* More typically I hear people offer very brief narratives of their house's history. When we were selling our first house, I mentioned I would write a history of our building it and send it along. The couple was lukewarm. I never sent it. In some ways I didn't want to pass on our history either. I remember once speaking with a newly married woman who had just purchased the home of another woman I had known who had recently died, in her '50s, of cancer. I remarked to the newly married woman how lovely it was that she could move into this other woman's house. Her immediate and acerbic response startled me: "well, it's not her house, it's our house now." She did not want to know anything about the previous owner, whose planted perennials she was, even then, caring for. She'd thrown up her own boundaries in this old house in order to grow her own thick mollusk shell. For this new couple, buying their first house, there understandably should be no equally vibrant past to the house, no hidden spirits. A new young couple, they needed their own story of Eden and their first house. Having swept it, having kept it, it was only theirs now. It's hard, even harder in our time of buying the new, to share the intimate space of an already once-inhabited house.

Mircea Eliade reminds us that even for those who prefer to ignore hidden spirits, for those who prefer to see space as entirely mundane, or "profane" (which, he reminds us, is a place term itself, meaning, literally, the place "before the apparition" of the numinous being in the temple), place resists (1957, 22-3). The married couple must occasionally have a passing and startling thought of the other woman's hands once touching a doorknob or digging in the perennial border. In that split second they know their hands will leave the knobs and the perennials perhaps survive them. They will know that they too will die, that they are not secure in their house on the earth, that another will one day be reading silent signs of their once habitation. Over my summers spent in the Maine cottage, summers filled with accumulated furniture and knick-knacks, I've had to carefully weave a path between saving signs of the previous owners, whom I'd known and wish to remember, and filling the place with new things. Always in the Maine house, with every stained cross-stitched 1930s laundry bag I throw out, I'm far more aware of the ways I violate the presence of the dead than I am while living in our newly built one.

When the poet W.B. Yeats purchased the old tower in Ballylee in 1917, he opened himself to history and landscape. And his neighbors helped him. One brought him the customary gifts of his place: "the 'seisin,' or symbols of possession: a bunch of grass from the field, a handful of thatch from the cottage, a stone from the castle wall, and two florins from the sale of a fallen tree."[27] The ritual must have reminded Yeats that the earth went before and would go after him. He was but its temporary tenant, one in a succession. Such a gift must have reminded him that he should reciprocate, give back to the earth. But another's bringing pieces of earth to him had to reassure him that earth was also greeting him in his tower. Although he does not speak specifically of the previous owners of his tower, in his poem "The Tower" he invites a procession of people he has known over time to climb his stairs one by one, as if they possess this place with him. The tower is the place of lineage and friendship. The poet turns to "images and memories/From ruin or from ancient trees" to ask them his pressing question: what to do with a decaying body? (1953, 195) For Yeats, the memory of those past reminds him of his own mortality.

Our contemporary rituals and our conventional language around buying and building don't support this kind of respect for and awareness of hidden spirits in house or land. House, land are "its" for us. When we decide to buy a house, the real estate "deal" is "executed" at a "closing," an affair punctuated by the sound of pens scratching at a sheaf of papers that needs signing. Real estate agents and lawyers orchestrate the order of events, telling us where to sign. We peruse the closing sheet, which contains all of the figures, and never read the full legal descriptions of those who formerly held title. People are, despite this show of orderliness, jittery. I've heard of arguments erupting. There is no place afforded the expression of intense emotions in this all but emptied public ritual. One merely walks in to the room an owner, and out of it a trespasser, or vice-versa. I've been at both ends, but never felt the solemnity, the terrifying rift in the passage of ownership, acknowledged. The day I alone signed off our ownership on the first house we'd built, the house I knew every square inch of, I remember walking to my car afterwards feeling all the life draining from my legs. At the least, we could have shared champagne, toasting each other and the house. If we shared a community history, we could have had a party at the house, with all of the neighbors joining in. If we shared a religious tradition, we could have offered prayers or "waked" the house. As it was, we were not close and knew no way to help us to come closer. It took me two years before I could drive by that house. I am still not ready to knock on the door, twelve years later. Now that it's been sold again, it feels like my hopelessly lost child.

Without the support of shared rituals to help root me in the hidden-ness, the otherness, of the emerging house on the land, living in a culture that encourages "my" sense of possession of the land, and so starved for a house, my desires became Promethean. Rather like the woman who wouldn't hear of her predecessor's planting what she thought of now as "her" flower garden, I became, for a time, caught up in some illusion of myself as the shaper of the place. I was following my hero, the woman who wouldn't get off the dozer. I was at the house site every moment, studying the mason or the plumber. I did not trust any of them with "my" house (I also, of course, did not trust my own knowledge in hiring them or in being able to discern that they knew what they were doing).

They, of course, sensed my anxiety. Their humoring me helped sometimes coax me out of it. I'd once told Clyde, our mason, how worried I was about Jerry, our plumber, a man he knew in town. Jerry one day had seriously proposed drilling a three inch hole in our six inch beam and I'd not forgotten this (this plumber had never plumbed a timber frame house before and I'd already heard enough stories about the divide between carpenters and plumbers). One day while Clyde was working on the third floor building the brick chimney and I was way out in the meadow, he started up his chain saw. He told his helper, "this will bring her running." Indeed it did. He had a good laugh, as did I. He was teaching me, I now see, that I could loosen up a bit, and I also now see that his feeling he could play this joke on me meant that he was trying to help me. I was fortunate that many of them did adopt me despite my tendencies to play the general. In a way, I suspect that my inability to hide my anxiety won them over—as did my being a woman whom most of them, traditional southern country Maryland men, were used to protecting.

Would I have been different in building the first, more leisurely, more aware of the power of place, of the land, less irritable and bossy, had I not been building as I was, in isolation from family members, other owner builders in the area, other women? Would that have been enough to make me less singularly possessive of that first house? Would that have made me more responsive to the spirits of those who worked beside me, spirits which did later inhabit that house? Perhaps not. I would also need a different culture, one that more actively and humbly loved land and honored working with others on it. David Kline, a contemporary Amish farmer, records the lovely tempo of his working life in *Great Possessions: An Amish Farmer's Journal.* Although his is not an account of building a house, his story invites a parallel. Early each spring, he says, he and his son, with the team of oxen, "turn the mellow soil, feeling its coolness and tilth. We take pleasure in the transient water pipits and pectoral sandpipers feeding on the freshly turned earth abounding with life. As we rest the teams, I listen to the joys and uncertainties of teenage years" (1970, xix). He is not thinking about owning this land. He is thinking about the birds and about the emerging life of his son. He sees himself as a steward of place. He has his community to support him, one which has trained his feet to move gently in the fields, his eye to notice the pipit, and his ears to hear his son speaking.

If I knew no supportive rituals to mark beginnings and endings of legal ownership and to help me as a new owner-builder, one sprung not from Amish roots but from Swedish and Dutch farmer roots now all but hidden from memory, I also moved under the spell of regulatory practices and language that could not nurture any awareness of "hidden spirits" in the land or in the new house. At the very beginning of the building process, I had to learn to negotiate the complex system by which the permit to dig the cellar hole is at last issued. As is true of the language used in selling real estate, so too the language used in the permits office has been emptied of all affective meaning. The once commodious word "land," a word suggesting its difference from "sea," and so a place populated with all sorts of animals and plant life, a word in ancient languages that means variously "enclosure," "church," "heath," "moor," is now vacant. The land from now on is termed a "building site," "my" building site, a thing looked at for the sole purpose of transforming it. Or, sometimes it is a "map" and "lot" number, a place defined solely by legal property lines recorded in the town or county land records. And so, we come to think that the house to come will be on a map that we know. We believe it is tangible, written up, secure, and small, owned by a bank, taxed by a town. As the house is nearly finished, at the other end of the permit process, that land will change its name again, from "site" or "lot" to a place lacking "landscaping." Without minimal landscaping (generally the planting of grass), one cannot get a "C.O.", or "certificate of occupancy," that for which every owner-builder strives. Without it one can neither occupy the house legally nor finalize any mortgage. "Land," in this language of the permits office, is designated as a passive receptacle, a thing defined by lack, waiting for all the appropriate parties to work on it: the building and landscape architects, if there are any, and the owner who orchestrates, builds and hires others. Completion is defined in these minimalist ways and, once achieved, the case is closed for the permit office, the bank, and the taxing authority.

Some owner builders work with architects who buffer the difficulty of navigating the permits office and so the emptiness of these words. At least architects are supposed to be the builder's advocate—and the professionally certified drawings will calm the anxiety of some clerk in the office who is anxious at suddenly having to perform mathematical calculations to determine whether your timber frame design meets code. Is the roof strong enough to withstand the area's snow? Are the floors strong enough to support people and furniture? For a more conventional house, a "stick-built" house as they are called, a house made out of 2x4s or 2x6s, there are charts for the officer to consult. But there are none for timber frames. And so the clerk needs someone, an architect, an engineer, to cover for his or her liability.

Architects also can begin to reorient owner builders to the land at least, if not to those who will build the house. But even the architect's relation to the land is as artist working with clay. The architect looks to gather the land up into the house. Architects typically speak of both land and, more rarely, the surrounding community as forces to be integrated into the aesthetic design of the house. For them the house is still primary, an other to be subordinated to their design, brought under their artistic control. Not now a commodity, as it is for the real estate agents and the banks, it is an aesthetic object. Architect Charles Moore, for example, has identified four ways in which the architect can view the potential house's relationship to the land, only one of which, the first, approaches some relationship of respect for the earth. At one end of the spectrum, the house can be made to seem to "merge" with the land, be inconspicuous within its surroundings. The house Frank Lloyd Wright designed for the Kaufmanns at Falling Water seems to rise up out of the waterfall beneath it as if it were a log thrown up in the air: the living room shares space with a large rock, and a set of suspended stairs to the stream beneath is visible through a glass hatch. This perhaps most famous of American-architect designed houses is perhaps also the best-known example of a house merging with its site. At the other end of the spectrum Moore maps, the house can be made to seem to "claim" the land, being "intentionally different" from it, often assuming the shape that Wright criticized as the box, with the strength of the claim dependent on the size of the house and the vistas it fronts. Moore gives as an example the large houses on Edgartown's beach in Martha's Vineyard which appear to sit on the dunes and beaches, radically different structures from the beach, with their angular height, their multiple windows which invite the outsider to imagine the views from within, and the various gables and Palladian windows which draw the viewer's attention upward to the peak. Moore names two other subsets of claiming: a house can "enfront" a part of the land, usually a street or a garden, when its architecture addresses some particular feature of that side of the house. The house can also "surround" the land when it encloses or partially encloses an outdoor space. Of these four choices, it is, not surprisingly, more traditional in our acquisitive culture to "claim" than to "merge" with it the land (1974, 188-9).

Witold Rybcynski's thought about designing his barn so that it will fit with the other structures in his neighborhood speaks of a different kind of merging, a merging with the community. He says that he did not start out this way. Rather he had intended to create a "modern" house, a house that expressed only him. He'd learned about "innovation" and to prize "difference" in architect school. A chance remark by an English painter turned him around: "'Your house doesn't look much like the other houses on the island'" (1989, 81-3). Fitting in is a powerful experience, both for the dweller and for neighbors, particularly if it is a pleasing, aesthetic fitting in. Some whole communities, particularly older ones, argues Jonathan Hale, had a finer intuition about aesthetic proportion. They saw in the "old way," a way in which each building was harmonious so that "one could walk down any street" and feel that it was "alive." Following uncodified but known rules of proportion and balance, these houses created aesthetic communities. Walking in this kind of community, one can feel the "mystery," the "promise," the "intrigue" and the interconnection among dwellings (1994, 1, 5). Merging, fitting, the old way of seeing: these open the door to some relationship between house and place.

While I was actively building either house, I did not think about what I was doing by building in a particular place. I was too anxious, overwhelmed at the house, to do so. But I did know, even at the beginning, that no one was addressing out-loud the invisible underground currents I was feeling inside. I was in contact with practical people, real estate people, permit people, whose task was to get the job done. The only moments at the beginning which opened me to another way of seeing the house occurred as I sat at my desk at the Shelter Institute. There we not only thought about things such as nails and wells, but also those larger questions, "what will be the place of your house in the universe?" "What kind of house will you draw to put on the land?" I struggled in my building journals after I left the space and solace of the class and began my own silent process with my seemingly unnamable and isolated feelings, of wonder, of curiosity, of agony for the destruction I was just beginning to know that I was about to cause. What new ritual could I propose at the land closing to solemnify this event and not risk being thought odd? What alternative could I offer for the asked-for "site" plan and not be refused a permit? I followed the rules. I walked away weak-kneed from the land closing and angry at the man I'd hired shortly thereafter to diminish the wondrous meadow, filled with fireflies, by remapping it as thin contour lines and a box of a house onto special paper, "Mylar," the blueprints from which he'd then ask his wife to print up, since he, as he put it, "was allergic to the dangerous chemicals."

I was, in my own faltering and largely unconscious ways at this beginning, becoming aware that this land felt qualitatively different to me from other places I'd lived since childhood, apartments I'd rented whose land I never bent down to study. At first perhaps it was only because I knew *I* was about to change this land from field to a house place. Something about my responsibility for this transformation I had set in play began to stop me, making me begin to bend down to study the timothy grass that would soon be dug up.

I did not at that point in my life, at the time of beginning the first house, think of myself as a religious or even a particularly spiritual person, although I was I think in these small ways beginning to acknowledge again, as I had as a child, the presence of an invisible world. What was under that grass? What would my building do? What would it look like from the sky, this about-to-be forever altered landscape?

Then too, alone, afraid as a young builder, once the house was underway I found that I had to be quieter and more attentive to each of my movements than I had ever been before. I had to do this just to survive each step I was taking—not only because the consequences of not doing so could be dangerous, hurtful for my body, but also because I did not know what I was doing. My husband and I had designated a space within the new house for a small meditation room. I would go to sit there even before I'd built the walls to surround it whenever I felt overwhelmed. I remember the day I'd called the plumber to begin his work. He came over to begin. He was astonished that I had no interior walls in the bathroom area to which he could affix his pipes. I would have to build them that evening. They were my first walls. They were small walls. They were monumental to me. I sat to meditate on the rough floor. I built them.

Perhaps the space in which one meditates is already sacred, open to the revelation of what Eliade calls "an absolute reality" (1957, 20-21). But I would not have put it quite that way, then. What I was more and more aware of at the beginning was a feeling, an extraordinary concentration of energy, in this single spot on earth. It was like a powerful magnet that stilled my mind so that I could get around my fear and move step by step. I had walked into the Shelter Institute class. I had begun to pick up new tools. I had filled a crude cardboard model with pictures from my imagination. And here, on one grassy clump of meadow, all of it, all those hours, all that dreaming, was going to become visible, not only to me, but to others and it would change this land. I'd never had any experience quite like this before. When I wrote, the page was visible only to me. I didn't think how I was altering paper. Eliade says that "if the world is to be lived in, it must be founded" (1957, 22). I don't think I was founding a new world in my writing then. But now I felt I was, for the first time, *founding* a world in which my work would be visible to others and it would have visible consequences for the earth. I was "undertaking the creation of the world that [I] had chosen to inhabit" (Eliade 1957, 51). I was making my center of the world.

It's not as if I thought I were building a temple. I knew that this house was too private for that. But I knew that it was at the same time an in-between space, in between my past experience of place and the few sacred experiences of place I had had. I later recognized this new in-between place as that Eliade speaks of as the place between the profane and the sacred, the threshold place. It is the place we all long to inhabit. It is the place of the "break in plane" between the two cosmic orders, the profane and the sacred. It is where we wait to step across. In building a house, I was building a door.

The story of growing into this in-between space by creating the place of the house is a jagged one. There is no simple trajectory. It happened, like heat lightning, flaring up here and there, seemingly without warning. To sketch this slowly developing consciousness, to tell of it, I need a whole new language and way of arranging the words. If I were graphically inclined, I could perhaps draw a series of changing "maps" of the land, maps sketching its geographical or botanical evolution, maps positioning it politically, socially and historically.[28] Or I could provide a series of mandalas, maps of my changing unconsciousness of the land. In words, I need to use a montage rather than a story. And it is a montage that is still assembling and reassembling because my experience of the land continues to shift. It is changing, even now, as I look at it, as I write about it all these years later.

I had no rituals, no tradition, no one bringing me a local version of the seisin brought to Yeats at the beginning to help support me, to help me open and accept this brand new kind of place. When most of us approach public sanctified spaces we know they are to be reverenced. We acknowledge that silent, not easily accessed spirits dwell there. We mark this acknowledgement and invite presence by behaving differently, often in small ways, according to actions we have learned from others. We take off our shoes. We lower our heads. We become silent. Perhaps we fall to our knees. We so carefully, conscious of the very nerves in our fingertips, put in our mouths the bread and hold so gently the cup of wine. All these are gestures signifying our radical humility and our readiness to wait. Through our special gestures in sacred spaces we properly "site" ourselves in relationship to these places as people who want to receive and who are grateful for that.

Not surprisingly, though, I initially walked the first "house lot" as if it were a nearly ordinary thing. I did not move, at that moment, with any intention. The listening began unsupported. Perhaps it is always like this for us living now in a spirit-vacated world. When Jung, on moving into the new house he built at Bollingen, heard the strange voices, he was not looking for them. He was sleeping or sitting one evening by the fire. Only when he fell asleep to dream of music, footsteps, voices, dark-clad figures, did he receive an answer: these were the spirits of departed folk. Later, when his daughter came to visit, she exclaimed: "'…you're building here? There are corpses about!'" (1989, 221-3). I think sometimes that the people who hear ghosts in their houses are yearning for this kind of contact with the silences, the past of their houses, their land. But to most of us these experiences come unbidden and so they disturb us. We know so few of the ancient rituals with which to intentionally approach land on which we wish to build a house and, lacking these to help prepare us, we also lack the spirit of receptivity.

There are stories of rituals from history and language that tell us that people once did accord the land on which a house was to be built the highest respect. Rybczynski chronicles some of these. The Ghanaian Nabdam farmers, for example, began the construction of buildings by consulting the ancestors and studying sacrificed animals in order to determine if the place were favorable. The Hindu, even today, dig a hole in the corner where the foundation will be and place in it holy objects, spices, water from the Ganges, this to acknowledge and ask pardon for the gesture of invading the land (1989, 78-9). Ancient peoples believed that every place was guarded by its own spirit, its "genius loci." This spirit they recognized as an "opposite," a "daemon," with which they had to come to terms if they were to dwell there. They had to understand what the place itself wanted to be. They tried to sense the "meanings potentially present" there (Norberg-Schultz 1979, 11, 18). We sense that they knew to ask Rilke's question, "Earth, isn't this what you want: to arise in us *invisibly?*" (2009, *Duino Elegy IX,* 337).

There is only one ritual from all of this now dimmed, rich history that persists into our famished time. This is the ritual known, but not understood,[29] by every framing carpenter: that of affixing a small evergreen tree to the last rafter, the rafter which completes the framing. In performing this act, the builder pays homage to the trees which gave their life for the house. Timber frame raising was a community event, a dangerous event, almost a religious event (Stilgoe 1982, 5-6). Once the roof beam was set, the carpenters pounded on the frame, calling for "wood." The master builder brought a fresh cut evergreen tree, women and children decorated it, and then paraded three times around the finished frame. There were minor variations of this—the saying of prayers and sermons, for example, about the builders' exalted calling, as well as toasts to the future of the house and family. When these were finished, the tree was raised, giving the frame the "life of a living tree."

I had to remind my builders to complete this ritual. I brought champagne. I knew it was important then. I know it is even more important now. They, I suspect, reveled more in the completion of the frame and the champagne. It was not, after all, their house. Perhaps if we had been a community building for each other, on land we all loved for itself, it would have been different.

I was not yet, in those early moments walking on that land that I thought might be house land, thinking of these things. I was thinking of the house itself in very practical terms. Would it be dry here? Would I have quiet? What would it look like in this place?

I was not, for example, thinking of the house as Henry Beston does in *The Outermost House.* Beston had a house built for him in 1925 on a fifty acre tract of dunes on Cape Cod. In writing about his house, his eye is most attentive to the house's surround. Though the monograph's title would seem to suggest a focus on the *house,* the description of the house and its specific location take up only several pages of the book. The book opens with a stirring, numinous description of the geological history of Cape Cod, gradually focusing in on the more specific and contemporary locale nearer Beston's typical vantage point of observation, which is the house and its immediate environs where he walked. Then Beston says, simply, "having known and loved this land for many years, it came about that I found myself free to visit there, and so I built myself a house upon the beach" (1928, 5-6). The ensuing description takes just a little over two pages. We learn only the number of rooms, the number of windows, a few details—the color of the wainscoting, the position of the fireplace, the method of getting drinking water, a few pieces of furniture, including a blue chest of drawers, and crockery. Then Beston quickly takes our gaze off of his house out to the four vistas it frames, "the four walls of the world" (9), dunes, marsh, distant cottages, ocean. Because he designed his house, his story is told in a different language and with different proportions than a professional architect would use. The house is not the center but the beginning, a warm, secure vantage point outwards to a seemingly endless horizon, a horizon that extends outward, upward, and downward. We cannot tell from his account if his house "seems to merge" or "claims." It is probably a "box" and so Wright would argue it "claims," but nothing in the prose suggests that Beston takes this attitude toward his dwelling. Like a field station, a tent, a cabin, it is not the house or even "his" fifty acres that consume him, but rather that which it fronts: "elemental things...fire before the hands...water welling from the earth...air...the dear earth underfoot"—all that we "lack" and are "sick" for (10). Beston's word painting is like Andrew Wyeth's *Her Room,* or Jamie Wyeth's *Fogbank,* paintings of houses which seem to be on the very edge of water, lookout houses. The painters draw our gaze through the open window, through the woman standing on the porch, out to the sea which seems to lap the very edges of the building. These are, like Beston's house, diaphanous, houses without boundaries, houses slipping into the ocean, as in fact Beston's did during a hurricane some years later.

As I approached the land for both of the houses I built, I was not so receptive to it, my house boundaries not so permeable. I did not see the house as a field station, a viewing point for the ocean of grass and trees about me. I did not see the land as already fully inhabited, by trees, animals, the resonant energy of the dead. Before commencing tree clearing (needed for the second house), I did not honor the trees, as a man I know does when he cuts them for firewood. He selects the tree, thinking less of its usefulness and ease of cutting for him, than of how the tree's absence will be felt by the other trees and by observers in years to come. He makes his choice, selecting a tree possible for him to cut, with good wood, yet one that is humble, one whose loss will be less marked, one whose life expectancy might perhaps seem shorter than that of neighboring trees or one whose being might prevent the other trees from thriving. He then performs an extraordinary gesture of love: he hugs the tree. Then he cuts it. Assuring himself of his solitude, he then falls to one knee and kisses the bleeding stump. He then finishes cutting up the wood and hauls it away, pleased with his work's being done, his needs met, yet regretting and remembering that his life requires taking that of another living thing. This man has seen the sacred in the tree. It is not that the tree is adored as a tree, but rather as what Eliade calls a "hierophany," a manifestation of the sacred (1957, 11-12).

I could have known of the power of tree cutting even though I met this man later in my life. I'd already read Frost and Hopkins.

In "On a Tree Fallen Across the Road," Frost writes: "The tree the tempest with a crash of wood/Throws down in front of us is not to bar/Our passage to our journey's end for good,/But just to ask us who we think we are/Insisting always on our own way so...." (1969, 238) Or Hopkins, whose anguished voice in "Binsey Poplars" seems to enter into the very pain of the trees on being cut: "All felled, felled, are all felled;/....O if we but knew what we do/When we delve or hew—Hack and rack the growing green!/....After-comers cannot guess the beauty been./Ten or twelve, only ten or twelve/Strokes of havoc unselve/The sweet especial scene...." (1986, 142)

But there was a veil between me and the anguish of the poets. My uncaring habits inclined me another way from any comforting ritual of honor and appeasement. And so I fled. The day the tree-cutters began to clear the lot for our second house, I hid in my childhood house across the field. I got in the car and drove away. Then I would have to go back to the lot, because our tree-clearer, now, ten years later, dead, would want to know which one next to take, which to save. I voted for saving many my husband wanted taken. He did not want trees too near the house. I'd rush to protect the young beech trees, remembering somewhere that their parent, the two hundred year old tree down by the stream in the back, had sheltered my childhood playing there. I'd tie red ribbons around their young stems, which seemed to me to be quivering with all of the noise around them, their fellows newly felled. Most of them were at least seventy five years old, seventy five years of patiently growing rings. I did not, however, hug them, or kiss them, or otherwise reveal my gratitude. I let them fall.

I was also, in arranging for the clearing, changing the view from my childhood house. First it began as a small clearing. Then it widened. Then we thinned the under story among the saved trees so we could see the far meadow. My natural tree house, my glade, was going, my once hidden place of retreat now more accessible to others. Settling, looking out, meant also looking in.

I walked in the same blindness when I witnessed the excavation of the patient meadow, the cellar hole for the first house. I knew nothing of the Pueblo Indians' custom of approaching excavations in the earth with reverence. I did not know that they knew these were dangerous, requiring prayers because spirits reside in the strata (Saile 1985, 100). The day the bulldozer arrived at the meadow of the first house, I was alone. I'd already imagined this moment many times as I'd sat in the untouched meadow, watching the timothy grass wave in the breeze. I'd imagined this noisy bulky awkward vehicle coming as a nearly sublime moment, a moment when all that had been in mind and in talk suddenly was to become bricks and mortar. I thought of the dozer as some divine messenger. Yet the moment it turned into the meadow to begin to cut for the driveway and then to excavate the cellar hole, I knew that we were also puny and noisy invaders. When John and I later crawled into the red clay cavern of the new cellar hole, whose musty, primitive smell I can almost remember now, something disturbed us. Not knowing to offer anything back to this gash in the earth we'd made, we had strange dreams for nights of pits and ancient deep monuments.

Perhaps I could not know more, do more, then. I needed to be focused on making a secure shell for my mollusk-like, woman body. I needed to imagine each shell as entirely free-standing, as continuing apart from either the field or hill into which they would burrow or the community of surrounding houses in which they would necessarily take their place. I was, I suppose, then closer to a radical "claimer" than a "merger," except that I wasn't, in staking my claim to the land, staking with chain saw and dozer, quite as bold as I could have been. I didn't feel I was carving my initials on trees as any school boy would have, or urinating on boundary markers as my dog does. I did not feel so entitled to territory. Rather I felt more like Woolf in *A Room of One's Own*, expecting to be turned away from walking any land at any moment, and so I rushed to claim some space for myself.[30] Like Woolf I could think only of getting into my house. This was as much as I could own—and I could own this *only* if I built it. As Woolf filled up her bookcases in her room with her reading in order to make it hers, so I knew I needed to fill the walls of my houses with my dreams and my sweat.

Perhaps it was not only my being a fearful woman novitiate carpenter that made me retreat imaginatively within my cardboard model, rather than opening out at that moment to the land and to the community. Perhaps no one can afford to consider the destruction one wreaks on the land in order to build a house—the upheaval of plants, the felling of trees, the noise to the birds, the disturbance of the deer's pathways, the breaking of ancient stones, the desecration of earth worms. George Eliot says that "If we had a keen vision and feeling of all ordinary human life, it would be like hearing the grass grow and the squirrel's heart beat, and we should die of that roar which lies on the other side of silence."[31] Perhaps one cannot ever fully contemplate the fragility of one's claims to own land that has always been owned before. Perhaps no one can fully think of the position the house takes within the community. Perhaps no one can move to build at all with a consciousness of all of these things. When the first timber frame in the Maryland meadow was being raised, my neighbor, who lived five hundred feet away, a man who later became my friend, would come over to watch. The timber framers had their radios blasting. I, who was sound sensitive, imagined he could not hear them. Nor could I think about how I was changing his view of an uninterrupted expanse of meadow, his only vista. I, simply, *had* to take up this space.

Now, however, having built the houses, having "unselved/The sweet especial scene," I need to try to "re-selve" that scene, now reconfigured, recognize the houses of my body fully placed in a landscape and a neighborhood. Having made the necessary shell, taken up residence, I can travel now through more space, can be *with* the acres and houses around me, the location. I can open the doors and windows, take a walk outside. I can expand my field of awareness so that I see not only "my house." I want to see beyond "mine." I want to be, in Martin Buber's words, in an "I-Thou" relation to this field and hill. I want to *see* the meadow and tree, the location, not as something that is an "impression," a whim of the "play of my imagination," but rather a thing that is "bodied over against me," something that "has to do with me, as I with it—only in a different way" (1958, 7-8). I need to know, in Hopkins' terms, the "inscape" of meadow and tree. "I" and "Thou" are fully necessary for each other, separate, yet connected. "Everything that lives is holy," says Blake.

And yet, human, we need limits, for each I, for each Thou. Edward Casey says that for each of us there is some invisible horizon, a boundary out there, at which our sense of what is our individual self stops. This is our place world, the world in which we know who we are. The house, within this horizon line, is for many of us one of our more important markers. Yet even it changes its nature for us. It sits on a moving horizon line. At times of our day or in our lives we see the house up close and it is good. It is a bounded shell, safe, lovely, private. This is the familiar, safe horizon. But at other times, harder times, the close house can threaten us. The house, Anne Troutman says, can assume shape as the sign of our primal fears, the manifestation of a terrified unconscious. The literary genre of the Gothic plays upon this fear of the corners of the house that is us. Troutman continues, "I imagine I am constructed of the various dwellings I have lived in over the years… To remember, to describe, to daydream about these spaces is one way I have of feeling whole, of grasping parts of myself that might otherwise be lost. The dwelling is a trust of my known and unknown selves." A place to expand our sense of self, a place to "defend the individual against the anxiety of being alone," this near place shifts shape (1997, 157, 149). At other times, we see the house from afar. This might happen as we view it from an airplane, or as we see it through the realtor's eyes, the one who is trying to sell it for us. We are always changing our viewing station, depending upon who we are at that moment.

The horizon line I knew beyond the Maryland house walls was coextensive with the property lines. The horizon did not extend out very far, and it did not go down very deep into the earth—because I wished to forget that cellar hole as the wood rose up to the sky. I would walk and re-walk those lines, planting one hundred white pine trees along its edges, as if to define my five acre meadow. I remember having little consciousness of the other houses around me except to notice their differences from my own. I would see that many of them were low to the ground, spread-out houses many of which were designed by one of the original residents, Charles Wagner, in the tradition of Frank Lloyd Wright. In fact, our realtor and Charles, good friends (he had designed her house), had taken us around to see some of these houses while we were designing and Charles looked over my drawings at several points in the two year designing process. We were being introduced to the neighborhood aesthetic. All Charles' friends, many of whom would become our friends, lived in his houses, one story affairs, with an open floor plan, minimally sloped roof, and stained wood siding--houses that seemed to merge with the land. Yet I resisted this subtle if loving pressure to conform. I insisted on an eighteenth century New England box, a cape forty feet tall to the peak. I had to have New England in Maryland. I was to pay for this, with a comment delivered at a party shortly after we'd moved in: "your house is too tall." I didn't care. After we built, someone across the gravel road built a similar house, another post-and-beam.

How is it that I could think, with this first house, that my horizon was the property lines? By what process do people develop these invisible horizons? I had longed for that first house for a long time. I had not ever "owned" property on which would sit my permanent residence, yet I had grown up among people conscious of ownership of land. My mother, after all, was a walker of boundaries herself, and I had often joined her. It was she who subtly taught me, on those walks, to look at all the corner markers, rusted out steel pipes driven into the earth, a tree, a stone wall. Since that first house sat on five acres in the Washington, D.C. area, an area in which I'd already, by then, lived for five years and in which I'd always felt crowded, I had a lot of walking to do. Like a person who walks up to another and establishes the appropriate distance for conversation, I was looking to remember, in my body, my own, peculiar appropriate distance to another house. My horizon line had to be at least five hundred feet from another house, the same distance my aunt's house had stood to my birth house. Finding that space, I needed to inscribe and re-inscribe that distance with my feet so I could feel safe, at home, again.

There were, however, even more complex, invisible forces at play in my marking of this horizon line. Some of these forces were local. The lot was located in a reserve, a federally protected area. It was also, de facto, a white area in a largely black community. Finally, it was a wealthier and more educated community than that which, at the time, surrounded the reserve. I knew only two people in the reserve, the people who had introduced us to it. I entered this community feeling already beleaguered, cut-off, in a precious, protected spot. I was content to roam over five acres in my imagination and no more, both because I was, somewhere, always afraid, feeling a bit encamped, and because I felt guilty at my privilege. I didn't want to look too far beyond that irregular rectangle that made up that legal boundary.

But underneath the more local forces that urged me to walk the line were larger, even less visible historical ones. I happen to live in an historical epoch of "enclosed" land, land in which the property line has a certain sanctity about it.[32] This property line has become an extension of our body's power in space, including power over others. This is why life-long feuds are fought over them. I have a neighbor who has been engaged in a ten year war with his neighbor over a two foot encroachment onto his land. Real estate laws are elaborate about what is called "adverse possession," in which one can lay claim to land by using it continually over a specified span of years as long as the legal owner has not verbally or in writing acknowledged that a trespass has occurred. The law, in other words, urges our vigilance to maintain the clarity of the property line. My neighbors and I in Maryland did not feel the need to establish the line to the inch. Our mowing habits visually conveyed where that line was, each to each, and reassured me where it was when I wasn't out there walking it. Other people, in city lots, put up high fences on their lines. Some go to other extremes to make the line seem invisible. In this way the expanse of owned property appears vaster to the owner than it is. The British Ha-Ha achieves precisely this: a sunken fence acts as a marker of the boundary line that is invisible to the one in the house looking out across the fields.[33]

Looked at in another way, however, I could have focused on the property lines as my horizon because these were a reminder to me in eyes and feet that I could know this much space within my body. I was, by encircling, working to contain the experience of something that felt newly sacred that was beginning to open in me, a meeting of body with meadow. By encircling I was, like the monks who regularly perambulated the boundaries of their abbeys, reminding myself that this acreage was a powerful, different kind of place that I could know.[34]

In Connecticut, my horizon widened. I was entirely unclear about the legal property lines, for one thing. They bordered the state forest on two sides, a boundary the state had never attempted to clarify. And, on the other two sides, they bordered other land that my brother and I owned. I did not need to be aware of the boundaries because there was no potential encroachment. Also, my mother had before me regularly patrolled the boundaries. That work seemed done. I could think, "my mother knew where the markers were." Though she often tried to show me, I do not need to remember.

I became more aware, living in the second house, of other kinds of boundaries. This time I began to see my house more as others would see it. My house became more relational. Even though I was in the woods, some five hundred feet from the nearest house, my large saltbox looked out upon two low, modest, ranch/farmhouses, those of my birth house and my aunt. These other houses I'd known as a child. I regularly walk within them now. I see my new house from their vantage point, through their windows, something few neighbors may be able to do and have the looking mean so much.

Beyond the birth house, the aunt's house, I also knew this town, this region, well. I'd been in many other houses, played as a child in them. My mother had been the tax collector and worked in insurance and real estate, so I grew up with stories of different houses. I grew as part of a church community, in which we'd have progressive dinners, moving from one house to the next for the appetizer, the main meal, the dessert. These processions wound around town, joining us all on a map I did not forget. My body, in coming home, felt familiar in a much larger geographical area. Nor were the houses on the other side of town abstract for me. Elementary school opened the doors for me to the house of a displaced Yugoslavian family, the house of Hungarian refugees. There were all kinds of houses I entered, large, airy, expensive, small, dark, smoke-filled, chicken-filled. As I walk or drive around town now, years later, I remember many of the visits I made there. When I lived in the suburbs of Virginia, I only knew the houses of my colleagues. I never learned any street names. I got lost all the time. It takes a long time to wear a path in a neighborhood and it takes people to open the door.

Yet neither of my houses quite fit in. People who drive up to each house are typically stunned, not by the enormity of the house, but rather because the immediate neighborhood hasn't prepared them. It's as if I were wearing some outfit from another time, but I was not nearly so bold in my own clothing. My house did the work for me. Surprised when they came up the driveway (a surprise heightened in the second house, in which trees obscure the house entirely from the road), people invariably say, "what space," "what light." Their vision of the house prompts me to be different—and larger-- than I ordinarily feel.

Yet although I did not try to fit in, I was also uneasy, particularly in Connecticut, about the other, less complimentary ways people might see the house. I felt the other houses saying to me, "you take up too much room." I remember that shortly after we'd moved into this house, there was a horrible house fire in our small town. It had started with a faulty hot water heater. The house was a hovel. I was related by marriage to the family. The grandmother would not leave her paraplegic son in his bed. Her grandson, thirteen, would not leave her. The three of them perished. We, as a church, a town, worked to collect clothing and find temporary housing for the remaining children. I saw their house in my mind's eye. I imagined them looking over at me in my large house, although they were three miles away.

Similarly, my uncle, then confined to a nursing home where his space consisted of some ten by twelve feet, half of a room, visited us one day at the new house when he could still get out. He had been a builder of two houses, one overlooking a large valley, the other overlooking the ocean. I saw my house through his eyes, as he thought of his houses now gone from him.

Perhaps it was really only in the course of building that second house that I began to consider the land, as well, as a place upon which I might more lightly walk. It was thicker land for me, land with a history that the Maryland land did not have for me (I'd known only that the woman who owned it, to whom we paid a check every month, had retrieved it as part of her divorce settlement. I'd imagined it had been farmed for tobacco, given the impoverished quality of the soil, but I'd no other stories of it and done no research.) I opened this thicker history of the Connecticut land the day I walked with another, then eighty-eight year old uncle through the woods. I'd called him to help me locate the driveway. This had been his business, and I knew he could advise me where the flattest and most pleasing driveway could be located. He was, it turns out, very skilled at this. He'd known some of this land before himself, having taken gravel out of a now overgrown gravel bank on the property. He would remind me of this gravel (and we would later open it up, getting all the gravel we needed for a 600' driveway from it and a pond, later, to boot). But we also talked that day. I asked him the question I always asked my father's relatives: "what was he like?" My uncle could not say too much, my father had been just a little too much older in a family of eight, in which the children inevitably paired off. A tear, nevertheless, formed in his eye. I had known that my father had often walked these woods, enticing chipmunks, tussling with skunks, looking for Indian arrow heads. I had also just recently been invited to dinner at the house my father had grown in. As we got our coats from the upstairs bedroom, I had quickly looked for what might not have changed, what he might have seen, the wide butternut floorboards, a patched ceiling, a particular view out a window. I knew in asking out loud the question of my uncle, as we stood on the house site, that I was implanting my father here. He was in my mind. I was, in my own way, beginning to acknowledge the prior history of this hill, that I was but one in a succession. For all I knew he could have knelt here often, to look at a plant or admire a view. (As chance would have it, the truck bearing the timber frame for this second house began its trip from Maine to here on what would have been my father's ninety first birthday.)

It was perhaps this opening, of speaking about my father while I was standing on the hill, that made me wonder about the history before him of this piece of land. I knew Pequot Indians had hunted here—I knew this from fingering the arrowheads as a child. But I could find no other record of them, neither on the earth nor in writing. There was, however, writing on the white colonists. Since they owned property individually (whereas the Pequot moved about within their own territories, camping in different places, building movable houses), these white colonists used writing to pass on "their" individual tracts of land. The prose of such transactions is suitably august, peppered with obscure and authoritative language: words such as "whereas," or "authorized," or "bounded and described as," with chapter and verse (volume and page number) cited. Anyone can research this written record, which, however incomplete it always is, radically shifts one's view of the land. One becomes aware not only of the solemnity the law grants to private ownership of the land, but also, ironically and paradoxically, of its ephemerality. "Ownership" masked coercion, in the case of the first colonists--yet those who once owned are now dead.

This very hill of the second house, for example: I can reconstruct its history. It is not an atypical story, but one whose retelling reminds me of my similar place. This very hill once looked very different. This land, near the coastline of Connecticut, was once more park-like in appearance. The trees were old and massive; the underbrush cut by the Pequots who roamed here, hunting animals that now no longer frequent these parts, particularly the wolf. It was a wilderness. But in the late seventeenth century the English began to settle here. One of them, a Simon Lynde, who had emigrated from England (from Holland) to Boston in 1650, "gave" a huge tract of land in a town in Connecticut far from Boston to his son. This town is now ten miles from this hill. For the new English settlers, this hill was initially area to be farmed—not lived on. And so trees were cut and cattle grazed. As this Lynde family grew, alongside others, some of the people farming this "North Quarter" began to live here permanently. They put down not lightweight movable houses, as the Indians had (Indians who had been driven into smaller and smaller enclaves, often forcibly), but durable, permanent houses, houses with foundations. Some years before this "North Quarter" was incorporated as a separate town, one of the descendents of Simon Lynde is listed as owning 279 acres. What is now our hill was part of that acreage. The man who is recorded as the owner as far back as I could trace in the town records was the son of the man who built one of the Lynde houses; he lived in his father's house and farmed our piece, which was a half mile down the road. Suffering from a lung disease, as many on those working dairy farms did (tuberculosis being the most common), he, along with other relatives, spent his last months in the then new state hospital built in the late 1800s. His land, land he had probably never intended to build a house on, land originally part of the 279 acres of his ancestor, land that had once belonged to the Indians, was sold on July 5, 1907. This date occurs a year before William died and almost six months to the day after my father was born in New York City, my father who would one year later move to the *same* house William had lived in, my father who would one day become the owner of William's parcel of farmland—a parcel which had, by his time, become separated from the house parcel.

The land, what is now "my" land, "our" land, was to have three other owners before my father, the first two of whom built no dwelling here but used it for farming or investment. Just before the third transaction, a strip of land to the rear was sold to the State of Connecticut (between 1927-1933) to make up what is now one of the largest state forests. And then comes Charles Lampe, the owner before my father. The evidence of the land, the age of the trees on "my" hill, suggests that Lampe certainly did not use this hill for grazing. Only the one large beech down by the stream, the place where the cattle would have refreshed themselves, is left from all that grazing time, shelter for them in summer heat and rain, a tree saved by the compassion of William or one of his ancestors before him.

At this point, the point of Lampe, I know more of the human story; the characters come into view through my memories of my mother's narration. Charles Lampe was a German immigrant who started buying parcels of land in the west end in 1896. He never married and had no children. As the story goes, he built three houses. He'd build one, live in it for a while, then another, and so on. One of the houses he built was on the parcel of land next to what was to become ours—a house and land he sold to Marie Heisler in 1933 (only Marie's name is on the deed, not her husband Emil's). Then, in 1934 he built our house, my birth house. It was a small house—two rooms heated by a woodstove, a porch to the north, and, most wonderfully, a greenhouse to the southwest that was heated by an oil burner! He had a barn and a few animals. But farming was not his main occupation. He was the night watchman at the factory where my father, who then lived up the hill in what was once William's house, also worked. Lampe was a small farmer—and he landscaped the property. All around the property he planted what must have been somewhat exotic plants for that time—mock oranges, weeping mulberries, peonies (which I've taken cuttings of for my gardens), a blue spruce, and spirea. The day he died a neighbor walked over and took the large orange tree houseplant that had thrived in the greenhouse, claiming he had given it to her. His plants were apparently coveted.

All the histories embedded on this land explode my consciousness of my place here. It is perhaps no wonder that the young married woman didn't want to go back at all. Going back also invites one to go forward: I could imagine the prose of the land records once we are gone, the house passed on, even as that first house, the Maryland house, is now written up somewhere with us as the one-time owners. Once I had opened this door, signaling that I was in the presence of invisible spirits, "house" would never be only "mine" again. When it came time to build, I would learn this in another key. For it was not only I who built the house. I built alongside, with others' hands, whose sweat is buried in the wood and the images of whose bodies I see even now around me as I sit here alone, the door locked against them. Their stories are next in time.

VII

Building the First Time

I placed a jar in Tennessee,
And round it was upon a hill.
It made the slovenly wilderness
Surround that hill.
 --Wallace Stevens, "Anecdote of the Jar"[35]

For the first time...my movements no longer proceed unto the things to be seen, to be touched, or unto my own body occupied in seeing and touching them... because for the first time, through the other body, I see that...the body contributes more than it receives, adding to the world that I see the treasure necessary for what the other body sees.
 --Merleau-Ponty[36]

And so the imaginary house begins at last to take root in the land, to take a visible place for me—and for others. But what is this thing? What is this new house-in-pieces that once was an iridescent, dream house, an imaginary house? What is this thing that is now a growing skeleton and an oh-so-slowly fleshed-out skin?

Although if I thought about it I would have known that the house was never really mine alone, that my desire for it was cultural and that the bank would own most of it, the house *seemed mine* alone as long it was only the dreamed house. That's how I wanted it to be anyway. In my dreams the house was solitary, as was I. The dream house had always been whole and perfect, perfect lines on a few sheets of paper, paper I could hide away when I wished.

But now, at the first moment of construction, of visibility, of tangibility beyond that of my fingers holding the drawing pencil, all begins to change. It is like the land which comes with its own history so that, once I begin to alter it, it begins to appear to me over and against me as a "thou" and no longer as an "it" to be manipulated by me. The growing house, slowly embodying outside of me, becomes its own, separate life. As it grows, it grows a history, a history that is not me. It is a history not mine alone, but a history of me-with-others. And it grows, as well, a future apart from me. It is also not perfect.

To ask this question now, at this point in this narrative, "what is this thing, the tangibly built house?, is not what many readers of house-building stories expect at this point. I'm confounding the plot by hiding the house holy grail. Now is the moment for me to display proudly to the patient woman on the stairs the completed houses, like trophies in a field, houses that *I* have made. Now is the moment for the aerial photo of the lovely, empty, timber frame house, like the long shot of the glassed-in house perched over the sea that ends the movie, "Life is a House." I've shown the woman how I gathered my will, broke through tool shed doors, went to school and picked up a pencil, walked the boundaries of place, got ready in short. Now I should be showing scenes, verbal photographs, of one triumph after another as I complete the houses. Here should be the climax of the comedy, or the heroic narrative, depending on how seriously one takes house-building. This is the moment for the marriage and the beginning of the happily-ever-after to begin. This is the reaching of the summit, the sighting of new land, the slaying of the monsters and the beginning of the reign of peace. I too have been nursed on these narratives. But this narrative doesn't unfold or end here, not this way. For me, the house "thing," the house rising in front of me and under my hand, didn't mean what it was supposed to at all.

I *did* see two houses through to completion. They do both still stand. They will likely stand after me. They are lovely. People seem to love to look at them and to sit in them. People rarely want to leave. And I *did* do a lot of the work to make the first, and the second, more than many people do on a new house, not as much as some other owner-builders do. I do acknowledge to the woman, yes, here they are, the houses. I can, I think, without disappointing her at this stage of my story, say at this point that I won't show her all the steps in the process. Others have written of this, broken down all the stages, and she knows how to read recipes. I don't think she'd be that interested in the details. What she's always really wanted to know is "however did you do this?," however did I put myself in this kitchen or sewing room that is the house-in-the-making? She wants to know the underlying conditions of the house's possibility, this large, durable thing, in me. She wants to know if she too could get there. And besides, as a teacher, I realize she doesn't need to have me at this point rehearse endless details and fatigue stories that might scare her away. She needs just to begin.

But I also know what would most please her, give her gratification, at this point in my story is a virtual tour of the finished houses, me standing proudly in each room holding a hammer and smiling. Much as my own crudely built house models reassured me throughout the building process that something was at the end, she perhaps needs a completed house to reassure her that she too can build one round herself.

Every supermarket bookshelf is filled with reassuring evidence of perfect houses. But I want to say now to that woman something quite different, something she may not want to hear, ask a larger question. "Now I want to ask you to reconsider what you mean by 'this'—as you sweep your eyes around my second house. What did you think "this" would give you, the reaching of this summit, this articulation of paradise? And I want you to reconsider your use of 'you' as you address me. You're implying that I am a discrete, separate person, a free agent, and that this, the free-standing house, is discrete as well. 'I' did 'it' you think. You perhaps think the house is just like baking a cake—you or I whip the eggs and produce the cake for us all to enjoy. You perhaps think that domestic life is this simple, this ordinary, this reassuringly regular, under control, and private.

House-building is not, however, like baking, or rather it is but this is because baking a cake is not so simple either. The 'you' or 'I' who beats the eggs isn't so simple (others have taught us, for example), and the cake itself is a combination of chickens, cows, trucks delivering the eggs, a company sending a new mixer to the house, the oven someone else built and installed, electrical currents, and on and on. And the cake, invariably, has too much salt or doesn't rise well enough or is too tough. Few cakes are perfect. And, of course, they are eaten all too soon.

The problem is in how we border a "thing." In this case the "thing" is house.

"I know," I continue to say to her, "that this additional complexity confounds your sense of a story. I'm not even certain you'll like how my story is going to go from now on. For one thing, it becomes less house-centered and more other-centered. And from then the story becomes more spirit-centered. I'm in my own small way a lot like Milarepa, learning through building far larger lessons about my place in the universe and the nature of made things. House building was for me but a way station, though I did not know so at the beginning.

"The one consolation I can offer you," I continue to the woman, "is that the less momentous and heroic you see the outcome, a finished, beautiful house, the more you might be more willing, less afraid, to pick up a hammer yourself. And perhaps, knowing the stakes, knowing what can come out of house-building, you'll see building itself as a far more important act than you now might."

One summer's afternoon I stood in the Maryland meadow looking at the first house frame lumbering its way up out of the earth, post by post, beam by beam, rafter by rafter raised by crane and sometimes lifted by eight young men. I was in a new viewing position and so the framed view was different. I was also, without then understanding it, in the powerful, and different, position of one who is watching others work on my house, others take care of it. I had a camera in my hands. Something was happening to "me" and to "house." We were being separated.

A different light slanted on it. Disappearing now in a blur of successive eye blinks was the simple image of house I'd been carrying with me in my daydreams for so many years, the glossy prints from realtors, the pictures of a dream house in a house magazine, my young glimpse from a boat of a house on the riverbank. The skeletal hint of house standing before me at that moment, if one could call it house at this point, was oddly shrunken, yet exquisitely beautiful. It was also terribly vulnerable, the free-standing timbers that had only lately been trees propped up by a few 2x4s and nails. Yet its power of place, of making place, was palpable. The house frame was oddly like Wallace Stevens' jar in that it was, in being placed there, making of the meadow, for the first time, a surround. At its beginning, the frame could also almost have seemed a ruin—perhaps, I thought, this is what it will look like at its end.

The house had escaped my hand. I could not hold it any longer like a set of drawings. It was too big, the meadow was too big. I was scared. Yet at the same time I found the feeling pleasurable in an odd, new way. I seemed to forget about the prospect of living in this frame someday or even owning it. Its rising peak surpassed my drawing, its thickening walls I'd never sketched enough, its weight on the meadow I'd entirely unanticipated. Peak, walls, meadow, the gift of trees and labor and an earth: not mine at all. "House" became in those moments rather only a location, a web, for a thousand movements, some always invisible, some visible only for a brief time, the time of construction. It seemed a fragile gift, full of nails and dirt and hot summer days, and I was its newly humbled recipient.

As the metaphoric brick by brick began to be laid, two images condense what I began to see. One came from a museum in China in the 1970s, by way of friends who had visited China as part of a pioneering "China-America Friendship Team." They had visited some of the grand palaces of the emperors that had now been converted into people's museums. Now, affixed next to each gilt object, was a sign showing how many people, horses, and materials were needed to make this one thing. Rich things were being redrawn, remapped for ordinary people. Watching the house begin to go up, I began to count people and survey stacks of material. And I began to see that the people and the material were caked with sweat and dirt, that they could tire, and that what would come of their labor would thus be imperfect, soiled, sometimes messy. And I began to marvel that they could be content, some of them particularly the independent sub-contractors, to receive only their wages—and not also some part of what they had made with their hands.

The other image comes from the Celts: the "Celtic knot." Strands of braid sinuously weave under and over each other, with no beginning, no end. Often this knot appears carved in stone. The house is such a knot of toughness and abrasiveness, a vibrating net of bodies, present, past, all doing different things all together, creating the whole that is the house. The house is the knot of place, landscape, social history, globally derived materials. When the house is done, it is still the knot, though the once noisy hammers are suspended in time in the now silent walls and the source, if ever known, settled into seemingly simple objects, banisters, wall board. I know some of the strands of the knot because I was there during the building. I can remember many of its parts and I can translate, into words, as a record for me, for them, for others, something of what is hidden in those walls. But I do not know it all. I cannot go back far enough or go out wide enough.

What was happening in me was a shift in how I saw a thing, the house thing. It happened physically, this shift, as my eyes focused and refocused on a house changing before my eyes because of all our labor. This is what the difficult yet fascinating epigraph to this chapter probes.

Imagine the "thing" that Merleau-Ponty is speaking of as a "house." Before, his "movements" (sight, touch, etc.) are narrowly focused on the "thing out there" and on his own body seeing (and touching) the thing, as if they, thing, house, body, are separate, in a closed circuit. Nothing, no one else, exists, and the thing is the focal point. The thing dominates. It stands "outside" him. This is us in our typical relation to the house, "my" house, me and my house, the house defines "me." Think of the photographs of the houses for sale in the realtors' office. This is how we are shaped to see houses—not me, no neighbors, stationary, there, fixed. This is the cold epistemology, the blurred lens through which we ordinarily see in a commodity culture in which everything is for consuming.

But then Merleau-Ponty's "movements" shift. Why this shift happens we are not told. Other bodies and then his own suddenly assume center stage, the thing itself receding into the background. He sees the body, his, other bodies, through what the body *makes*, the body as the active, important force, not the thing itself. The thing changes from a thing in and of itself to a thing that is there *for* the other, and *with* the other. We can remember the movie *Witness,* in which we see not the house, but the moving arms of the many black-clad men at work on the frame of an Amish barn. Bodies, many bodies, make the treasure. The treasure is not encapsulated, fully contained, in the thing that is made. The treasure spills out: is the process of its making. This, this process, cannot be bought and sold. To translate: many bodies make the house thing. The treasure is in the bodies making. It's a fundamental perceptual shift, a difficult shift. It's a radically new field of awareness for us. This photograph is never in the house magazines or on the realtor's window. It's not what I, as a young woman, filled with house desire, saw from the boat on the river.

To return to Heidegger's idea of dwelling, dwelling is not simply owning or having a thing, a house. We need, says Heidegger, to "take measure" in order to "dwell." And "taking measure" involves reflection, memory, and often writing (and building). What we reflect on, remember, is the thing, the house, as a *gathering* place, a gathering in Merleau-Ponty's terms of *bodies making* the treasure.

We need to see the "thing" as not a momentary, congealed, separate instance, but continuous, flexible, intertwined. Because Heidegger says we are depleted, objects are depleted, we need to work to "thing the thing." We need to see "thing" as a verb. This "thinging" involves memory and intention. "Dwelling" is not about "a" dwelling, a thing, but is a continuous act, an intentional, remembered, and remembered-again act by us. *We* are the ones who dwell. The thing, the house, doesn't do it for us. We need to remember our houses as *treasures made by many for the world.* We may continue to live in private and not in common in houses. But the things become, as we contemplate them, vessels of ours-with-others' work. There is, then, no center that is just "mine."

In this way the house, the landscape, as we listen, becomes alive with the ghosts walking the perimeter, up the stairs, into the rooms, in time before, in time to come, ghosts of the land, spirits of the neighborhood that memory calls up. Their spirits are noisy. They are Yeats' "rough men-at-arms, cross-gartered to the knees/Or shod in iron, [who] climbed the narrow stairs...[who] come with loud cry and panting breast/To break upon a sleeper's rest" ("The Tower"). No castle that is ours alone, our houses—they have been others' castles before and now and will be again in time to come, as many walk and will walk the halls loudly. The house is but a way station, a toll house, a place we pay to stay in for temporary shelter. By thinking of it in this way, we can imagine the often invisible lives of others not only on this very spot of our house, but also others alone in their own rooms, their own houses. I think this is why after I built I would love to walk down a strange street in the evening and, glimpsing a lighted kitchen or dining room table, begin to imagine with a newly thickened joy the density of another's nest.

Heidegger uses the image of the bridge to help us understand how a "thing" is not in and of itself, but rather creates a "location" for crossing, by people, a "location" which needs to be *remembered*. He shows us how the "thing" requires *us*. It is important that there be a real bridge. This is not the issue—daydreaming of one is not the point. But the bridge works as a "bridge" in its fullest sense when we think of what it does. The house too is a bridge, the visible house. Yet this now visible house, to be full, requires us to remember it as a crossing place, a thoroughfare of sorts—but with walls and locks rather than planks and railings. Another word for remembering is "staying with."

> *Even when we relate ourselves to those things that are not in our immediate reach, we are staying with the things themselves.... If all of us now think, from where we are right here, of the old bridge in Heidelberg, this thinking toward that location is not a mere experience inside the persons present here; rather, it belongs to the nature of our thinking **of** that bridge that **in itself** thinking gets through, persists through, the distance to that location. From this spot right here, we are there at the bridge...From right here we may even be much nearer to that bridge and to what it makes room for than someone who uses it daily as an indifferent river crossing.... To say that mortals **are** is to say that **in dwelling** they persist through spaces by virtue of*

their stay among things and locations (1971, 156-7; emphasis added).

Building, and then writing about building, making a memory container, a house jar in words, is a way to make the house continue to be like the fully experienced bridge. Elsewhere Heidegger says that building a house does not guarantee "dwelling," just as repeated bridge crossings don't guarantee one will know fully what "bridge" means. But building, like walking across the bridge, gives one a better chance than, say, if one were thinking abstractly of "house" or "bridge." We need a specific house, bridge to help us remember our bodies' motions, other bodies' motions. We'll feel the fatigue in our legs that way—and the fatigue in others'.

I mark the beginning of my seeing my house as a bridge, a thoroughfare, and not a simple thing out-there-for-me-only on one day, in which I changed the way I referred to the house in speaking with others. Before I built, I would say "my" house (all the more odd since I was married and my husband was also going to help me build it.) Yet shortly after that first day in the meadow watching the wall rise up, shortly after the frame was complete, after the rafters were affixed, after there was an early sense of "roof," I started referring to it as "*the* house." Clyde, the mason, may have triggered this. One day I heard him say, "no one will ever tear this house down." He then began a story of a demolition crew being unable to pull an old timber frame apart. The house from that moment had a life span different from mine. And to Clyde, it was "a" house—not just *mine*.

Perhaps because of Clyde's offhand remark, one hot day as I was wheeling my red wheelbarrow around collecting the day's voluminous building debris, ugly things really, soda cans, cigarette butts, candy wrappers, I had a thought: in time to come another I do not know will walk around this yard as well, mowing, feeding the lawn yet to come out of this detritus. Then, as friends came by, some curious, some eager to try their hand at hammering for a few hours, some of these friends built a few walls. I took to calling the wall, "Peter's wall," or "Pat's wall." There were moments, as well, when I began ceding ownership over to what I once had called God and soon would again. "My" house was becoming no longer mine in any way I could before have imagined. In beginning to "thing" the thing, ironically, to grasp the house more fully, in an entirely different, denser, thicker way than it seemed before, I was on the road to separating myself from it, the need for just it--and on the road to something else that lay ahead of me, the second house, and beyond.

To not forget the thickly being there, being there with others, to not forget the bridge of the thing, to "stay with" it, we need words. The signs are hidden now, the frame, Peter's wall, covered over, my early prayers for larger help, sometimes out loud, carried by the wind. Even my own body is changed now, its building traces effaced for me. My once stronger right hammering arm now blends in with the rest of my body.

Even while I was building when I could read the signs on my body, many could not. Many of us have no "grammar" for this. George Simmel says that primitive people wear their art on their bodies—not as exchangeable ornaments, but as tattoos and paints made of the earth's natural dyes. Others around them could see these tattoos, know of what they were made. My tattoos, visible to me, weren't even recognizable to others. After a day at the lot, I'd go to the university to teach my summer school class on Woolf. No one appeared to notice my blue-black nails. If they did, they would not attribute it my marks to a wayward hammer. They did not know the grammar of manual work, nor perhaps were they easily able to place a woman doing it. Berthe Morisot's painting, "Woman with a Red Carnation," shows a woman with large hands, working hands, holding a small flower. My suburban students often found her unattractive. I heard a rural man, however, at a funeral speak of his father's work-worn hands. He read them for us in the language of his love, told us how his father had used those hands in the factory making jet engines, hands he would later place gently on his son's shoulders. Working hands, painted, described, need this son's kind of "thinging" of them for those who cannot read them. All the building photographs need it too, the ones in my album, the ones others now look at. They are insufficient by themselves. What is "in" them, by way of a bridge, needs to be told in words.

  These are some words about those days building the first house, some of which are frozen in photographs. The journal I wrote helped me then to stop, to pause. Now that journal helps me to remember all that the photographs leave out and the many signs I might now myself not notice. These are entries from a time now over twenty years ago about some of what is buried in the cellar hole, the concrete, the walls.

Saturday, April 4, 1986. Accokeek, Md.

In a photograph I see my husband John and me standing over a pile of 2x4's in the Maryland meadow. The bulldozer has not yet arrived. It is coming in a couple of days. Our still bodies don't show the tension, the fear we alone know—or the awe of this moment. We were, that day, trying to set "batter boards." We'd never done this before. A carpenter, who ordinarily does this part of the job, could have finished the task in a quarter of the time it took us. But there we were. I'd wanted to do this. I felt I had to do this. It felt somehow primitive, like the ancients cutting a foundation furrow, or my Puritan ancestors in New England walking out of their old meeting house to "set the stake" for their new one. This was part of the "stake setting ritual."

The week before we'd spent four hours measuring, checking diagonals, pointing the compass, as we set the four corners of our house, driving short pieces of "rebar" into the sodden spring earth. It would be wonderful if this were all we had to do. If we were going to put our house on posts or cement columns, we wouldn't have to do anything else. But because we wanted a basement (alas it couldn't be, by the building code, a wood-lined hole lit by a descending candle), because we were following our New England custom of wanting our house to sit not on the ground, but to come out from it (anathema to Frank Lloyd Wright), we were out here today once again building these strange little nests out of wood and string, mini Stonehenges they looked like, or a little like the fairy houses visitors to Monhegan Island in Maine are fond of constructing out of little twigs on the woodsy path out to Pulpit Rock. Holy markers, all, they seemed to us.

We needed to build these wooden structures from a practical point of view because we would, eventually, have to take last week's painstakingly set four pins out of the ground. We had to do this because the excavator needed to move the bulldozer around in a hole much bigger than the house's footprint, which the pins marked. And yet we and our mason would need to know, later, exactly where these corner pins of the footprint had once sat. For once the hole was dug and the footings poured, the wider "shoes" on which the thinner legs of the basement walls would stand, the mason laying the concrete block for the walls would need to know exactly where to set the first perpendicularly laid blocks. We would have to pound a nail into the footing marking the precise corner. These "batter boards" would help us do this because we would cut a small saw kerf in each cross piece marking where intersecting strings met over the corner house marker. Then we could take the pins out, yet find the place where they belonged later on.

The batter boards have another function as well: all the cross pieces have to be level with each other. The excavator will use these cross pieces to tell if the hole is dug both to the right depth (indicated on the plans) and if it is roughly level at the bottom.

I was flooded with excitement and anxiety. I was participating in a derivation of an ancient ritual. Once "batter boards" were used to establish the slope of stone walled houses. Now they had been reconfigured (who thought of this?) to ensure that wood frame houses would be level and square. Could I mimic this practice? I thought of John Donne's sonnet, "Batter my heart three-personed God"—same word, slightly different origin, but no matter, the power of the wood felt the same as Donne's image of a battering ram opening a besieged city. And, as in Donne's sonnet, more was being opened at that moment than the gate into the undisturbed earth, in our case.

Last week was intense enough; obsessive we were, checking and rechecking so the pins in the earth would be set exactly on the square. We knew that if we were off by even a half an inch, we'd pay in money and hours of labor, for cabinets that wouldn't seamlessly meet in the corner, for flooring and wallboard that wouldn't square up. Every day we'd see the evidence of a non-square house! But this week, we had to measure yet again, as we created around three feet away from each corner pin two sets of 2x4 structures set at 90 degrees from each other. Then we had to measure, this time using a transit, to be certain that all the cross pieces we then nailed up to the web of three vertical 2x4s were level with each other. This way, we could string strings across the cross pieces, making sure they met exactly over the corner pin (using a plumb bob), notch saw "kerfs" in each cross piece at the exact point where the strings crossed in order to secure them in place. The excavator could then use the tops of the string as a benchmark for his own transit (woe to him and us if he dug deeper than he was supposed to, or if the floor of the basement hole were uneven, for no good house will stand on "undisturbed earth"—that's a wonderful thing, a divine thing it seems to me: house must stand on a rock!) Then, when he's done digging to a level depth, we can drop the plumb bob again and reset the pins, this time in the floor of the cellar hole! We can then mark the lines for the footing trenches on either side of the pins (with a chalk line and lime), take out the pins once again, invite the backhoe to dig the trenches out to a depth of 12" and a width of 18" (just the width of his bucket) (in So. Md. the soil is clay, strong when dry, so people rarely build forms for footings), and then reset the corner pins on the footings when they are cured. This time we'd use a single small nail which the mason will use to set the cornerstone. Thus the power of a measuring tape and a little nail!

In our minds we knew all of this, knew how important this task was, how seemingly small yet crucial it was. The photo doesn't show any of this. Nor does it show John lifting a sledge hammer over his shoulder again and again to pound the trembling stakes into the ground, stakes I was holding in place. The photo doesn't show the stakes quivering, or his body's tensed energy, or release the smell of the pine wood. This little thing, the house corner, was a nest of body movements, a Stonehenge, a new station for new sightings of a new world.

We had begun our house. It was not irrevocable, not yet. We could stop now. We didn't yet have a gaping hole that would have to be filled. But, all the same, we had erected these strange shapes that signaled to anyone who knew that "house" was happening here. And we had done it, with help from books, from the Shelter Institute, from my husband's bodily strength, from my fledgling confidence. It felt like a sacred act, this humble beginning of the house. Crudely sharpened 2x4s, a primitive sledge hammer, a *measuring tape, string, a saw, a tool with a water bubble in it by which we could see "level": ancient, simple materials and tools, lying around in most sheds in people's back yards. Like an infinitesimal egg and sperm meeting by chance, with them we were building a house. The land will never now be the same—an untouched meadow ready for its own spring. It was a grey, rainy spring day. I said to John after we finished, "here I am, walking in our back door."*

April 24, 1986.

In another photograph stands our 8x12' shed in the distance in the meadow. It too has an invisible history. On this Tuesday I straightened it for the first time. And I tidied what's left, after our hungry foraging deer, of the hundred white pine saplings my mother and I planted two years before around the perimeter of our five acre meadow---my first garden here, and a garden at the boundary at that. It was rainy and cool. I was all alone, acres of space around me. It was delicious. I was dirty and thoroughly happy. I loved sorting out the odd tools we'd assembled, arranging some of the materials I knew we'd need in the days ahead. I am happy restoring order, planning the tools I think we'll need, and sweeping up what's left of the visible plywood floor of this shack we made a year ago in preparation—our first building project. Then, my work done, I sit on the stoop of the shed and look at the dome of the sky over this softly blooming meadow. I'm happy that is, as long as I can be patient, become it, flow with it. I keep remembering an elderly carpenter friend,

Pappy's, advice, advice given to an old boyfriend who'd passed it on to me: "just go out and sit in a swing and think about the problem a while." I've no swing in the cherry tree, but I've this stoop at the end of one day. Pappy made me my first tool chest ten years ago, fitting it out with a small saw, a hammer, a square for marking saw cuts, and a few screwdrivers. He little knew what would come of all of this— but, remembering the knowing gleam in Pappy's eyes, perhaps he suspected where I was headed! Two years later our neighbor will offer to hitch the shed up to his backhoe (we built the shed on skids rather than a permanent foundation) and drag it to permanent footings twenty feet away. The shed, the meadow, the invisible presence of all the others in them, and of my sweeping: needing thinging in the photograph.

April 29, 1986.

    I've a photograph too of our doors, one of the front door, the other of our cellar door. The first door, the beautiful one, began fifty miles away. Tonight George, our timber framer, called to say they had started to cut the frame and the custom insulated door in his shop. Our house and door is beginning far away from me, worked on by their knowing hands as they plane the oak timbers for the house frame and sand the Arkansas pine used in the door. Meanwhile, I too, ten miles from the meadow, start my own door, the one for the cellar, in the basement of our rental house. Converging lines. I used Shelter's plan—tongue-and-groove pine set within a 1x6 frame. Each side of the door is this, with an air space and foil for insulation, and then the sides are covered with 1x3s. It will be hung with strap hinges and a latch and bolt for security. It is crude—my screws don't all quite match up (I should have made a pencil line first) and they are not countersunk because I don't know yet how to do this. But since it's the door for the cellar I will not worry about it. I began to use the circular saw to cut the pieces—my first time. The high-pitched whine of it scared me. I remembered the power it had to gouge out my father-in-law's leg (he'd stupidly removed the guard). I was slow and careful. I wore my goggles and hearing protectors. I supported the boards on the back brick steps (fortunately my landlord next door in suburbia is a carpenter and so encourages me.) I remembered to square up the door—something I forgot when I made my first bookcases six years ago! People like the door! When I see the photograph of the door, I see that I am getting better with tools—more gentle. I see that I move more with them. Building treasure in the doors, Bill's hands from George's crew, my inexperienced hands: the doors still stand, vessels of our work.

June 1, 1986.

We drove out to the lot tonight in the old green pickup truck my brother gave us. I've a picture in memory of us standing by it. The day was too hot. It was the first time we drove up on the new "driveway" together (it's barely even that yet—only a cut in the meadow) and the first time we stayed until dark (8:45). It became deliciously cool and breezy, with honeysuckle clinging to the air. A heron flew over to the left—a good omen, John said. I imagined us spending evenings on the future porch—it's hard to believe we could have such evenings ahead. All there is now is grass and sky and driveway and batter boards. This place does not exist any longer. This memory is buried in a time before the house.

June 11, 1986.

Underneath the basement floor, on which someday will stand another's boxes and suitcases, is another series of movements in time, like photos of earth and of heart, if that could be done, arranged in sequence. This place does not exist any longer either. This memory is buried in the time before the house.

First there is a shot of an open, clay-colored hole in the earth. We have walked in it, sat in it, spent hours in it that felt like years: this five foot deep 40 x 40' human made hole. Into it the backhoe has carved out 12" deep and 18" wide trenches. The earthen pit troubles me. I've never been in one before. How do miners breathe? I understand now why throwing prisoners into a pit is a form of torture.

In the next frame John and I are holding each other weeping as we sit in the pit. This frame is only in memory; there was no one watching us to take the picture. That day, Sunday, it was 91 degrees and humid, no shade. We'd been out here for fourteen hours. We'd been doing necessary, and invisible, work, work that will ensure that our house can stand for centuries on strong "feet." I'd learned from my reading that one of the reasons there are so very few old timber frames standing now in New England, when there are many in

Europe from the fourteenth century, is that the colonists did not understand how to build good foundations in American soil. So I know we need to have the foundation deep and rock-like. And so we pound short lengths of steel into the undisturbed earth. It has been known, since the middle of the nineteenth century, that adding steel to concrete exponentially increases its strength. As we pound, we make sure the tops of all the pieces are level. John has borrowed a tool from his father so he can tie with wire 6 and 8 foot horizontal lengths of reinforcing bar to these short ones. John had worked in the factory alongside his father in college summers. There he had learned this gesture, one he'd forgotten he knew, one he never expected to use again. I'd bought lengths of reinforcing bar short enough for my 6' truck to transport (hanging off the end). I'd then rented a bolt cutter and tried to cut some beforehand but it was too hard for me to apply enough pressure and I was alone. Frustrated at my hands, at the same time I learned in my hands the reassuring strength of the steel. I finally found a place which would cut them for me.

The history of objects: when we were done, we had rebar 2" from the bottom and 2" from the top of the footings—this so that the footings would be strong in this weak clay earth. Then we'd another project. We had to set a small section of drain pipe in-between the rebar so that later we'd be able to attach the interior drains we were going to put under the slab to the exterior footing drains that would later encircle the house's footings. ("Water:" said Pat Hennin, "the great enemy of all houses.")

We had to do all this, the leveling, the drain, in one day, the same day the footings were dug. The photo does not reveal any of this. One day: because the fragile clay could collapse with a rain, and the consequences of this were unimaginable to us. The concrete for the footings must be poured on top of undisturbed earth. Humans disturbing the base, it turns out, would fatally weaken the house.

With no rain in sight, at the end of the day, our work done, our hands sore, our bodies caked with dirt and dried sweat, John and I sit in the earth of the cellar hole and put our arms around each other and cry. John had cut his finger a little in handling the wire and some blood has seeped into the trench. We remembered somewhere hearing that blood in the foundation is auspicious , a primitive partnering perhaps, our blood, the foundation. It feels this way.

In the next frame, concrete is frozen in one moment, as it pours out, like lava, from chutes angled high above the trenches. The truck's wheels are hanging over the edge. It did not fall in. There are phone calls behind this photo. I'd ordered concrete, the special strong "footing mix," for the next morning, early. I had to use my charts from Shelter to help me calculate the right quantity (you order the concrete, it's yours—too little and you have potentially messed up your footing if the truck can't come back right away; too much, and they have to dump it somewhere on your property so you have to prepare for where the excess can go!)

There were other phone calls. John thought we needed professional help. I wanted to try it alone. But we called our excavator who recommended James, who has worked on highways for the county. A moment before the first of three concrete trucks arrives, James drives up in his black pick-up truck. He jumps out, looks around, and goes up to the driver as if they were friends. He organizes John and me and my colleague Pat Story, who has come out to help us. James shows us how to move the concrete about, break up air pockets, and ensure it is level with the tops of the pins we'd set in place the day before. James then, just at the right moments, drags first a 2x4 and later a metal float he's brought along across the tops of the footings as they are curing. They shine as the concrete gets harder.

At the end of that day, Monday, James, the trucks, gone away, there is one photo I took of Pat and John looking at the silvery grey band of footings. Lovely they are. To think soon they'll be covered over and no one but us will ever have seen them. To think that what we are looking at the Romans developed the recipe for (a recipe lost for hundreds of years and not rescued until the early part of the twentieth century)—Portland cement: lime, silica, alumina, aggregate (Benson 1988, 116).

The moment does not fully close. It never does in building. There's always a problem that pushes you forward to the next frame—time and the growing house are not the only motors. The drain got squashed a little during the pour. How will we figure out how to attach a fitting to it? And, there's more: the footings aren't level because I didn't use my transit correctly. We are each of us, John and me, terribly scared. It is the non-chalance of the others that reassures us. "You'll find a way with the drain," and "the mason will correct your dip in the front of the house." They are right. John *figured out the drain on his own one day, and I got a mason whom nothing bothered.*

June 26 1986.

    The cellar wall is half built. Mounds of block sit off to the side, waiting. This photo, since I'm taking it, does not reveal much of my relationship with the mason Clyde. He doesn't say much. But he confides, delivers swift judgments on his helpers, and in effect supports me. And the photo doesn't do justice to his skill with the trowel: one, two plops of mortar between the courses, just the right amount so that the wall is hardly ever off of level (and he taps it to meet his string as he goes along), then a quick swipe or two against the vertical surface and the mortar is neat—the excess thrown on either side of the wall for me to clean up after it dries. He never pauses. He keeps time with his trowel.

    Two full days I've worked with him and his sometimes resisting crew. We're in a terrible rush, or rather I am because Clyde never is. The timber framers are soon coming with the house. And because we have to reinforce the wall vertically with more rebar packed in mortar (a new edict from the county following the collapse of a neighboring block wall), the two men mixing the mortar have to work all the time in this terrible heat. They've barely time to run to their truck and sip the vodka they drink all day long or look longingly at the huge snapping turtle they caught this morning and have placed in a barrel with some water—soup for them later.

    I see I'll have to help if we're going to get done, given this extra task of rebar. As Clyde places each top block, I climb on my ladder and trowel mortar into alternate holes of the block alongside him and then stuff in the pieces of rebar. In between I take my truck and travel the winding country back roads to the lumberyard to get what they need, always more mortar mix. The drive is my break. I love these shaded, winding roads, like the rural roads of my childhood. And I can cart long lengths of lumber in the short pickup truck when I need to since I never have to worry about anyone else being on the road.

The wall has all of this in it. It is lovely, this emerging wall, its smell, its rough texture. I will go home, forty five minutes away, shower off the mortar, and then drive another half hour to teach a three hour seminar on Virginia Woolf. When she says writing is made of bricks[37], I feel her metaphor. My writing fingers are caked with mortar mix.

July 2, 1986.

All these photographs are not only of frozen, incomplete moments, "unthinged" things without the story of what each thing gathers: the story of shared work. The photos are also usually utterly uninteresting to most who see them. "House" is not for them the footings or the cellar wall. These are, for most, rather like the mud in which the lotus flowers. I too began this building process hating the cellar (a far better word than "basement," "cellar," one of the most beautiful words in the language says Poe). I couldn't wait for wood. But the longer I worked in the cellar, and it seemed to take forever, the more I came to see the beauty of the mud—and why the lotus roots there. (I couldn't help remembering as well Yeats' line about the human body: "Love has pitched his palace in the place of excrement.") Without a good foundation, a house rots and dips and is the whim of hurricanes. Without a good cellar there is mold, rodents, and cold. When we feel a house is good, it is partly the solidity of the good foundation that we feel intuitively.

But now there is a photo, many photos in fact to reflect this rising out of the mud: one truck, two trucks, piled high with timbers and large white rectangles, "sandwiches" of insulation flanked on one side by sheet rock, the other by plywood—these will wrap and so insulate the timber frame. I heard them coming before I saw the two 40' flat bed trucks come around the hairpin curve of the gravel road. They barely made it. The house at last, coming around the corner. They set to work, piling the timbers and the stacks of wall panels on pallets we had spread out for them on the ground to the north side of the foundation. Some of the stacks were thirty feet high. They spread plastic over them to protect them from damaging rain.

Then they left. A wind, presaging a storm, blew up, lifting the thin plastic protecting the drywall. We knew what that meant: its ruin. John remembered how to use the forklift we'd rented for them and he showed me how to move the forks. John then climbed on to the forks themselves, I worked the levers as he taught me, and he rose up to meet the top of the stack. From there he could crawl up onto the top of the pile and secure the plastic before the rain came. A thing, a motion, he'd learned years before was now opened for him again, for us, a saving motion for the house. I'd earlier in the day had time to rub some of the massive mixed red and white oak timbers lying on pallets on the ground with a linseed oil and turpentine mix I made up.

I loved stroking their knots and cracks, each one distinctive, each a tree. This treatment would protect the timbers over time and deepen their luster. It was far easier to rub them while they were lying on the ground than when they were in place 8 or 12' off the floor. I managed to get to almost all of them rubbed before the rain came—one of the hot, tired men mixing the mortar, in an act of such unanticipated kindness, helped me. The rain that day spotted only a few of the timbers. I saw those stains for years after as I looked up from a chair.

Today, Monday, George returned with the full crew and they have begun to assemble the "bents"—the three vertical posts and horizontal carrying beams that make up one wall—on the ground. We've rented a crane for them to use later to lift the heavy bents in place once the first floor deck is done—in earlier timber framing, each post would be hand carried into place..

July 5, 1986

And now, today, miraculous this day: the first wall. There is something about a wall—and this one I didn't want down. George finished setting the first floor joists around noon and leveled the house. Then after lunch John and I learned to walk (gingerly) over the open joists over the cellar pit (how marvelous to be out of the basement at last!) and began to apply beads of glue to their tops, so that the subfloor the crew was laying down and nailing behind us would not squeak later when one of us got up in the night. By 4:30 we had a deck! Pat and our friend Steve were out there too—Pat waterproofing the west wall of the foundation before I can glue up the insulating board later, Steve hauling 12 inch block away from where we will backfill (and we need to do this soon: the house is so high it's hard to get into it now—the crew is complaining!).

Then at 4:30, George wanted to raise the west wall before they left to go home for the weekend. He too wanted to see what the frame he had been cutting in his shop looked like against the sky, my pencil, his saw, joined here. This, this wall: it was like nothing I'd ever known. It is our first wall, our living room wall. It is the birth, the house going up to meet me. This is the wall I'd seen only in my mind for a year. Here it was, out there, in the meadow, out there for others to see. It was no longer "mine." I took a hundred pictures marking this, this, my jar placed in Tennessee, my jar in a Maryland meadow that once grew tobacco.

July 13, 1986.

The frame is complete. I find a small fir tree. George tacks it up to the top of the rafters. We gather for the photo, champagne in hand. The prayer is unheard. I toast the crew.

The power of this frame cannot be photographed. I want the house to stay open this way. I want the wind to pass through it as it does now and the meadow to be entirely visible through it as it is now. I wish I could glass it in. I understand Philip Johnson's glass house for the first time. I understand Thoreau's complaint about his house "never pleasing [his] eye so much after it was plastered" (217-8). I think anyone who has framed a house must know this.

July 22, 1986.

One member of the crew had hooked up a video camera. From the time the frame begins to rise to the time the last window and shingle is applied, we've now a moving sequence of pictures. These show more, but only movements across time.

The swathing of the house in panels: it looks like a Christo project. From outside the house, the viewer sees in the video the tip of a chain saw poking through one part of the house that is now a closed box. This is Bill. He's beginning to cut out a hole for a window, the window of the dining room. In another moment on the video, I can see the men hoisting the window into place, nailing into the 2x6's they've "let in" to the sides of the hole so there's something for the window to be nailed to. The video does not, however, show me looking out from inside the house at the suddenly new view. I'll sit every day at the table and see just this. I think: how important the frame of the view. I will come to know this particular swath of the meadow better than all others, because of this frame. And I'll remember this view long after I've left here—more easily than I'll remember the view of the whole meadow as I stand outside in it.

The video camera moves out. We see Dave kneeling on the roof and hear him tap tapping as he nails another cedar shingle on. He's making us a roof, on which we will so depend in time to come. The video doesn't show how I feel—the tap reminds me of the thinness of this membrane, of how little separates me from the sky.

Then the camera shifts positions again, to the cellar. Its eye is on me, kneeling on the cellar stairs. I'm thin. I'm wearing shorts and a turquoise gauzy blouse, white socks and sneakers. Silver earrings dangle from my ears. I'm utterly concentrated on the new 20 ounce framing hammer I'm holding in my right hand. I'm trying to nail long finish nails (called "16d," or "16 penny" nails) into southern yellow pine. I've taken some scrap flooring from our second floor and cut it into lengths for the cellar treads. Tap, tap, ten times for each nail—humorous for the knowing viewer and the crew, who hear that I'm a novice hammerer (it should take only three taps). What this moment on the video doesn't show, however, is that I'm the one who has cut the stair stringers, the long, notched boards that the crew has set in place on the diagonal, to receive the treads. This cutting of the stair stringers was a major carpentry breakthrough for me, a crossing. I hadn't planned on this. I knew entire books had been written on stair layout—it's that complicated. One uneven rise, one too wide tread, and someone could stumble, our feet are so knowing. George one day said, "you can to this." We hadn't contracted with them to cut the stringers and we were all tired of climbing stepladders to get from floor to floor. George, also an engineer, checked my calculations (again derived from my Shelter notebook). Allowing for the variations at the top and bottom, I marked off with a pencil each V for a riser and tread on each 2 x 12. I used my framing square affixed at each end with specially made screws for marking the end of each riser and tread (so each would be the same). I then held the still new circular saw and began the cut, as Shelter had taught me, finishing off the very inside corner of each with a hand saw. The thing is, once I knew I could cut stair stringers, I knew I could do anything.

In the last video scene, the house is quiet in the meadow. The frame is up, wrapped, windows and doors, roof on. I now have an entirely open box inside to fill in with walls, by myself. What comes next is the long silence, unrecorded since I'm largely alone for this part of the job. I am like my colonial ancestors, many of whom hired a professional to design and supervise the planning of the timbers, make the house weather-tight outside, and then leave the inside work for the farmer to do in the winter. It is now nearly August. Winter is coming. It's a good vessel.

Scenes from a thing-in-process. We moved into that house, center of these scenes, seven months later. The house was not finished. We'd no "finished stairs." We'd no trim around the windows. We lived out of boxes in the kitchen because we'd no cabinets yet. And the house was imperfect. I knew where the bent nails in the stair stringers were. I could see the timbers stained by the rain, the ones I'd been unable to rub with turpentine and linseed oil before the thunder. For months, until we finished the trim, I could hear the wind moaning as it passed through the window frames, reminding me I was not sealed off.

And once we moved our old furniture in to it, life, messy, complicated life began to happen, again. All those months of building I had concentrated on doing the job as right as I could and on getting the job done. And that's all I saw. I didn't call or write to friends. My husband and I didn't go to the movies. We didn't talk life over dinner and a bottle of wine. He sat in the den and watched television in the rented house. I sat in the living room, my building books and papers spread out in front of me. Only a sight line in the doorway between these rooms connected us for months. And during the days we worked there, it was just like the fourteen hour day in the trench—except we stopped hugging each other and weeping at day's end. I was birthing the house and its birth was a long labor, a lovely labor some of the time, but a long and difficult labor. And it was a lonely labor. I gave it all my concentration, all my worry, all my love. Shelter had warned me: it's best if couples take the class together. It's best if both are obsessed about building. It's best. We hadn't. He could only come to one class. And I didn't press him. This was to be an immaculate conception. This was going to be done, whatever the cost. And it cost.

    The day the old furniture was arranged in the living area, near the west wall, the first one I'd seen raised that July 4th weekend the year before, John and I sat facing each other. Our furniture came with a history. We came with a history. I looked at him, and he at me. We didn't know what to say to each other. We'd not sat like this for a long long time. I remember feeling at a loss—and so I began to cover some wall switches with scraps of wallpaper for the bathroom. Better to have a project in such moments of silence and vacancy. Better to move as I was used to in this space: work. Later John would tell the story, "I told Eileen that if we didn't spend some real time together, we'd be getting a divorce; her response was, 'oh and on your way home would you buy a box of twenty-penny nails?'" This was true, he did say this and I probably did say this back to him. The photographs reveal nothing of this kind of conversation either. I was building a house. I was not building a relationship to live in that house. I wasn't then thinking about right relation with my husband. I was still trying to make the perfect vessel, and I believed I could. I saw nothing but the vessel. I saw nothing but what I thought I was making of it. It was my idol, first above all else in my life. I thought this was how I had to do it.

One of the first nights that we slept under the sloping rafters, I dreamed a wall of fire came within ten feet of the front door. It did not come further. But it was there. I had nothing to do with stopping it. The unconscious, I have come to believe, is very knowing. It would take walls of fire at my door to wake me. Or perhaps this was another kind of wall of fire, the kind the Hebrew prophet Zechariah speaks of. Zechariah's vision is of Jerusalem and not a house, but the house had become by then my own secular Jerusalem, and, like it, would have to be undone. It would come, over time, my house, to have entirely new kinds of walls like those the prophet of Jerusalem speaks about. Jerusalem, he says, "shall be inhabited like villages without walls...For I will be a wall of fire all around it" (*Zechariah* 2, 4-5).

A couple of months later, we stood with friends on the new porch in the summer twilight. We were watching the massed fireflies in the May meadow, the magic of their lighting up here and there, where one could never predict. As we sat for a long time, we began to hear the thunder in the distance. Gradually the lightning irradiated the sky. As sound and light came closer, I knew the way I always do, having been inside two houses when lightning had hit them, that this was an ominous, terribly powerful storm. We went inside. The house was spared. I was not sure it would be. We'd no lightning rods. I was a lightning rod.

Several hours later the phone rang. It was a friend. John's best friend, Carl, had been at a park with his wife and infant daughter. They lived in Baltimore, an hour away from us. The same storm had sprung upon them, as suddenly. As we were watching the miracle of fireflies, they were gazing at herbs and listening to someone tell of their history. When the storm hit, they all took refuge in an old stone chapel, whose windows had long been gone. A ball of lightning, we were told later, came in one of those windows and hit Carl head on. It stunned him unconscious, and injured a number of others. He was in the hospital. He was not expected to live. Someone had had the presence of mind to turn his infant daughter around before she could see the fire hit her father.

The following afternoon as we sat at the table, John picked up a wine glass. It shattered in his hands. We remembered the wine glass Carl and his wife had smashed at their wedding on another summer's afternoon. We later found out that Carl died just about that time.

Life and trouble and death were filling the house, the new house, the house that was to be perfect, perfectly walled up against all of these messy, uncontrollable things. Like the wind in the windows, we couldn't keep life out. We limped through months of John's grief--and through months of marital discord. Alone in the building time, he was alone in his grief. We had forgotten how to be together. He wanted me to be there at the moments when grief can be shared, but he'd lost trust I could. I wanted him to continue to help me build our house and not go off inside. We were walls, acres apart. A critical break had happened, a turning moment in our marriage.

We never quite knew how we managed to go on but we did. That seemed out of our control too. We lived through months of taking ginger steps back together, months of slow healing from all the wounds to us. I learned in that painful time of our earliest months that the house alone would never save us. I learned that driving home through wet leaves on the road at night and pulling into the driveway would not promise a warm fire. I learned that sitting in the living room or the den, backing up to the beautiful west wall, would not be times of peace or joy. My house building had blinded me to that which I never should have been blind to.

My father-in-law, who had visited us from Connecticut from time to time in order to work beside me in the early days of the house, visited after we moved in to help us finish it. He wanted to paint the cellar walls. He would paint for a couple of hours, then drag himself up the stairs and look at me and say, "I don't know why I am so tired—I've worked so much harder than this in my life." I would urge him to sit on the sofa with an unaccustomed book. He slept. He read it in fits and starts. Within the year he was dead, of congestive heart failure.

One day I stood in the garden, the garden abundant with tomatoes and squash and cucumbers, the garden abundant with bugs and heat. The telephone rang. My mother reported that she'd "overdone" it. She said she'd been helping my brother roll logs down the hill in Connecticut, the same hill we would later build the second house on. She said to me, when I asked, that both her left leg and left arm were limp. I said, "you have had a stroke." She went to the hospital. They did tests, put her on medication. It was a "temporary stroke." She was to live for four more years before having another, fatal one. I knew as I hung up the phone and wandered back out into the garden that day that this was the beginning of her end. My house could not hold them, either of them either.

  What got me through these years of real life in the house was meditation in the now completed meditation room. I'd begun, in a way, this spiritual practice as a child. In the summers of my teenage years, I'd sit in the hammock and read Norman Vincent Peale's *The Power of Positive Thinking*. I remember he'd recommended that one try to empty one's mind for fifteen minutes a day. I would sit in the hammock in the yard, the summer traffic speeding by on its way to the lake, and try to think of nothing. It was almost impossible. But the trying to think of nothing was something new. It was a coming to ground. It stilled me and the traffic's sound was deadened. It anchored me in the hammock, outside the small family house. I looked forward to it.

  I stopped this practice, an early form of prayer although no one told me I could call it that then. I read and wrote instead to cultivate my quiet, my solitude. It was not the same. Years later, shortly before we began to build, we had also, both of us, begun to meditate. I found the practice difficult at first. I'd crawl into the attic in the rental house that my husband had converted into a meditation space and try to sit cross-legged. It was cold. I was uncomfortable. Once a week we'd often go to a local ashram for a program of meditation and chanting with others. I found it all strange—and strangely compelling—the orange-robed monks, the sounds of the Indian instruments, the smell of incense, the pictures of Indian gurus on the wall, and the quiet of just sitting, and sometimes the surprise of what would happen within me as I quieted my mind. I would wake out of meditation and feel my eyes swimming and see the largeness of others' eyes. I did not know it then, but I was preparing an inner house, an inner place, one that would go with me, wherever.

This is how both our new houses came to have small meditation rooms. In fact, we couldn't settle on the design for the first house and a friend said to us, "do what the Japanese do: design your meditation room first." We did, and the design all came together. It was a small space under the eves, just 6x8', and it was dark. I would go in there to breathe, breath in, breath out. In this way I finished the walls, saw the next step to take care of, and became less anxious.

Gradually I found myself meditating more and more. When my husband and I acknowledged our distance, I crawled into the quiet of the meditation room to be alone with myself. When we started to come together again, we began to get up at 3 in the morning every day, meditate for an hour, and then chant for another hour. I always felt this time was the healing time between us. We followed these spiritual practices for a whole year.

I was, without quite understanding what was happening, turning to build another kind of house, an inner house. The outer house, exquisitely lovely, did not suffice. I was learning the fragility of the vessel, like Jeremiah's potter (18:1-6), that I had made. I was beginning to feel I was in the middle of some holy conversation that I couldn't yet hear. I had more to do. I had more right relation to grow into, more travels with God, much more inner house building to do. I was only beginning. It would take, among other things, other events, other people coming into my life, leaving this first house and then building again to lead me there.

VIII

Leaving

...the anguish of seeing the mobility of places aggravates still more the mobility, already so frightening in itself, of our being.[38]

No, I'll never get the house back, not if by 'getting it back' I mean holding a deed, owning a key, crossing the purplish shade of the porch to enter the side hall, slamming the screen door behind me. I must content myself with another kind of possession altogether. My task is to house this house, which has vanished from the waking world, as it once housed me, to grant it the deed to my dreams.[39]

--Nancy Mairs

But is not a moment of self-dispossession essential to authentic selfhood?[40]

--Paul Ricoeur

Perhaps we are all, unknowingly, a little like Proust upon waking: sorting the objects that slowly coalesce before our eyes, placing them in one particular house and not another from the past or from the dream world. So we locate, emplace and still ourselves. So I would every day, after I meditated, perform another kind of "house-keeping." Though I had learned I couldn't stop the little airs of death from entering the front door, all the daily rituals, wiping the counter, mopping the floor, pulling out a few weeds as I took my early morning walk through my gardens, coffee cup in hand: these comfortingly built the house round me again and again. I was the monk walking the boundary again, the dog circling my nest. *Stabilitas*—staying in place in order to go on.

We redraw the house's boundaries every day, not just once and for all at the moment of building them with wood and nail. Leaving their daily care for a time, to travel, we return to the restful comfort of these rituals' assuaging rhythms.

But what if there is no return? What if the place that had been our shelter night after night, the place about which we have told stories, the place we remember through all its coming-to-be: what if this place is lost?

One of the losses rarely spoken out loud is the loss of possession of a house.[41] I once asked a friend who'd lived in a house for twenty years before moving to our town how he managed. I knew him as a man who tended his property with deep affection, for I'd seen him garden and repair and mow his lawn. This now elderly man, reserved, shy, stood suddenly still. His eyes teared and his face reddened. He said, "I just walked away and didn't look back." He could say no more. This particular grief has no public currents. We grieve openly with those whose houses have been lost to hurricane, tornado, earthquake, fire. We should grieve for those who sell. They don't lose photos, don't lose everything. And those of us who sell have perhaps made a free choice. But one who leaves any house for any reason knows this breach that cannot be repaired.

Emily Dickinson, who never left her family home, imagines the shock of severing her body from a once loved house. She approaches the old house, "and now before the Door" "dares not enter." What if a "Face" she "never saw before/ Stare stolid into mine." This other face, it could be a new occupant, maybe in time ahead, or time past, it could be her old self. She imagines this other asking her what is her "Business there" and she answers "'My Business but a Life I left/Was such remaining there?'" The other does not answer. Who could answer such a question, even one's older self? The speaker's body crumbles. "Leaning" upon "Awe," "lingering" with "Before," "laughing" a "crumbling Laugh/That I could fear a Door," she puts her hand to the "Latch," then "moves" her "Fingers off/As cautiously as Glass." She flees "gasping from the House." What is on the other side of that door? It compels her yet terrifies her. It is the unredeemable past. It is a sign that maybe she was never there at all. She imagines the building round her broken.[42]

Looking back can be deadly. Anna Akhmatova in "Lot's Wife" explores the price of this in her rereading the Genesis story. God spares Lot, telling him to leave Sodom and Gomorrah before God destroys it. God's only prohibition is that Lot and his family not look back. But his wife does. And she is turned into a pillar of salt.

...a wild grief in his wife's bosom cried,
Look back, it is not too late for a last sight
Of...the tall house with empty windows where
You loved your husband and your babes were born.

She turned, and looking on the bitter view
Her eyes were welded shut by mortal pain;
Into transparent salt her body grew....

Who would waste tears upon her? Is she not
The least of our losses, this unhappy wife?
Yet in my heart she will not be forgot
Who, for a single glance, gave up her life. [43]

Too much looking back to the abandoned house, too much grieving could kill one. Lot's wife turning into a pillar of salt was not a punishment, but a necessary consequence of that look. Perhaps my elderly friend was wise after all to not look back and to be silent about the leaving. And yet look back, imagine, dream, grieve we do.

On August 15, 1914, Frank Lloyd Wright's house in Taliesin, Wisconsin was set on fire by a disturbed employee. Wright's sister, Maginel, said the house was timeless, magical. She claimed that she could feel Wright's presence from the scents, of wood, of herbs. Seven people died in the fire and the house was destroyed. Only Wright's studio remained. The house failed to provide safety. People combed the wreckage looking for signs of the house that was. Survivors retrieved from the ashes shards of porcelain and rebuilt them into the concrete pillars of the rebuilt house.[44] On television people who have lost houses to tornadoes and earthquakes similarly peck among the ruins, looking for shards to put in a new foundation. Was a life remaining there they ask?

Earlier peoples, far smarter than we about the curative private and public power of ritual, practiced destruction rites. It was not enough, for example, to burn the building before moving on (not always as a punishment to the invader but also a sign that the houses belonged to particular people). The house would also be unmade, ritually. When a town or a foundation was made, the plough would cut the boundary. When a house or town was to be destroyed, or unmade, it had to be "unploughed"—the initial carving into the earth filled in, the plough turned in the other direction.[45]

Once John and I decided to move to Connecticut, I struggled for many months trying to figure out how we could keep the first house. There was no way. There was the cost. There was the three hundred mile distance. There was my unsuitability as a landlord. I couldn't take care of this house and another. The gardens were dying. Once I accepted the inevitable, I cast about for rituals to help me leave.

I could find none. And, even worse: few people wanted to talk with me about what I was feeling. Some of them were people who'd never moved. All were people who'd never built. Some, good-naturedly, offered practical if unconsoling advice to me: you will go on to build another, better house. I loved this first, as I would love none other. It alone bore the marks of all my forty-year old fledgling building strokes. It alone greeted me with evidence of the turn of my life.

The ritual I devised was private, by me, for me, alone. Part of it was my writing of a "leaving journal" to complete the "building journal" I'd written on the way in to the house. The leaving journal was my private demolition rite. It was a way to pick among the ruins of the house to come, a ruin for me, for shards I could take along in my pocket. The journal would become the memory container, the jar, which the house had been. It was another kind of building round.

We had decided to stop renting out the house while it was on the market. I moved back in during the several days a week I was in the Washington area teaching. The seasons passed one complete round as I looked out its windows and walked in its meadow. I lived there largely alone in that time. I had four or five pieces of furniture in a 3,000 square foot house: an old maple table I'd refinished, an antique chair the side of whose seat was worn as if it had been used for a sawhorse (or so my mother had said), two wicker chairs I'd purchased new for this time, a hide-a-bed sofa we'd left behind for our tenant, and a bed borrowed from friends. I brought a few books with me. Several vases of dried flowers and a couple of plants reminded me of the many others once filling the corners of the house. A white and blue patterned hooked rug warmed the foot of the sofa, and another like it the foot of my bed. Most of the rooms, guest room, our studies, den, were empty, echoing chambers. The house was going to have to sell itself, speak for itself the beauty of its internal skeleton, its oak timbers, the quality of the light from the meadow streaming in the windows and skylights onto oak floors. White walls and honey-colored oak it was, all of it. Someone who once stayed in the house had said, "angels live here." Perhaps they did—I thought so more now in the echoing emptiness of it. Waiting it was—waiting for me to be ready to let go, waiting for someone unknown to walk through its door and call it home.

28 January 1997

How big the sky is here! I always forget until I return on Tuesday evenings from Connecticut. As I walked from the garage to the house this cold, dry winter night, it came to me again all the splendor of this wide open meadow now stiff with frost. And when the moon is visible (it is not now), as it was in late December when John and I were here together for a few days, the whole landscape is lit with it, as if from within. We would love to stand together and look up at it through the sunspace skylight. In summer moonlight I would take the dog out on his leash and walk over into the high grass to be nearer the subtle light eerily softening the full large oaks all along the meadow's edges. There always seemed to be a summer breeze, as there is winter wind now. Always wind here, wind that, at the house's beginning, groaned through the timbers and that still, at times, greets the house with high-pitched wisps. As I go to bed at night, under the massive oak rafters, that wind continues to greet me with that same far-off noise, something banging, that I've never been able to track down in all our years here. It's become my prelude to sleep.

Will I ever be ready to leave all of this, this wind, this meadow, that skylight, the bed nest under the eaves? I do not know. I know that I feel a new kind of gratitude for time, for time to be taking care of it, living here so sparely, so lightly, until the very end. Mine, mine, I say sometimes, still mine, though I know it never was.

3 February 1997

As I push open the thick pine door into the house's solid silence, I feel at times great sadness for all the life lived here that is now so past. Our marriage repaired here. I finished a book here. Friends and guests stepped through this door, sitting many long nights at our table or around our fire. My father-in-law spent weeks here hammering beside me, sharing our morning thermos of coffee. He is now dead. My mother planted trees with me and hung out our laundry on winter days from our porch stoop. She is now dead. Our puppy lived his best years here. When we brought him home, we set him on the lawn and he was suddenly happy to be just here. He is now aging. Leaving a house signifies these passings as probably nothing else does. As I stenciled the entry again I thought: "blessings on the ones to come" and, then, "I know every square inch of you, know it with my fingers. I have painted all of you, all of you."

22 February 1997

    And the moon has come around again, full face through the sunspace skylight. I could mark each month as we lived here as the monks marked time, although I chose not to. I do now as I count my time. I can understand more now how counting moons oddly opens out some other kind of time. In the moonlight, I can see the deer grazing in the meadow and on the lawn. I no longer worry about them, what shrubs they are eating. They can have their fill. The serenity of their quiet movements, the nod and brush of their heads reclaiming land that was theirs long before it was ours, is reassuring.

23 February 1997

    Another sun-spilled morning sitting in the wicker chair in the sunspace. I move the chair from place to place to catch the light. All reddish golden, the light making its angular shadows by the hearth, the plants serene, robust. A cardinal, could it be the same one every day?, perches on the window ledge and peers in at me. Sometimes he pecks at the window.

    Will the ones to come, I think, sense our life that was lived here? Will our spirits gracefully haunt this place for them? They do not yet even know the life ahead of them here, nor do I, nor can they ever know what was left behind here. This is a mystery of our separation from each other, not to know such things.

25 March 1997

As the Washington spring begins, always so deliciously early here, I grieve for future of the trees we planted, so vulnerable they seem. I try to think of these cherry trees in a hundred years—some of these trees will make it on their own, spared from blight or axe. Perhaps I overestimate my role in their survival. What do the planters of trees do? Do they live on at all in the planting? Around my birth house, Lampe planted weeping mulberry and mock orange and peony. I know him only in this way. But is not this something?

Four trees here hurt most: the magnolia, the Shogetsu cherry—planted as but saplings by our hands, and "Joe" and "John"—the maple planted by my father-in-law, now dead, and the blue spruce I planted because John loves them. Would that I could take the trees and shrubs, especially the ones we planted—I care less about the ones the landscapers put in. And yet they all grow apace, apart from me. They are too big to move. They belong here. Their robustness reassures, even as grieves me.

And yet, a nagging thought as spring approaches: this garden, this 40 x 60' garden that I tended so carefully for so many seasons, a garden brimming with tomatoes and peppers and eggplant and squash and lettuce, along with the beneficial insects, ladybugs, lace-wings, preying mantis, is now fallow, waiting under mulch. It waits for other hands. This land needs a better steward now that we've planted our humanity here.

17 April 1997

What is hardest is coming suddenly upon people being "shown" the house. I drove in today only to find a car in the driveway and a prospective couple. Rather than being eager, I found myself assessing them: would they care for this place? I hardly cared what they thought! The realtors have already made their assessments. How odd to find one's choices criticized: the entry is not good enough, the washer and dryer shouldn't be in the kitchen, there needs to be a closet in my husband's study. I become hostile when I hear these things, uncomprehending. It's humiliating to have our choices evaluated by all of these strangers. I am being trespassed against.

20 April 1997

The lawn is freshly cut. The dogwood's leaves are beginning to turn brown and shrivel, the viburnum about to open. Each unfolds in its turn. There's no stopping them. The lilac will come after. How well I know these pages turning every spring. Can I do this again? Plant more shrubs? They will take ten years. If I didn't build the other house now, I'd have only a "young" house to die in—and young bushes. Mature ones somehow seem more appropriate. Is this consolation enough for leaving?

2 May 1997

Two small miracles: Five or six years ago I planted a wisteria that an elderly man had given my brother. He has now killed himself. He faced a terminal illness. He lived alone. I lost track of the wisteria. I forgot all about it, in fact. Today, as I was driving out, I glanced up at the trees by the side of the driveway, and there it was, in full bloom! How did this happen? It had been taking all this time to climb slowly up the tree, and all of a sudden there it was, blue and pendulous, as if lilacs and grapes had crossed!

And the other: two years ago I think it was I planted a clematis, "Nelly Moser," by the side of the outside stairwell. I had hoped it would climb the lattice as the other clematis in the front had done. But I lost track of it as well, forgot about it also. And then, there it was one day as I turned the corner, flowers saucer sized, pink and white, sun smiling.

6 May 1997

A splendid spring day. I sit on the porch grading final papers. Wind. Birds. Grass in the meadow, sinuous. How can we let it go? But I think we are both not here, and I am here so little. I think the house is waiting for a fuller life again, its garden, its rooms filled. I think I walk too lightly in it, and so I console myself with my thinking and my writing.

The golden locust is splendid now, like golden rain, large, perfect to shade the porch that had too much morning sun. I find myself beginning to dream of a sunspace in the next house, whose foundation, poured this winter, is waiting for us to resume—after we sell this one. Only the waiting foundation, waiting for a house, and the pull of Connecticut, and the pleasure of designing, dreaming new spaces pulls me gently forward, inch by inch. Perhaps all change is like this, inch by inch, a tug away and a tug toward what is coming.

I find myself remembering what the minister said at my mother's funeral: "this house is not our home." And Jesus, "you must give up all and follow me"—and they did, Peter, Andrew—even houses.

8 May 1997

And now someone is interested. I find myself checking the stove more earnestly these days (to be certain it's turned off)—fearing my subconscious. I understand the desire to burn one's building behind one. It makes emotional sense. Efface the past, the structures that would otherwise withstand to remind one that one has moved on. I wonder if people used to pick the people they wanted to buy their houses—this would make more sense. People could line up and one could choose the right one.

24 May 1997

How could I have forgotten the fireflies in the meadow! Will, then, the chuck-will's-widow come next, nesting always it seems in the same corner of the meadow each summer? With the summer's full trees now blowing, comes an old memory of one unrecorded day, a summer evening long ago, when I walked up the hill from downtown to the church in Connecticut and glimpsed all at once a full canopy of laden leaves in the late heat. It was I think my first young moment of fullness. Am I preparing myself, or is my memory preparing me? And my husband's hair, more salt and pepper. And all day my mother has been very close. Can it have happened that she died? I am always stunned that this is a fact.

29 June 1997

Fireflies, again, in the fog and blowing trees all around the meadow. And the dream: the answering machine was not blinking but I pushed it anyway. My mother had left a message about where to find a veneered board. I heard her voice. And she's been so around me in these solitary days here in the house. Some say the house is a mother. It is a little over a year now—and I am selling this house as I grieve her passing. Interlaced griefs.

30 May 1997

Twilight, and that old dark tug about the heart. The restless lost time of late afternoon. Yet I want to face the setting sun.

Perhaps this will be my last weekend alone in this house. It is not mine. We brought it into being, but it has its own life—we husband it only. Water attacks it, sun fades it, the weeds try to invade, and, too, it ages. Are the panels aging? Does the dry wood age? Little used now, it rests. It seems serenely to be choosing our future and its own. Reading J.B. Jackson's "The Necessity of Ruins": those who restore houses, he says, need ruin, for they need to "reproduce the cosmic scheme and correct history" (1980, 102). I go another way, in always building new houses—on ancient earth. What way is that?

1 June 1997

Living in this house now, it comes over me, my mother's wonderful concern about our comfort and well-being. When we were ill her voice was so soothing, her hands spread open with soup, with tea and maybe cranberry bread. When I was confused or upset she would speak with such calm and sweet reason that I, lullabyed, was calmed and sweetened. I always wanted her to need me, but she always evaded me, wore a self-possession about her that stands me in good stead now. It becomes me. Her once having yielded to great loss, was that its source? Or being so on her own all her life? For whatever, she wore her dignity and own good counsel wrapped around her. Even in dreams now, so many dreams in this house, her presence envelopes and calms me. Is she this house?

28 June 1997

Can I build another house? My body ages. When we built this house I felt immortal—at least it seems so now. But I've crossed a divide since she died. I feel as if I can make it through this hurdle— the various breakdowns of the body—I can go on into another use of it. It's another threshold.

3 July 1997.

And now, as I'm back in Connecticut for a couple of weeks, when we least expect it, comes an offer. When I'd heard the agent's voice on the answering machine in Maryland I thought, this is it. And it was. How do I feel? Floating. Adrift. Perhaps I at last understand Dickinson's describing the way she removes her hand from the latch "as cautiously as glass."

27 August 1997.

And now, the house is sold. I've one more month to live in it. As I sit in the big window in the sunspace and watch the buddleia, scraggly this year, I think about eternity, the eternity of this moment in the late summer breeze. Bachelard says, "houses that were lost *forever continue to live on in us; that they insist in us in order to live again, as though they expected us to give them a supplement of living,"* And he speaks of Rilke being in fusion with the lost house: *"I never saw this strange dwelling again. Indeed, as I see it now, the way it appeared to my child's eye, it is not a building, but is quite dissolved and distributed inside me: here one room, there another....thus the whole thing is scattered about inside me..."* (1958, 56-7). *It will be like this with me. I'm glad they've gone before me to tell me this is what it will be like.*

3 September 1997.

The end of my time here is upon me. Perhaps in another life I shall inhabit this house. Do I want to build the other house now? Yes, I say, with growing heart. I don't love the air here, the landscape, the place, as I do Connecticut. Here is the place that reminds me of it, but is not it.

There have been moments I dreaded. My mother's death. And now this. Then to come: the others, husband, brother, friends—will they go before me? Dread is a terrible thing. Lot's wife was promised salvation if she did not look back, if she moved ahead, fleet-footed. It's the same about looking forward—one can't look there either. Keep one's eyes only on the path right there.

5 September 1997

A day so like the many I spent here alone at its beginning: sweeping, tying up endless bundles for trash pickup. But this is one of the last here. As it was in the beginning, so now at the end. John is here. I so welcome that. He helps me put into thought the beauty and place of this house in our lives. It hurts less to do this. We wonder what will be left of its spirit. Generations to come here. What a thought! My mortality. I stood in the shed door just a few moments ago and decided to sign our names in a hidden place on the door jamb: 1984. Eileen Sypher and John Yrchik, owners, builders, designers. I have to leave a signature. At that moment of looking out, having signed, I remembered being twelve and standing in the barn door at home, wearing light blue corduroy jeans, and thinking, I will make myself remember this day all my life because time is passing so quickly.

And now I must get back to it, get back to sweeping us out of here—and see to the poor hummingbird that I cannot help who is beating his life out in the upper window of the garage. How I hate the cage of roof trusses now, that keep me from him.

6 September 1997.

I have met the new owners. They will spare the trees. They picked the house because it reminded them of New England—they saw this one on the realtor's board after a quick decision to take a drive. Just like that.

7 September 1997.

Now the house is empty. It is as it was in the beginning, before we moved in. In my end is my beginning. And the end of all of this striving is to arrive at the place we started and know it for the first time. Eliot is so right. Fare forward. You are not the same person as the one who got on the train. And Heraclitus: you cannot step in the same river twice.

8 September 1997.

It is early—got up around 4:30 a.m. and meditated. Now the darkness is breaking up. These are the moments of being in our lives—those of transition, when we recognize transience of place, objects, self. I am now sitting in a new place in the house and sleeping for the first time on our hide-a-bed which we are leaving for the new owners.

10 September 1997.

I am moving in numbness, yet I feel a light step. I am focusing on being still, on doing the task just ahead of me—and on sending my blessings to these and all inhabitants of this house in time to come. And for me, in the next space I imagine, refuge, childhood, *mother, father, a New England perennial bed, no need to recreate New England. I will be there.*

Tonight I go to sleep with their furniture, some of it, now settled here and there in the house, like sentinels. It came while I was away. First I felt like fleeing. Then I focused on cleaning out my things. I began to see the beauty in the carved wood of their pieces, the child's pink toothbrush in my bathroom, a few art objects. Tonight I am in-between two worlds—my last in this house, edged out in a way, but I chose to go. And I feel their benign presence to come.

17 September 1997.

I said goodbye to the house this morning, as much as I'll ever be able to say goodbye. I will not, chances are, live in it again. It will now slowly retreat into a place inside of me, in dreams. I've so dreaded this moment but mixed with it I feel that relief when the dreaded thing has finally come—and the surprise that I can go on. It will be interesting to see, when the house fades from actual sensory experience, where it goes in me. It will have different, vaster boundaries. Will the new one supplant it? I doubt it can, for this has all the marks of the "first." Its aging is as dear to me as my aging body, some of which was worn out building it. The new one will take time to ripen. Now I must devote my energy to giving it a good start. This will be my best cure. I am a builder at heart.

I made up my own final leaving ritual. I entered each room. I hugged myself and as I did I drew into me all of our private memories in that space, leaving the energy that is the house's for the ones to come. I said prayers in what was our meditation room and then said prayers as I walked in a circle around the central hearth. I walked out the door, locked it, and got in my car. I did not look back.

IX

Building Again

A boundary is not that at which something stops but, as the Greeks recognized, the boundary is that from which something begins its presencing.[46]

— Heidegger

When a dog, like the setter, turns round and round, it's flattening the tall grasses into a clearing for a bed. It's a temporary nest reenacted from memory and the fields of the past. The nest is a part of the field, and the field reaches out to the hills and hills to the mountains and mountains to the sea, and you have a land...[47]

I did build another house. Within a week of closing the door on the first, I traveled three hundred miles on a well-known roadway to face the shell of the garage rising up in the Connecticut woods. We would have to wait almost four months for our second timber frame to arrive from Maine. The trucks were as large as those that carried the first, but this time the road did not offer any impediments. The second house was, in almost all ways, easier in its coming.

Unlike Milarepa, I did not take apart the materials of the first house and reset them upon the earth when I turned to building the next. The first house still sits in its meadow, silently bearing the traces of our work. I am not the agent of its mortality. I took it apart only by standing in the middle of each room and gathering it into my memory. I took it apart only by writing of it and taking that book with me.

When I built the second house, I did not design a radically new shape for it, as Milarepa did. But Milarepa's story isn't really about changing the house's shape. "Shape" is a metaphor. Each house is always new, different materials, a different ground. The next house is never a repetition. The experience and so the meaning of each house inevitably change.

I watched the first house go up as if it were my painting and I were the only one in charge of the brush. It was, as a friend once critically put it, "my monument." But when I began to build the second, I no longer stood at my metaphoric easel in the meadow trying to coax "my" vulnerable thing into being. The meaning of house and particularly its "mine-ness" changed. The second house began to leave its protected position as the object of my painting, my framing, of it. The "this" the woman on the stairs pointed to as she asked me her echoing question, "however did you do this?," was shifting in meaning once again. The second house is a very different "this."

Once dispossessed of a first, a second house is never so much one's own. Paradoxically my second house might seem as if it would make even deeper inroads on any claim I might make to its being mine. The field from which I watched the second house rise, three hundred some miles from the first, was not one I'd bought from a stranger. I'd been a child on it. The field stretched between my childhood house, where my brother still lives, and this new one. Nor was the field bounded by the land of strangers, new neighbors, but by relatives whose own house history I well knew. And yet this "I" in relation to this second house was never just "mine"—nor could the house be. In a way, "I" could not really watch this house--I was already, in effect, being "watched" in my memory, watched by a familiar place, by family, by a community. My new house was already a part of a history I knew too well. Perhaps it is our cultural habit of wandering from strange place to strange place that feeds house possessiveness. If the walls of our house are all we know, they thicken.

"Before I built a wall I'd ask to know/what I was walling in or walling out."[48] Frost's advice—about the need to know--was difficult for me to carry out. What did this second house wall in or wall out? What kind of boundary is possible between one's adult and child selves? In returning I confront the child I was and am so often surprised at the continuity between them. In returning I re-enter the always complex familial and neighborhood network. History is thicker here. I don't think I could have presumed to build this second set of walls in this place had I not built the first. This ghosted land threatens always to be so much larger than I am. Its memories could so easily paralyze.

When I was a small child, my father's feet walked the land that now lies buried under the footings of the new house. He would bring back from its then woods the odor of skunk on his leather jacket or a sapling maple to shade our house for years to come. From my childhood bedroom window I could look out at the frost-tipped meadow that stretches now between the two houses. With the trees bared, I could then see the very contours of this hill. I might even have seen him once in the distance, sometime in my first four years while he was still living.

Years later, one of my last memories of my then eighty-year old mother working outdoors, work she continued to love, was of her carrying cut up logs down this same hill of my now house for her firewood. One day I helped her load the logs onto the truck. This is now the place where the daffodils I have planted grow in spring.

On my mother's and my last woods walk together, on the ribbon road, now rutted, unused, that winds through the state forest that backs the house, she and I stood at a small bridge over the stream and looked just this way. The new house did not yet exist. She did not know it would be exactly where it now is, nor did I, though she knew it was in the coming. And yet, it is precisely from this point on that bridge on that path, and only this point, that the cedar garage and roof of the house is now visible in winter.

While our excavator, Pete, was carving out our driveway with his own artist's knife, his backhoe blade, I had told him that we'd once had a gravel pit on the property. He began, while I was away, to dip bucket after bucket from it, filling his truck ninety times—to cushion the 600' driveway so we would be able to drive over it without puncturing tires on tree roots or tips of rocks. When he was done digging for gravel, he smoothed out the hole, and then went deeper and deeper, allowing the water from the water table to rise. He thus made us a pond, deepening the shallow water where I once had searched for tadpoles as a young girl and making a place where now frogs chant all night long, spring through fall, and where I can skate in winter. As I look from the backyard of my childhood home into the pond's surface, I see reflected my second house on the hill.

I did not plan any of these things. All I did was walk the hill and then, at one moment, know that it was "here, just here." From the beginning I was not in charge.

I felt, in saying, "here, just here," waited for. I felt I was taking my place, my place among many others, family, my child self. I feel as if I am, here in this, the second house, at the center of converging vectors. I feel at the same time that this house radiates outward. This second set of house walls does offer some stiffening of me, but the walls are more porous too than those of the first house.

A boundary seems such a simple thing, a line in the dirt, the red ribbons surveyors use, iron stakes marking corners. Our system of property division enabling taxation and the selling of real estate depends upon exact lines. If you say to anyone now, where is the boundary, people most likely point to the iron stake in the ground.

But what of different kinds of boundaries—porous, inexact ones, are not these also real? Heidegger speaks of a boundary as not the end of one's property, but the beginning of some "presencing." If the boundary itself "presences," it isn't inert. It suggests there is some other out there meeting one at the wall. Under these circumstances, our speaking of owning the land to this boundary loses some of its certitude. "Boundary" instead begins to become a moving horizon. As Frost goes on, the "something" that "doesn't love a wall" "sends the frozen-ground-swell under it/And spills the upper boulders in the sun,/And makes gaps even two can pass abreast."

Frozen ground swells and spilling boulders are this boundary at the second house. Ken Wilbur offers a perhaps less violent but equally unstable image for this other kind of boundary. He says that real boundaries are more like shorelines, which change shape all the time with the tides. There is a difference between shore and sea. There is a difference between what is out there and me, my house, my land, but each, shore, sea, depends upon the other to be what it is and the line that divides one from the other is always shifting.

It is, however we choose it, important to use the right visual image for a boundary. A fixed line, a closed line, and much follows from that. One thing that does not follow is "dwelling," dwelling in the sense of being *with* persons and things.

Perhaps because the boundaries here are so blurred, I think of my second house more as offering me shelter after a walk, than as a fixed monument. Because I looked out on this hill as a child, looked out at it in frozen winters at its desolate trees, a forbidden place it was, the place of fox and skunk, as well as the magic place of the strange, eerie night echoes of owl and whippoorwill, because I saw hurricane bend the thin trees and ice weigh and snap the limbs, because I was returning here and had no berth any longer in my childhood house, I needed above all to shelter myself in this place that was far more powerful than I am, to make a place to sleep, to wall in my childhood tree glades. This house was always a becoming and never a certitude.

Rilke says that when he was in the country he loved to be out-of-doors during a storm because there he could feel, as he could not in the city, that the storm "sees a lonely house" (Bachelard 1958, 42). I can see my lonely house when it was still unbuilt, still unimagined, from the storms of memory. I needed as a child my own house, needed it, but couldn't build it yet. There is a delicious as well as terrifying starkness in remembering the loneliness of the house that could not then be quite seen. It's like standing outside in rain and being able to see the outlines of a protective roof ahead, a roof of just the right slope and material. But that is all there is, the outline of roof. Walking toward such a roof, in rain and dark, we feel what Tillich calls the "contingency of our spatial being" (1952, 44)—we are here, in this place, in this time, for a little while only, and we do not know why. Walking toward such a house, seeing that roof and that light we hope shines in the window of the house, we hope for rest in place just ahead. I was walking toward this house's promise for a long time, without knowing it. And because I waited so long, its boundary was never fixed, was always presencing.

When we were building, I was preoccupied with wind and rain, with the roof's ever-so-slowly-coming-to-be a roof. I'd stand in the boxed in timber frame shell watching the plastic covering the future bay-window area (this area would have to be constructed with 2x4s when the interior partitions were built). The plastic held out wind and rain, its membrane almost gauzy and thin-seeming but durable. I'd stand in the empty shell in the rain to hear it pelting the skylights. I was preternaturally aware of the bare plywood that would later hold the siding and the white rigid foam insulation under that. I remember putting my hand on either side of the wall, the inside and the outside, feeling the warming shelter this otherwise nondescript white Styrofoam offered the inside of the house. I studied the ragged channels grooved within this Styrofoam for the electrical wires, wires that now power this computer (so allowing me to talk about sheltering at this very moment). I would touch the dry wall on the inside wall, a wall that is now painted, here where I sit, a blue-purple like the morning sea. And I fingered the hard ridged 8" red bolts that secure these wall panels to the massive timber posts and beams they surround, the posts and beams I can touch at this very moment. This boundary's porousness remains in memory.

And sometimes the boundary was literally porous. I remember, looking up at the roof over my bed every night as I crawl into it, the place where water once poured in to the valley before the shingles were applied. Puddles of water sat on the floor. I remember days and days it seemed of pushing water into the drain of the basement slab because we hadn't yet put up rain gutters or graded the earth to slope away from the house—so inviting all the water to seep into the basement. I take nothing for granted, neither Styrofoam, nor bolt, nor drain, nor slope, nor gutter, all humble, seemingly small things but each one crucial. Many urban and semi-urban people in history have apparently taken to building primitive huts for themselves (Rykwert 1981, 82). Perhaps they do so to know shelter in this way—to know it by building it, to know it by working to patch holes where the rain came in. Even now many of us love to sit in a room with a tin roof, or a room in a cottage in which the ceiling has not been insulated: this way we can hear the rain pelting on the window and feel our own dryness. I needed the complexities of this kind of boundary, here, in this place.[49]

  I had, in short, aged with the years, with the return to the land where many are now dead. My sense of house was different even before I began the second. *That* was the shape of the second: the house was leakier, as was life. But there were other conditions of this second building that changed the nature of the boundary. Building in this small town, in the town where I grew, building as many before me would have done before the great migrations, westward, or to the urban north that began at the end of the nineteenth century, influenced the boundary here. This difference in this boundary became clear to me when I went to the town office building to propose a subdivision of my brother's and my property so that my husband and I could build. Although I needed to record this proposal in the usual way, observing traditional surveyor's boundary markings, and although it would subsequently be recorded in the usual way in the town assessment records, these acts, superficial boundary notations, were superseded by my own memories of that town office building, where my mother was once tax collector, and by my knowing the town clerk who recorded the deed. My knowing the place, the person, humanized the recorded boundary line. Earlier property descriptions had been written in longhand, perhaps even by a relative. While this is no longer so, I could understand the power of the hand, the person, the room in which it was done. Furthermore, my talking to others about the location of the lot was different in this home place. When family and old-timers, people who had stayed, asked me "where" I was building, I would describe the property in terms they could understand. I would say, "on land that belonged to Lampe." The surveyors' boundary markers, the red tape, the iron stakes, used to mark our "subdivision," meant so very little in their older language.

Even the building events became changed because of my being in this particular textured place. In building the first house I'd hired others, strangers, and worked beside them. I knew that they had helped make the boundaries of the house, that these were not really all "my" boundaries. I knew that their labor, and not only the materials, was necessary to that house. Yet, at the same time, I hired fewer people than I did for the second house, I did not know them before, and I did not know them after.

In the second house, almost everyone I hired, and there were many more, had some relationship with someone else, either one of the other subcontractors, or with someone I knew in the town, or, more powerful yet, with my family. In other words, the web of relations, the web of those working at constructing this house boundary, was dense. I seemed to myself but a small part of it.

I remember encountering this within one two or three day span. A man named John, whom I'd hired to take care of the foundation work on the second house, had ordered the concrete. When the driver, whose name I now forget, pulled up, he began to talk with me once he heard my last name. He'd known another family member some time ago. We chatted for a few minutes while I tried to work out where she fit into my kinship map. A couple of days later, after the foundation was poured, I'd asked my father's cousin, who was a dowser, to dowse for our well (although we were putting in an artesian, or deep, well and so probably didn't need this, I wanted to ask him; my father had hired a dowser and I decided it wouldn't hurt—and the well-driller was not at all surprised, in fact knew my father's cousin and respected his mark). After he dowsed, a mysterious process in which I saw the willow bend of its own accord as he tried to steady it, he and I talked. He told me the cement truck's driver's story wasn't quite right. The story was about his sister, although it turns out he knew the driver, and told me where he was from.

  I knew from these kinds of conversations, placing stories, not only that I could feel more confident about the quality of the work on the house (since everyone's reputation depended upon it since we all knew each other, and way back as it turns out), but also that this house was in some odd way not mine, not mine at all. Oh, I would live here. I would eventually collect their keys. Yet at the same time the house was taking its place in the history of my family and the history of this town. It would be talked about among people who knew someone I knew. Nothing I could do here would be unnoticed. Their presence within the boundary would emanate long after they left the scene even as my house would live on long in their memories.

My second house building experience helps me to understand Casey's understanding of what it is to be "in place." We may think that persisting through place means being near our own things, in our own private rooms, in our houses isolated from the outside. We may think we can move from house to house, carrying about our own belongings, and lose nothing. But being in place means something far different for Casey. Place is the "scene of the face-to-face encounter" with the other (1997, 276, 282). Knowing place means knowing the *location* of the house. Casey is not talking about a plot plan. He is not talking about the realtors' mantra: location, location, location. He is talking about location within an invisible web of social relationships. He's talking about location with a history that is palpable to one. He is talking about living in a community.

For some peoples, Casey says, dislocation can kill. The Navajo have no word for dislocation. They have sickened and died in experiencing it. Casey suggests that we too, although we do not know it, suffer like the Navajo from dislocation, from not knowing others around us, from not knowing the earth--and from not knowing our very own skillful bodies whose labor emplaces us (112). We too, he says, suffer disorientation, memory loss, feelings of homelessness, depression, and estrangement from self and others (38). Our word for the enclosed space in the home, a "room," is also the same word we use when we wish to open a wide space ahead, to "make room." Yet our sense of a "room" has shrunk. We need to know the "making" part, the opening of that boundary, the exertion of our bodies in doing so.

Being in place does not mean, however, being fixed. We are located within a shifting shoreline, a porous horizon. We are, essentially, as Melville puts it, "not down in any map; true places never are."[50] If it is not a staked piece of land that determines a "place," then what is it? One determinant is the network of informal social relationships, everyday relationships, recounted through stories. Kent Ryden says that storytelling, telling stories about the people in a place, bounds a place; where the stories stop, the horizon ends. I know this because here, in my childhood country, I have a sense of a region; beyond the river, north of a certain point, I have few stories. The people on the other side do not feel as if they belong with me in the same network. Schools, theatre groups and choral groups help create these storytelling boundaries. The deep history of a place does too. Although many do not know this, this town I live in was the far border of the original settlement of the British in the 1600s. Our region still maintains some of the same invisible boundaries. Of course some of the story boundaries will be individually inflected. But, whatever, the storytelling parameters we each do carry within create some invisible map of belonging the longer we stay in a place. We recount kinship lineage, tell stories with others of events of years ago, speak of past inhabitants of houses, so that our map of our location is always enlarged and reconfigured. My new house, on this map, is now part of a story-telling sequence—people tell stories of my house being built, or now of being at my house, and I of theirs, and so we map our houses on a community map, rather than the surveyor's monad-like grid.

Memory told through story provides the horizon not only for us laterally, in the present, but also vertically, as we remember and tell of the depth of our own past. For those who build, the storied history of the building is also always a part of that experience of place. For those who do not build but who invest much in their relationship to ancestral objects, the horizon line can be particularly deep within as well. This boundary of the house disturbs the property line, focusing us on our unending boundary with the past. Proust reminds us that as we care for special objects, we unlock the spirit of our ancestors. The Celts, he says, believed that objects can hold the souls of those we have lost; happening to pass by them or possess them, we unlock them and they "start and tremble...[and] call us by our name" (1928, 61). These are memory objects, objects that, held, looked at, open up the vista of the past.

In both of these situations, the one a porous lateral horizon of community, the other a porous vertical one through memory, there is no absolute fixing of a boundary. We never know the limits of the familiar, for the transgression of the alien always fronts and infiltrates it, the ground swell always happens without warning. My childhood home across the way looks different to me across the field now than it did when I was visiting it from afar as an adult. Memory is so uncertain, unpredictable. Proust bites into his madeleine, not even an ancestral object, and unlocks an otherwise forgotten memory of his childhood at Combray. "Something start[s] within me, something that leaves its resting-place and attempts to rise, something that has been embedded like an anchor at a great depth" (64). At length, the visual memory becomes attached to the taste memory. An accidental encounter with the place-world, with a cake made by his mother, an ephemeral object, a slight thing, pursued, concentrated on by Proust, changes everything. So it is the objects, yes, the familiar things—but also following the memory out: this deepens, vertically, the place world for us. I linger here over a stone in the path, one we did not move with the bulldozer, and I wonder who lingered by it before. I can almost remember some familiar presence, a mother, a father, brother, perhaps me once.

I moved into the second house two springs after my mother's sudden death. I ended up carrying some of her things over to the house that my brother didn't want, linens, silver, some of her dishes. When I hold a teacup in hand and look out the window at was once her house, I remember some story about that teacup, probably more forcefully than if I could not look at the house at the same time as I held it up. The wall between us seems very thin. When I pull out one of her recipes, written in her hand, I invariably look out the window to her once house. So near it was where she once pulled them out of the recipe box in her own kitchen five hundred feet away.

I added new things to the new house, of course. I chose door latches—but find they remind me of the Yankee ancestors on my father's side. I placed my cellar door in the middle of the house, and then remembered this door is in the same position in my birth house. I push up on the double hung window as I did in my childhood bedroom down below.

But there is more than mother and father and grandparents in this new house. The others who built here seem to have an audible presence in the house even now. Because there were so many in this house, because I knew more of their stories, because I built beside these others, I imagined them more deeply. I imagined what their hands were feeling, or the rhythm of their work day, or the fatigue of their bodies.

Sometimes I would even push myself to build more than I expected so that I could be among them, try to feel what they might be feeling, so that we could all be together in this house. One day, at the second house, built eleven years after the first, to get my body into this house, beside theirs, I put my now fifty-year old body to the test. Perhaps this was one of what seemed to be an increasing number of tests I put myself through as my body clock ticked. The house is silent about all of this. This is invisible in photographs, invisible to visitors, invisible even to my husband John who wasn't at the house that particular day.

I'd covertly been planning to undertake a small task while I was alone in the house shell, a solitude I was most looking forward to. I'd contracted out more of the work this time around, including the building of the often tall partitions. The house, another timber frame, was enclosed against the weather and most all of the interior walls had been built. The people who had completed the interior framing were not returning, since our principal carpenter, Rick, would shortly be coming back. He was recovering from numerous injuries at our site, including a broken back. He'd fallen off a slippery roof one January day. The clatter of the ladder, his heaped body on the ground: I will never erase these images from memory. But before Rick healed and returned for the finish work, those in the other trades had to complete their work: Guy, who installed the duct work for the heating and cooling; Bernie, now dead, who put in plumbing pipes; and Richard, who ran all the electrical wiring through the partitions and under the floors; and then Norman and Don who cut and screwed the sheet rock to the now filled up walls and applied one skim-coat of plaster. But in between this march of the other trades, a few carpentry jobs had to be done. I would do them.

  Guy had run the interior sheet metal ducts for our geo-thermal heating and cooling system (750' of pipe, buried 6' underground in a closed loop would bring 50 degree air into the house all year long—this could be circulated for air-conditioning or heated slightly for the winter.) These ducts, where they ascended through the floors, needed to be covered with walls. These are called "chases." These walls would provide not only a covering for the ducts, but a place for Guy to install supply and return vents, as well as walls for Richard to affix outlets and switches. I needed to make, in effect, wooden "boxes" to cover these sheet metal ducts. These could be closets in some cases, in others merely concealing boxes. I could design in storage space where possible. This was my project, to build on what they had started, to prepare for their return. It was ten years since I'd built my last wall in the first house. And I was ten years older.

  This would have been a simple job for someone with a nail gun or even someone who was comfortable using a cordless drill (with which one can also set screws). Though I may by then have bought the drill, I had not yet become comfortable with it, which wasn't much in use ten years before. And I didn't own an expensive nail gun. So there I was faced with building four "boxes" of open studs, each one approximately 2'x3'. I would have to build as much of it on the floor as I could and then raise it. But I could see also that I would have to plan the task *very* carefully. I knew that I would be unable to strike a hammer from certain angles within that small space (I still had my 20 ounce framing hammer). So I pulled up a chair in front of each of the four areas and thought each one out. I made drawings. I thought about the nailing problem. I also had to think about design issues: where did I want the boxes to begin and end? Since two of them were framing the open entrance to the dining area, they would look like large columns—how much should they match each other? Even if I'd hired others to frame these boxes out for me, I'd still have to make the latter decisions. Framers nail the studs up exactly where you tell them and then that's that; you've a door opening where you've marked it, and there it is for years and years to come. These seemingly small decisions, where to mark a door opening with a pencil on the chalk line on the floor, resonate for years, affecting not only where you can put a piece of furniture but also the feeling of the threshold and the view of the room and the window beyond as you cross the threshold. Then there were other details: I'd have to think ahead to Norman and Dan, the dry wall people: they would need "nailers," wooden blocks to which they could affix the sheet rock (something I'd learned the hard way after I'd built the interior partitions for the first house—I didn't have nearly enough and had to scurry around with them waiting for me as I hastily nailed some up, with a hammer that I could barely maneuver in some very tight spaces).

It took me one whole day to build each box. I suppose some would think this was a waste of time. I had the money by then to hire someone else. But I had to do it for me. When they were done they were perfect. They were in the right place. There were enough nailers. I'd not gotten myself into any tight nailing spots. And I'd remembered, from ten years before, when we'd built the first post and beam house, to make the walls 3/8" or so shorter than the distance from floor to ceiling—so that the walls could clear the beams and rafters overhead when I raised them up. They were plumb as well. And, best of all, not only could my mind still work, still think through all the parts of this task, but I knew that my body had remembered when my mind hadn't how to hold the circular saw, how to hold the hammer, what size nails to use, to get the nails started before lining up the different pieces of wood, and how to use my feet to keep the boards aligned as I nailed them together. I hadn't made much demonstrable progress in the house in that day. But I'd shown myself that I was still a building me, that I brought along with me things I once knew. Looking at the finished job, I could see myself, an older self resurrected and carried across in time. I still, unbeknownst to others, pat those walls almost every time I walk by them. And what I see of them is not the painted plaster walls, the clock, the painting. What I see when I am looking at them or reaching in one closet for a skirt or another for my writing paper is the now invisible box underneath, the box that only I know, the box that no one else may ever see again. I built, once again, a part of myself into the insides of this new, second house those few days. I emplaced myself, permeating the wall between my body and it. My body could still spin its own shell.

As I stand near that box now, some ten years later, my body does begin to remember again the angle of my arm, the bend of my back, the hammer's handle. The circular saw sits in the garage attic, collecting dust, but I can still remember how to set the depth of its teeth for a 2x4.

My body is not, however, the only body in the walls of this house, as it was not, as well, in the first. Although now I am often alone in its rooms, the material house stores the prints of others' hands besides my own, a thing I know because of those days I worked too. In sitting and standing and walking throughout the house, I remember and so live beside all the others in my body memory. Whenever I think of my arms and hands sawing and hammering the duct chases, when I remember bending to sweep the floors, raise my hand to paint a ceiling, the presences of the others using their arms and hands on that very spot at the same moment of time come forward before me. I need not wait for a Jungian dream. Our movements often had to work in concert. Guy had to have been there before I could close in the ducts. Richard, and Norman and Don, had to come after me before I could paint those duct chases. I waited in time for them, and they then waited for me. But now they are out of time, remembered as a concert that is now over but yet is an echoing whole playing itself out in internal time.

Yet who sees and hears this daily concert that is every new house under construction? What do outsiders know, people who do not move around on construction sites? In housing tracts, the more common kind of construction site, "no trespassing" signs appear to protect the property, to limit liability. On custom house sites sometimes retired neighbors walk down the drive, but only if they know the owner—and how many people now do? In some parts of the country a hundred years ago an entire neighborhood would come by to watch and even help build a house. Now the house site has become as off limits as a factory with locked gates, a site in which that which is made, that which we absolutely depend on, is entirely hidden from our sight. And so as a culture we turn to books and films. But few books, save Tracy Kidder's and Michael Pollan's, tell others much about the whole concert. Novels and films about house building usually devolve instead around other axes—romance, crime. All the reader/viewer has left is a few glimpses: the carpenters all together throwing out of windows the frames they've been constructing (this after Cary Grant, in *Mr. Blandings Builds His Dream House,* when asked, says, without a clue, no, he does not want rabbeted joints). *Witness* is a thriller. *House of Sand and Fog* is more about struggling for a house—not the building of it or living in it.

Were I to make a video of the building of this house, the presences would arrange and rearrange themselves out of temporal order. On one day Guy could be working on ducts in the cellar, beating on sheet metal. Rick, and Mark, his partner for a while in carpentry, could be sawing and nailing flooring on the second floor. Richard could be outside on a ladder quietly pulling wires through for our flood lights. Yet their sounds and movements may not have occurred all at the same time. Memory disconnects these moments from time and reconnects them in another pattern. When I think in this instant, for example, of the four humble duct chases that I built, perhaps in May, duct chases I can see down the hall from where I sit now in the library, I simultaneously see in my memory Ed and Dave one March day building the wall to the left of my chair. I still can hear our conversation, how we discussed the desirable size of the double French doors (2'0" for each, which I'd designed, "wouldn't be good," Ed said; "you'd have to open both doors to get through"—he was right to make each 2'4"), and then I watched them lay out the wall and nail it up. I remember worrying about a twisted stud and I remember where it is now. Or I can see Rick up on his ladder installing in the library in August the birch bookcases he'd built in his shop or the delicate mantel and frame he put around the gas fireplace to cover the rough edges of the floor tiles my husband had had to use to border the opening. In the library above me rest the second floor 4x6 Douglas Fir joists, fastened by black metal plates to the larger carrying beams with chrome screws that I painted black while standing on a ladder. These edges of these joists and the beam the Hennins "had champhered" (beveled) and then rubbed with penetrating oil before putting them on that January truck. The Hennins, Pat, Gaius, and another helper Chuck, then used a crane stationed in a single position to raise them in place. Place, in other words, connects these bodies out of the sequence of time. Place nourishes memory to connect. Perhaps what Pascal meant was that a room is restful because it evades time as it gathers all together. Such would be my movie.

This second house is a memory house for me, holding many. But what is it for the others who worked on it? Are they in this place in more than my memory? Did they, do they, too feel in any way emplaced here by their labor? Do they even remember this *particular* house now, several years later? I try to imagine how this house now is in their memory and what their bodies remember of it from their time here. Rick, certainly, will always, remember in his body that he fell here, one icy wintry day, fell off the roof. But what about their other bodily memories of this place? Are there good ones for them? Certainly they wouldn't experience, even though they worked here day after day for months, the same kind of enveloping, protective wholeness that I did as I nailed each nail and observed the others doing their part to help shelter me and my daydreaming, as Bachelard says all houses do for us. They knew they would not spend hours alone here. They knew they would not sleep or make love or be ill and heal here. Shelter though this provided them on rainy days, it was day shelter, work shelter. They did not, any of them, even oversee the whole thing (I did). So it can't be even that kind of mirroring, and possible pleasure then, of a temporary "whole" in memory that they'd experience. They knew only their own jobs and the parts of their jobs that they needed to in order to help others.[51]

They do remember the help they gave each other in a small community, where everyone knows everyone else. These subcontractors had their own dense web of relations, a web that would continue on into other houses after mine. I'd heard horror stories of wars between the trades. At our first house site, where the web was not so thick, our plumber got into a sawing war with the carpenter at an adjacent house site. He didn't like where the carpenter had put the floor joists. He sawed them off to put in his pipes. The carpenter returned to take the pipes apart and reset the floor joists. I don't know who finally solved this dispute. The plumber did not obviously know or care about his reputation with the carpenter, and vice-versa. Admittedly, those in the mechanical trades, as they are called, are usually closer to each other than they are to the carpenters. Guy would talk with Richard about his electrical needs, and Richard and Bernie, who hadn't known each other before, would have coffee together.

Interconnected as they were once on the site, do they, however, remember this house? How stiff is this boundary for them? Does it now, locked, shut them out from it in memory? They'd hundreds of other walls, hundreds of pipes, hundreds of wires, miles of ducts behind them and in front of them. How could they remember this one?

But some of them do. One evening I was sitting alone in our first house a couple of years after we had moved in. My husband was out of town. There was a knock at the door. It was the man who had installed our wood flooring. I was at times afraid of this man. He'd a tattoo of a knife dripping blood on his arm and a long knife gash on his cheek. Our plumber said that he'd once gotten into a nasty fight with him in a bar. But at the same time I trusted something about this big, burly man. I could tell that he was a protector of women, for one thing. But I also knew that he loved his floors. I let him in. He was doing a floor at a new house down the road (on our recommendation—the same one that had had the joists sawed off by the same plumber) and he "just wanted to stop by to look" at the one he'd done for us. He walked around head bent, his face aglow. He paid no attention to anything else about the house. He arrived at the hearth and stopped. "You need to trim that out." He'd picked the one part of his job that we'd yet failed to finish. I took care of it the next week. Ten years after wiring our second house, our electrician can walk into this, our second house, and remember where he buried a wire in a wall so that we could eventually use it for a new alarm system. Pete, our excavator, even now as I write these words, is whistling outside as he adds more stone to the driveway. We've just gone around by the concrete wall because he remembers writing the depth of the septic tank on it. I know he is happy being back at this house. Rick showed up on Sunday to show the house off to prospective clients; he points out all the things he's built to them—forgetting only the small mantle he'd made over the fireplace, delighted to discover it again. I, who have no single angle of vision on any house but mine, having no special skill, find their memory astonishing. It's as if each now remembers the house from an entirely unique and partial perspective: floors, bookcases, wiring, ducts, retaining walls and septic tanks.

    I want to know what they see and how they feel now about their work, and what they felt then. But I cannot know much, try as I might to read the few signs I have. I can't see what each of them sees, know what their bodies know, know what they feel, know how this house is in them. They are divided from me partly by the specificity of their craft. But they are also divided from me by the nature of their relationship to this work place. How critical is our different position? To what extent is our relationship to our bodies as we make something and our relationship to the things we are making dependent on our ownership, our possession, over the eventual product? To what extent is this relationship dependent on the organizational and inter-personal conditions under which we work? To what extent is our attitude toward work dependent on our own internally derived attitudes, our psychic disposition, or on our spiritual perspectives? How critical is a supportive community environment, those both organizational and interpersonal? How critical is one's own attitude toward one's work?

A book like *A Way of Working: The Spiritual Dimension of Craft,* asks these questions. One of the writers, Jean Kincaid Martine, in her essay, "Working for a Living," meditates on a way of working that "feeds" inner hunger—so that in working we feel "uncertainty, risk" because we know something is "at stake": one's very being. But she also thinks about working *situations* in which we can be supported in this approach to work. The medieval priests and guild masters regularly reminded the cathedral builders of the purpose of their work: service to God. Prayers punctuated the day, and workers mingled with each other, eyes and hands meeting—whereas today "little is 'handed' from man to man,…eyes rarely meet, and the human voice cannot always rise above the noise of machinery;…men in their isolation from one another begin to feel a kinship only with their particular machine." We live, she says, in a time of "mass forgetfulness that we are under any authority higher than that of our boss, whether he be the factory foreman, the president of the company, or oneself" (62-3).

I hoped, especially in the building of the second house, to help create a perfect place not only for me, but for the builders. I brought with me years of reading utopian novels and hours in coffee shops in the 60s and 70s talking socialist work ideals with social scientists. I'd carried along William Morris' image in *News from Nowhere* of happy workers, haying in the morning, reading in the afternoon, people relaxed and proud of their work. And, from more recent years, I'd brought with me work experiences in a spiritual community, an ashram, then a church, communities in which work is equal, all necessary, all offered selflessly (or that is the aim).

I knew the limits of creating that perfection here. We couldn't talk about it because they weren't these kinds of talkers. We didn't share spiritual pathways. Nor could I ask them to complete the rituals many of them knew now only a small part of—rituals that I knew would bind them and me together such as not only tacking the fir to the rafters but finishing by encircling the house saying prayers. But there was even more behind these limits. Our power relationship was asymmetrical. I was, after all, hiring them to build *my* house. We weren't together as medieval co-workers or people in a spiritual community, building a public cathedral. Since I had the power to hire, I also had the power to fire. They knew it even if I forgot.

But despite these very real inequities in our power relationships, I could try to make this work site not only as pleasant for them as I could, but one in which their own craft had center stage. I wanted to try to support their work feeding them as much as it could, even though they wouldn't own the final product. I'd an image of the artist: dreaming and then painting, loving the painting, then selling it for money to another—as I had my first house.

Some of the things I did were small, like bringing coffee and donuts up every day for the Hennins or the temporary carpentry crew we'd hired while Rick was healing. Some were larger ones (and far riskier for me), such as agreeing to payment by the hour for those who wanted it (at one point I had to negotiate a cap because some of the carpenters in the temporary crew were turning the framing of the bay window into a costly work of art). In this way I hoped people could focus on doing a good job, on practicing their craft as they were pleased with it. I was also in a position to pay everyone promptly, since I'd arranged my own money, borrowing here and there. And critically important I think, I knew enough about what everyone was doing that I could show a knowledgeable appreciation of their skill and offer praise. And I was relaxed enough (during the second house) not to hover suspiciously and anxiously over their shoulders.

In trying to cultivate a good working place and time for them, I also hoped I would cultivate a perfect building place for me. I've always believed William Morris' observation that one cannot be content unless others around one are. The spirits of the subcontractors that I met by day should be proud and pleased with their work. I would at some point have to gather their keys, shutting their bodies out. We needed to get on with the business of living in the house and they needed to get on to other jobs. But I wanted to try to ensure that they, bearers of the place's "genius loci," would contentedly promenade around the house's perimeters in my daydreams ever after.

I cannot know how they really feel, what their bodies remember, what stories they tell of this house, if they ever told any. They aren't talkers, many of them, and in any case wouldn't be apt to tell me anyway. I am sobered by a carpenter friend's remark about his years of building houses for others: "I loved building houses, but they broke my heart." Was it the nature of this work he was referring to—cheap materials, speeded up production either because of the contractor or the owners' pocketbooks? Was it the others on the job—one of whom tried to strangle him one day until his dog rescued him? Was it the fact that he was building for another and not for himself?

I can only make inferences about how the others experienced working on the house—inferences rooted in my knowledge of the sociology and literature of work, in my interpretation of the few building narratives we have and in my intuitions and casual conversations with others. I am not, of course, an unbiased student of this subject. I want my house to be a treasure to others. I want this partly for good reasons, because I believe in good work--and partly, truth be told, because I do feel some guilt about the loveliness and size of my house.

Both houses are modest in size by some standards—2500-3000 square feet (given that we've no children, however, they are far more than modest). Both houses sit on five acres of land, one in the Washington D.C. suburbs, the other in the Connecticut woods. Both houses are, to my eye and to those of many others who have visited them, strikingly beautiful structurally, with oak or Douglas Fir timber frames, numerous large windows, and plentiful skylights and irregular ceiling heights. In this second house my guilt is even greater than it is in the first. I'm older. I'm more aware that many of the people who travel through it live not in such a space. There are the neighbors, my uncle, the people down the road in their poor house that burned one November day. But even those who worked here: some of their own houses are lovely, well-kept, others more modest and yet I sense contentment. Many of them, in fact, seemed to accept the size of our house for the two of us (their knowing my ill mother-in-law would be moving in made the size a little easier for them I thought), comparing it favorably with some of the egregious mansions some of them were working on (9,000 sq. ft. for one person, someone reported). Yet one day I heard the wish of one of the workers that his child, his little boy, with whom he lives in an apartment, could have such a yard to play in. He will never be able to afford a house like this. He was still living there five years later. One day he spent the whole of it, in the heat, jack-hammering out some improperly applied bluestone for our patio. He made no money that day. They'd made the error, not out of sloppiness but out of lack of experience with laying bluestone in wet cement (it shouldn't be done) and they had to absorb the cost. But it was hard for me to see him working that day. All is not perfect among the spirits in this house.

And yet, I know that work on this house had to be more pleasurable than work on most houses is for craftspeople in our time. Most new housing today is constructed by large contractors, who work with developers. Farm land is subdivided and houses are constructed before an owner purchases them. Sometimes they are not finished until the purchase, at which time the owner chooses faucets, carpeting, etc. The construction process itself has become as streamlined as it can be to minimize costs and time. The house as work site is a relative latecomer to the assembly line (or as close to one as it can get—not easy because most American housing is completed on site—manufactured housing has not yet thrived in this market). The market for the single family house doesn't really develop until after World War II. But now it is becoming increasingly supplied with factory-based products. "Pre-fab" houses, "pre-fab" trusses, "pre-fab" decks, etc. have been transforming the industry ever since Leavitt introduced some of these techniques into his Long Island suburban development in the 1950s. Leavitt would have many of the parts of his houses made in his shops, off site, and then truck them in to be quickly assembled. Also, on many house sites, the conditions of work are coming to resemble those of the assembly line. A worker on these jobs might spend all day installing baseboard or adjusting roof trusses.

Both of my houses, in contrast, were built in the shrinking portion of the housing world which is called "custom." I, as an owner builder, doing all the contracting myself and some of the work, occupy an even tinier portion of the custom market. It's the least efficient way to go according to those looking to maximize profit. But working on custom built houses is potentially more rewarding for those hired to do the work. Every work site is, of course, dependent on the particular relations among the people involved and therein lies the danger for the subcontractor. I as an owner-builder-contractor won't necessarily ride herd on my subcontractors the same way a contractor of an expensive custom house is apt to do in order to meet deadlines or contract costs (if any part of the job is hourly). If my sub is working by a contract price, he or she will self-monitor. They need not fear, either, that not showing up or taking longer than they need they will irritate the large contractor and so lose future work. My smaller custom house can, in this way, be more desirable, I imagine, from the point of view of the people who work on it in terms of offering maximum autonomy and ease of work pace (unless of course they've too much work out there, which many, particularly plumbers, electricians and heating contractors do). Several of the people I hired, in fact, I know will not work for large contractors; they prefer to be their own boss.

On the other hand, working with an owner-builder as the contractor can be a difficult proposition for the subcontractor. One is faced with the owner who is far too attached to the house and is potentially a nervous wreck over costs, who can inexpertly supervise by hovering overhead at every moment, and, who, if ignorant of any part of the process, can fail to secure permits or order necessary materials on time, so slowing up the whole job. Sometimes the owner builder will choose inferior materials, which upsets those who take pride in their craft.

Do I really know that the people who worked on this house derived satisfaction? I've my experience with the man who came to see his floor in Maryland. I've other moments I thought I knew, particularly in building the second house. Were we luckier? Did we locate "happier" people? Was I more confident and so calmer? Could the network among my subs have helped here—everyone seemed to know at least two and many knew some relative of mine.

I'd come home, back to my mother and father's territory, and I always felt that for some of them I was welcomed, like a prodigal returned. I can still hear Richard, the electrician, whistling as he opened his van door in the morning, see him smiling at me broadly and wishing me good morning (but he is also a relative). Or Guy, who always seemed cheerful, full of concentrated energy as he'd walk through the front door and head immediately down to the utility room after refusing the coffee I'd regularly offer ("Thanks, I've just had some.") Bernie, the plumber, was never distressed by anything that I could tell. He brought his carefully prepared lunch every day, including his thermos of soup. Though the carpenters would occasionally express distress, Bernie approached every part of the plumbing job with calm and made me feel that there would never be a leak anywhere (there hasn't been). Pete, our excavator, neighbor, and family friend, once joked that people were asking him if he lived here because he parked his dozer here for so many months. The head of the timber frame company that erected our first frame seemed to be pleased I'd asked him to sign the frame. He knew where to do it: on the attic beam. He hadn't been asked to do it before, but knew of the custom and had his grandfather's stamping kit. All eight names of the Timbersmiths' crew to this day face the new owners as they go down the attic stairs, even as they are imprinted on the beam of my memory.

With the carpenters it was, though, a little different, more complicated, but they are the ones who are with you the longest. There is something about carpentry that is different from all the other trades. Does the Biblical elevation of the craft, in the persons of

Noah and Joseph, reflect an ancient tradition of reverence or create one? Carpentry is, at any rate, *the* synecdoche for "craft," as electricity and plumbing and excavating are not. Carpentry is the stuff of artisan culture. One of the first words I learned when I went to Sweden with my mother to visit our remaining family was the word for "carpenter." The word was pronounced with reverence by my great aunt as she spoke of her father who'd built the sideboard I'd admired. Hardly anyone (except Pete) finds a newly excavated ditch beautiful.

Carpentry is in fact the first thing people think about when they think about the house. Carpentry is also the part of the house building process most written about. And some carpenters are very verbal about the meaning of their work. I have talked with our timber framers, from Hennin Post&Beam, about their love of the work. I've known them for twenty years now. This love irradiated the course they taught at The Shelter Institute. They prefer not to do a whole house, only erect the timber frame and the insulation panels. They were with us for only three weeks. It is not as easy however to talk with people who will be with you throughout the building process. It seemed an intrusion. Owners enact a kind of marriage with the long-timers, and, like all marriages, especially if one is around day after day, one begins to see the many sides of the person. Silences are sometimes necessary. Particularly with the carpenters, I could feel their worry as we neared the end about what the next job would be. Plumbers are called in the night; rarely carpenters. The toilet needs repair. The wood doesn't.

Carpenters have also built more of themselves into the house, as they spend the most time here. They might design bookshelves or mantles, all of which is very visible, like art works. I feel I've seen the pride in their faces. As they near the end of the job, however, like someone about to sell their painting, they have to separate themselves from their creations. They have to refocus on their skill and withdraw their attention from that which they've already created. The more experienced they are they learn to view their creations with detachment. And yet, it is the carpenter who brings prospective clients by to show off the craft.

Always an outsider to what the others felt, I turn to literature to try to patch together how carpenters might feel about their skills. Some of this literature is written by observers, some by first-hand participants. Yet I know that even when written by a participant, desire and the need to mold the fact to the narrative can shift, distort, the real thing. Every story reshapes the material. Maybe they don't know the truth either.

In her 1859 novel *Adam Bede,* George Eliot opens her first chapter in a 1799 carpentry workshop in the Midlands, a workshop belonging to Jonathan Burge. Although Eliot herself was not a carpenter, her father, as overseer of several estates in the early nineteenth century in England (a job Adam Bede, the novel's hero, takes on later in the novel), would be apt to frequent such scenes and would tell his daughter of them. The scene she paints is idyllic, colored perhaps by the lens of distant memory, inflected perhaps by nostalgia for pre-urban, pre-industrial England, nuanced by "Adam" and the Biblical associations of the carpenter's shop. In this work space, there are five carpenters and no supervisor. They do not own the shop, "Mr. Burge" does, but he is never present nor does he ever check up on them. They are in the process of making doors, window-frames and wainscoting, each one apparently completing his own task. They probably know whom the doors are for (it's a small place). It is quiet and clean in the workshop, lovely in fact. They are using hand tools, planes, screwdrivers, hammers. A dog is sleeping on the "heap" of "soft shavings," the afternoon sun and the scent of pine-wood and elder-bushes envelope their room and their bodies. While Adam carves a shield in a wooden mantelpiece, he begins to sing. The narrator, admiringly, goes on to describe his carpentry arm, "likely to win the prize for feats of strength (50)." The workmen then proceed to tease Adam's brother Seth about the panels he's forgotten to add to the door he's been making. The only hint in this passage that Adam is not still in Eden occurs when the workmen throw down their tools at the stroke of six in order to go home to "play" and Adam chastises them for their fear of "'doing a stroke too much'" (55). The clock is the only sign of constraint upon them. This is a narrative celebrating pleasurable work, skilled work, work that hones the body, work among good-natured friends.

It is surprising how this trope is repeated in more modern literature. Even when the workers are part of a construction company, harbinger of today's more typical house site (though in pre-union times), even when the novel has a political purpose, that of advocating for "combining" (or unionizing) through socialism so that jobs can be more secure and better remunerated, the attitude of the workers toward their work is similar. Robert Tressell's 1916 novel about the building trades, *The Ragged Trousered Philanthropists,* paints scenes of workers, left on their own, wanting to use their skills. The foreman, who sneaks up on them hoping to find anyone slacking off so he can fire him and replace him with a cheaper worker, can find no wrong. When he argues for one coat of paint in order to save himself money, one of the workers, with the others' approval, dilutes the paint when he's not looking so that when he goes to show them that one coat will work, the workers prevail. They know that two coats will look better. Two contemporary narratives in which the carpenter builds for others (although not for a large and greedy contractor) offer remarkably similar portraits of pride in work. Tracy Kidder's popular ethnography on custom house-building, *House,* published in 1985, traces the building of a single house through the lens of the three groups most involved in it: the owners, the architect, and the carpenters who are also the contractors. He devotes most of the book to the story of the carpenters, seemingly actually recording their conversations, although only at rare moments does he announce his own presence to us. That announcement reminds us that they are speaking to an outsider, representing themselves to the world (and Kidder tells us, as he has presumably them, that he has not changed any names), but the rest of the time we believe, as we do in Eliot's vignette and in Tressell's novel, that we are getting a "true" conversation, a private conversation among themselves. Although Kidder shows his carpenters experiencing far more worry and anger in their complex relations with owner and architect than does Eliot, their self-representation of their feelings about their work is remarkably congruent with Eliot's. "The three partners could foresee a full and interesting summer of building from scratch. They were eager..." (24). On the first day: "This is great...Building a new house is fun" (103). They fuss with the house—it "deserves it"—it will "sit here a hundred years, at least" (140). These carpenters, like those in Burge's shop, also have a complicated but generally genial relationship. The pace of their work is self-controlled. They take great pride in their work and will go to extra lengths to do the job well, for the sake of the house itself. The descriptions of the building site even bear many of the same traces as Eliot's: "The day is fine. The trees are in new leaf...It is a sparkling blue morning, with a clearing, chilly wind out of the northwest, a day to make horses and carpenters frisky. It's May 17, 1983, the first day of carpentry on the first new house Apple Corps has touched in nearly two years" (102-3).

Don Snyder's *Cliff Walk* is a memoir, and so in the first-person, about his transformation from a college professor to a carpenter. His is a much darker story: he did not choose carpentry. In fact he thought all such work beneath him for a long time after losing his college teaching job. But again, as in Eliot, he represents the work as ennobling him, the pleasure he takes in his body's newly developing skill altering his depression. In the past, before he got his first carpentry job, he would perform small acts of sabotage against the wealthy whose success he bitterly resented. One day as he's pitching a drain pipe through the concrete forms on the house he's building, he realizes that a year ago he might have sabotaged this rich man's house by pitching the drain the wrong way; the drain would be buried in concrete and only after a number of flushes would the toilets back up into the house. Now he's running back there, after hours, in the heavy snow to remove a scaffolding plank so it won't fall and break some of the new windows. No one told him to do this. He won't get paid more. But he's taken it upon himself to make a good house for the sake of his own self-esteem and the house, if not for the rich man whom he never comes to know. In fact, a friend says to him, "'in a true sense, the edifice will always be more yours than his'" (231). Snyder's story of his discovery of the value of such work occurs within a family drama, in which he comes to understand his blue-collar father for the first time. It is hard to know how much of his elation over building is connected with this need for re-connection and how much is connected with the work itself. Unlike Kidder's story and more like Tressell's, we are more aware of Snyder's desperate financial circumstances. We know that part of the pleasure he feels in his house-building work derives from his being paid a living wage. In this way his narrative also far extends Eliot's vignette, in which there is no payment mentioned (later, however, the reader will learn that Adam cannot marry unless he advances in the shop but his *pleasure* in the work seems disconnected from the money he receives).

Are these narratives merely the continuance of a literary tradition of the artisan myth? Or are they true accounts of at least some people experiencing pleasure and bodily/spiritual transformation in building other people's houses? This is hard to know. I would like to think that those who built here, who worked on our houses, brought something good away for them. They may not be able to open the door at will and revisit this, partly their treasure.

That is a consequence of our social system of private ownership. But I hope their acts of building help remind them of who they are as builders. I do know that their embodied selves in this house are a treasure for me. This house, this building, is but the enduring expression of all of our building movements.

In building the second house, on childhood land, among others whose lives as well as labor settled into this house, whatever their feelings about it, whether or not the house settled in them, I come now, here, to the edges of possession. The house is less mine than was the first. I legally own it, yes, but the house belongs not only to me but to the others before, the others who built, and to others to come in the future.

Such may be the consequences of building on native ground, where memory is thick. Or perhaps it's aging, or having had to sell the first house. Perhaps Dylan Thomas is right: "After the first death, there is no other."[52] After the first house is gone, there is really no other. This second house is even lovelier than the first. But it is not the first. And I know now it is not mine.

The fruit of this new relationship to house was my beginning to inhabit and work on another kind of house entirely. I began to feel more at home in a house we call not our own, what some of us call God's house, a church building. Standing as it has now for eleven years on a Connecticut hill, amidst beeches and rocks and a stream, my second house, my private house, began to take up an entirely new position within my interior landscape. The porous quality of the material house's walls, a porousness paradoxically created by the density here of memory, of private and public history, of storytelling, a history of a child returned to a landscape filled with ghosts, moved me out of the house. I no longer needed this shell. I needed another, one bigger, one set on different kind of land.

X

A House of More than My Own

My God, I read this day,
That planted Paradise was not so firm,
As was and is 'thy floating Ark.
                             --George Herbert, "Affliction V"

Where there is no temple there shall be no home
Though you have shelters and institutions,
Precarious lodgings.[53]
                  --T.S. Eliot, "Choruses from 'The Rock'"

Like living stones, let yourselves be built into a spiritual house.
                                              --I Peter 2:5

The three epigraphs that introduce this last chapter, though all seated within Christianity, are disjunctive in their meaning. They are connected paradoxically as the different kind of house they describe is itself paradoxical. My narrative turns to the next stage of my building it round me story, the story of the third house. It is not a house I built. It is a house I helped build. It is a house I continue to help build. It is a house that is always being built. Really, it is not a house at all, though, at least not in the usual sense. It is a house built with bricks and mortar, wood and glass, yet also this physical house is not *the* house. Nor is this house an "inner house," if by that one imagines a tiny house carried around inside of one. This other house is the church. My building round, once, twice, led me at last here, to this house.

Bachelard says, "maybe it is a good thing for us to keep a few dreams of a house that we shall live in later, always later, so much later, in fact, that we shall not have time to achieve it. For a house that was final, one that stood in symmetrical relation to the house we were born in, would lead to thoughts—serious, sad thoughts—and not to dreams. It is better to live in a state of impermanence than in one of finality" (1958, 61). Bachelard knows that for those in love with houses, there is can never be a last house. What he means is that the thoughts of a "last" would remind us of our mortality. But when he thinks of the "later house" we shall build, "much later," he is probably not referring to any other kind of house than one made of wood and glass that is ours alone. He is not, I think, talking about church "houses."

I think, however, that I am done building Bachelard's kind of house for myself. I no longer dream of a next one for me. I no longer doodle imaginary plans on paper napkins in restaurants. When people ask me, "What would you do differently," I tend to stare blankly at them. I have no answer. On others' houses I will help, but no more of my own.

Perhaps this is the way many of us go as we age and count our years, months, minutes more carefully. When Yeats was young, he wrote of wanting to go to Innisfree to build "a small cabin there." When he is old, living in the tower he bought later in life, he calls up his "images and memories" of friends and writes his will.[54] When Wittgenstein was young, he went to Norway to build his cabin. When he was older he gave away his money, and designed a house for his sister to live in. He retired to the "barest of rented rooms."[55] When Patsy Hennin of the Shelter Institute, who taught me so very much of what a woman builder can do, was young, she built house after house, with her husband, with her family. In April of 2004 she and her husband built one together in the Caribbean. In May, she returned home to Maine, feeling younger than ever, then, all of a sudden, feeling so very much worse. Her breast cancer of the year before had returned, with a vengeance, spreading to her liver. She didn't plan another house. Before she died, she went back to the Institute to help teach the classes that teach others how to build.

Knowing more what being fifty meant, in a way I did not so understand forty, I said to the builders of the second house, "I plan to go out of this one feet first." They found nothing surprising or morbid in this. My mother, as she'd hoped, went feet first out of hers, carried out the very front door my father had perhaps once carried her into. My grandmother did the same. So did my aunt and an uncle. They weren't building houses for the sake of moving and improving. They were building a house for life, and for death. That is the way for a lot of old-timers in this town. Houses are for keeps—until you can't any longer take them along with you, until you begin to see Emily Dickinson's "cornice in the ground," the gravestone house.[56]

But the energy to "build it 'round one" goes on and on in one, even when one is done building the last house. We imagine Milarepa standing there all his life with his hammer in his hand. We witness with Jeremiah, standing beside God, the potter throwing vessel after vessel as God destroys each one. These images show us the life's work: to keep building a house, to keep throwing the pots, no matter how transient they are, no matter how transient we are.

But the vessels themselves, houses, can change not only in number but also in their very nature. This is what the above epigraphs point to. These epigraphs suggest that when we are talking about church we need a radically new definition of boundary and indeed a different sense of architecture itself. These epigraphs change the terms of ordinary architecture, whose object is a known material thing, a house, a school, a church *building*, a free-standing, separate thing. The architect may try to "fit" the house or church with the neighborhood, the church building may stand in relation to other buildings and other historical churches for some architects, but there's no questioning that the church house is no ordinary building.

These epigraphs pose a challenge to the familiar idea of a building. The first, from Herbert's poem, is perhaps the easiest to grab hold of with the mind, however much it does not make sense to us home-bodies planted amidst our gardens and secured by our gates.

On the surface, Herbert might seem to be arguing for houseboats over houses with foundations in the earth. In a literal sort of sense, this is right. But the metaphor runs deep in these lines. One of this book's epigraphs, from Rykwert, alludes to the archetypal primitive hut in us, the hut which informs all our dreams of houses and all architecture. Rykwert roots this imagined hut in Eden. He says that we cannot imagine a garden without a house. We need to *house* Adam and Eve. And although Adam and Eve did not need to be sheltered in that place of no rough rain or hot sun, they did, Rykwert says, need a huppah, a sacred canopy, of living trees and woven vines. They needed this image of their conjoined bodies. That's what their house is. And they also needed, he goes on, a mediating place, a place that sheltered their own bodies in the face of the great world, and the great God, outside of them. Their house would help them make sense of the vastness out there. Adam's house (and Eve's, though Rykwert oddly calls it "Adam's,"), helped Adam and Eve place themselves in the center of the map of paradise (1981, 190). Our inherited, mythic Edenic house mirrors us to ourselves, helping remind us of our central place in God's created garden. Rykwert's interpretation of such an archetypal house is radically different from our more familiar Cartesian-based house: "I dreamed it, I made it, it's mine." Or, "my shelter is my shields interlocked above me, protecting and fortifying me."[57] Adam and Eve's house is not an echo chamber for each of their own egos, nor a weapon for their survival in a hostile world, but a porous place through which each gathers knowledge of their responsibility to God and to the whole creation.

Herbert's reference to the Flood with its radically different kind of house, which God calls for in the cleansing of Eden, offers if not quite a counter-image to Rykwert's vision of the Edenic house (since the open huppah, is, to begin with, potentially movable on land), then a new inflection of it. Herbert's holier house, enclosed now, is on water, an ark, buffeted by rains, led hither and yon by God. It's a house of trust. Noah is called to build the ark, and it had better be weather-tight so he has to exercise his skill, yet it's a moving house, a house he takes with him as he makes his watery pilgrimage. Herbert's poem wrests from us our golden-age nostalgic fixation on Eden, our vain attempts to "get back to the garden," our fixation with a solid foundation for the houses we build, and urges us instead toward faith in the unknown waterways. It returns us partly to earlier people's conception of the house as a moveable, transient thing. But it goes even further with the stormy landscape. The ark house is never fixed on one point of land, even for a moment. Herbert takes away the foundation of the house and emphasizes the fragility of our water-moving shells, the fragility and the special kind of trust in God that grows only when we know this vulnerability. I have always loved the stories of people looking for pieces of the ark.[58] They, these pieces, seem like lifebuoys that we can grab onto.

The second epigraph, from Eliot, however, turns us *toward* a house on land, and so exists in some counterpoint to Herbert's. In this way, Eliot's image of a holy house, a God house, may be easier to hold onto, especially when contrasted with Herbert's. But Eliot's tone, his assertion, would be radical, disturbing, for some. For Eliot questions the solidity of the foundation of our ordinary private houses without a temple at their center, a church. Eliot's image is decidedly geographical. That is, he implies a physical temple in the midst of houses, much like a church in the middle of the town green, the design favored by my Puritan ancestors. For Eliot, this church/temple isn't just one building seated among others, "fitting in" aesthetically with them as some architect might design a community. Without the temple at their center, says Eliot, that to which the other houses must "fit" in far more than an architectural way, the private house is endangered, "precarious." Eliot is implying there is no restful dwelling in the private house unless there is a temple to which it is intimately connected. He adumbrates Pascal's idea that we need to learn to be at rest in a room. For this to be possible, we need more than a room of our own, a house of our own. The one, the private room, the private house, gains its solidity and restfulness from the other, the temple, the meeting place of worshippers.

The third epigraph shifts the terms of this third house, this church place, once again. In the first letter of Peter, our bodies become the "living stones" built into a spiritual house. We, our very bodies, become the foundation stones. We each do not individually become a spiritual house. There is an image of community here—all of us together found the house. Yet the house, despite the physicality of our bodies, is not a physical house. The house, the spiritual house, is the assembled body of believers, the gathered people. The physical house itself is nothing. John Calvin chastises his followers about such attachment to the place and the house: "It is wrong that a love of walls has seized you; wrong that you venerate the church of God in roofs and buildings."[59] The structure is but a reminder of the covenant and promise we have made each unto each.

What is uneasy in this triptych for those of us who turn to such a third house, the church, is that there *is* a house of God, a temple, a *domus dei,* a special place where God seems to dwell, and there is also *not* a house, not a place, a *domus ecclesiae,* house as only the gathered people. This tension, between the physical church, the building, and the members, the changing body of believers, is difficult. It has haunted the private lives of those who know the church. It has haunted church politics. It has fueled religious wars (to what lengths do we go to protect the physical sanctuary?). It has troubled my life of late, these twin views of church, as I return to my birth home place and my birth home church. What is it if the church place itself becomes so filled with personal memory, of self, of family, as this church place is for me? What is it if one starts repairing the physical body of the church building and becomes attached to the repair? How are these attachments productive of spiritual growth, or how limiting of it? As I enter the third house, reside in it more and more, in me grows yet another, new understanding of both "building" and "me."

The birth house I grew in was not on a town green. The church was not in sight. In fact it was three miles down the road. My house, built in the 1930s, was built too late for the green. And indeed the first version of the church building, on the green, had burned and been built somewhere else in town, by the side of a road on a hill overlooking the village. The church building I knew and know again was too late for the green too. In our attachments to particular church buildings many of us forget that there were probably several church buildings for a particular "church."

But it might as well have been next door, this other house, the church house. The two houses, our house, church, "temple," met at every turn, as if each threw a search beam and they inter-arched. We knew, my brother and I, as we were driven there by our parents and grandparents, to this other house, exactly when on the drive the heater would kick on in winter and how warm we would be when we turned into the church drive. Our very bodies could tell the turns of the road to get there. I have often felt I could drive this road blindfolded and know what to do.

I grew, however, on stories, not of driving to church but of walking to it, stories that profoundly anchored "church" as *the* destination point in my yonng mind. My grandfather told of his weekly five mile walk to church and then back when he lived in the small village in Sweden where he was born. In all kinds of weather he would walk. The walking was his compulsion to go to the other house, and the compulsion of others. When my grandparents, from that same small village in Sweden, met for the first time in the small Connecticut town to which each had emigrated, they repeated his pattern, this time with a shorter walk, a two mile walk to the Swedish Lutheran Church. On the way I imagine their minds clearing, their hearts opening. I imagine them thinking of who they would see at church, but also of the prepared table, and the pew in which they would sit to listen to the preacher. This walk, this imagination, of table, of preacher, would be unlike anything else in the week past or the one to come. Though "held in the cycle of days," as Gordon Lathrop puts it, Sunday shows us also to mark our days. "Sunday makes us aware of the week" (1998, 40). I imagine people walked together. Yet I imagine they were often quiet. The walk was a ritual procession. On the way they would have noticed a bird in summer, the icicles in winter, seen the smoke rise from a chimney, contemplate a flower in the summer beds. But the church was the true and purposeful destination. And it would give its own light to all that they saw on the way to it, and on the return. The jobs they walked or later drove to—these trips would have been different for them. These trips were only necessary to support the family's needs for food and shelter; there was no rabid consumption of things, and there was no debt. My family did not work for the bank. They might have had worried thoughts on the way to their jobs, about the paycheck, about the social relations and these perhaps consumed them. The church walk would have been different—not always tranquil, for there would be conflict there too. But the walk would give them time to "solve it by walking," as Augustine said, "salvitur ambulando." Much as the monks walked their boundary, they were walking the thread, the line that bound home to church, walking to it and back from it.

  We who so walked and then later drove to church (is this really the same though?) dwelled, then, in that birth house, all five of us, perhaps in the way Eliot alludes to. Our lodgings did not feel precarious in any way except the essential one. And we knew that one, how we knew it. It is true that we owned the house, farmed the land, we sewed and knitted and were well fed and healthy. We did not fear dispossession or hunger. But we knew, still, our essential precariousness in that house. We knew, my brother and me, that our grandparents had left other homes in Sweden for good, homes we never could know of. We knew our house was a gift from Charles Lampe, a gift that he passed on one day in the driveway when he handed my father the deed. We knew how much depended on that simple paper passed hand to hand. And we knew that the house could not stop the little airs from creeping under the door and claiming my father's life one June day. We knew, in other words, oh we knew, how precarious we were in our little house.

Knowing, *and being able to face knowing*, this precariousness: this is the deeper dwelling. This is what Eliot means. This is what I have been heading to here so far, as I've told of building what I thought would be these solid houses whose boundaries were after all porous to others and place, to history, to the future. As I've told my building story thus far though, I have not spoken of the place of this other kind of house. It was now, this other, to begin to loom down the road for me when I moved back home. It was to become a different order of consolation. We knew, my birth family, and knew we could manage, this deeper precariousness of the first house that we all felt because we had this other house down the road apace. I had not really confronted this deeper precariousness yet in the two houses I built along the way back except in a humanistic way, through the imaginations of poetry and philosophy, and its consolation that I was not alone among my fellows. I would need deeper consolations, from another order of things, in order to admit to this deeper precariousness of all houses.

When I was a small child, every night my grandmother would lull me to sleep with the rhyme imprinted on so many of us as children. Every night she would recite with me as she tucked my arms under the blankets, "Now I lay me down to sleep, pray the Lord my soul to keep. If I should die before I wake, pray the Lord my soul to take." Every night even as a child I was so reminded of my transience. Every night I would say hopefully to my aging grandfather, asking him in effect to deny his own mortality: "I'll see you in the morning." And he'd unfailingly reply, "I hope so." And every week as I was taken to church, these night-time thoughts were confirmed. Death was spoken of everywhere—as was reappearance, in the form of repetition and resurrection. I learned of an unseen world beneath the seen in which all was not as it appeared, not at all. There were readings, on houses being destroyed, and rebuilt, on God's command. There were stories of plagues and pestilence, of tribulation lasting for years and years, of pits and darkness, with promise at the end. There were anchors for images, God as the only rock, God as the light. I knew that all these people who lived so very long ago lived no more, and yet I also knew that they somehow continued to live here, as their stories were told. I knew I was like them. The language that wove through my life was of these other shelters of a living past, other shelters than the house, a shelter we could not see or touch or walk to, but one that meeting in the church building every Sunday connected us with, as if it were here, indeed it was here now. The stories changed for me the meaning of time and place. They made a word painting that would color and rearrange the landscape of the week behind and the one ahead. I would no longer see things in quite the same way I would if left to my own, if left to the influence of the secular world around me, the profane world not yet opened to the sacred.

More than Sunday's words made their way into our house. The rhythms of the house of that church three miles away defined our own. Everything in the week leading up to Sunday pointed to it, everything following alluded to it. Our rhythms at home existed in relation to church rhythms. There was to be no work on Sunday, no washing, no ironing, no baking, no bookkeeping. If you had asked my grandparents if they understood the Biblical reason and textual sources for this day of no work, this day of rest, they probably would have said no.[60] It was just that way. The other days of the week the house was a jumble of ordered activity, the usual household domestic clock of my grandmother ticking away, the washing, ironing, baking, and the other rhythms of my mother and grandfather who went out to work during the day and who gardened or cut brush when they got home. When people went out in the evenings, it was to church meetings always, Trustees' meetings, Search Committee meetings, Deacons' meetings. Or they would go to repair the building, paint, mend it, or cut potatoes in the kitchen and knit wool mittens on a summer's night in the easy chair for the annual Christmas fair.

As Sunday approached, all of this seemingly ceaseless rhythm, a rhythm that wrapped itself around us as if to lull us into forgetting our cosmic position in the house, would come to a full stop, abruptly. Come Saturday evening, after supper, it began. It was bath time. We had an order, a procession into the cast iron tub in the single bathroom, which my mother would scour after each use, and my grandmother before her. I, one of the young ones, was somewhere in the middle (my grandfather usually had his first, because he needed time every evening to dress his amputated leg after removing his artificial leg and bathing it.) When I'd go in for my bath, my mother would knock on the door and ask if she could help, wash my back, help with my hair. I would say yes. I loved her ministrations. They were our profane baptism, every week. Then I would gather my curlers and bobby pins and sit in front of her on the hassock so she could pin my so straight hair up for church. We'd watch Lawrence Welk on the television. I would consent willingly to go to bed with the hard curlers on my pillow. On Sunday morning we'd gather for breakfast, which always included my grandmother's fresh "vetebrod," Swedish coffee cake spiced with cardamom, and then we would dress up for church. We would take time for dressing. My grandmother would, for this special occasion, place one dot of rouge on each cheek and apply a little lipstick to her mouth. Then she would don her large hat and she would be ready. Sometimes we'd take a photograph of one of these pre-church moments. We'd stand in front of either door and my mother, usually, would snap the photo of the four of us, grandmother, grandfather, my brother and me. After church we'd come home for our ample, simple, delicious, Sunday dinner, perhaps a rib roast or a pork roast, a dinner to which we'd sometimes invite the organist or youth minister, who lived farther away. The rest of Sunday was a rest day. We would take a ride, or a walk in the woods, perhaps a relative would visit. We'd sit on the porch and talk or, more usual, I'd read quietly in the hammock out in the yard. My grandfather would watch his growing garden from his chair in the front of the barn, or in winter sit in the living room and read the paper. The house was utterly quiet. Only after supper, after sundown, would we turn the television on to Ed Sullivan. George Herbert speaks of Sabbath: it is, he says, the "couch" of the world's week. It was a deep and utterly restful couch. It was not a couch of forgetful sleep. It was a couch of alert rest.

Sabbath day at the house was another house entirely. It was a house out of time and space. Our usual domestic rhythm, abruptly ceasing, transformed the house for this one day. We would collectively recall, although we would not speak of it, that this house could change, that this house of the weekday world was temporary, precarious and that another kind of resting, because of this other house, was there all along for us, wherever we were, in whatever house.

One does not forget the early rhythms. I never forgot the preciousness of Sunday in all my later years. I remember saying often to myself as a child, "I hate Saturday. I love Sunday." I retained that dislike and that preference. But I lost sight of the other house. When I went to college, chapel was no longer required after my first year. A new place, new people around me, my old rhythm fell away. Sabbath lost its place.

Perhaps it was daily meditation years later that was to prepare me for a return. Or perhaps it was my regular attendance with my husband at a local Catholic church in Maryland for several years before we moved back near my birth house. But Sabbath time began to insist in me again, slowly. It had been over twenty years.

Perhaps it was returning to the same place, to a house I'd built next door to my childhood one, that, as if I were sleepwalking, turned my steps again to that same church. That was not, however, the specific reason I gave to myself for going back. I would come to say two people waved me back. One was a minister and friend who stood on the deck of our rising second frame one afternoon and said, quietly, he was not so interested in houses anymore. I was stunned. His gentle statement fell like a plumb line dropped deep within, stirring long quiet folds within me. In that instant, I remembered, again, not only the precariousness of the house that I'd already been learning about through building, but also the spiritual precariousness I had known in my bones as a small child. Not be so interested in houses? Whatever could he mean? Yet I knew what he meant. What did I really think I was doing by spending so much time and money building these houses?

These words, blending with old memories, connected with another waving hand that gently pulled me back, to drive the same road to that same church and to walk the same sidewalk. When we returned to Connecticut, I started walking, first with my brother, then alone, through the church doors of my childhood church. I went back there because my mother had died. There I could be with others who had known her. I could hear them say at coffee hour, "oh your mother...." Some of them would even call me not by my own name, but "Elsie's daughter." As I stood in the pew near some of them to sing a hymn, I could remember the sound of her voice in my ear next to me, a memory I could recapture nowhere else. I went, at first, because the church seemed a place where my mother still lived.

Much as I, as a small child, would open the door of the nursery school room several times in an hour to see whether my mother still waited outside the door for me, so now it seemed that she pushed open the church doors of a Sunday to see if I were here again.

And I do believe that my mother in some odd way brought me back here, invited me back in to this house. One day I was vacuuming under my old childhood desk in the second house, a desk I still use, and a letter got stuck in the nozzle of the vacuum. The letter, neatly typed, was now yellowed and frayed. It was the first letter my mother had written me at college. It was filled with church news, who played the piano at the potluck supper, what she found out about a new baby while peeling potatoes in the kitchen. She had enclosed a church bulletin within the letter. It was, I felt, her call.

My mother had placed me in the church as soon as we moved into Lampe's renovated house, placed me in that nursery school. When my father died, the church became the center of her life. Her friends were from the church. Her activities were at the church. She arranged our photograph albums around the church calendar. There's a photo of me in my new Easter clothes, one year, then the next. There are photos of me on "Children's Day." There are photos of my confirmation. There are no photos of me inside the sanctuary. We did not take pictures inside then. The first set of photos I have inside was taken at my wedding in that church when I was thirty four. In looking at me standing in the front of the chancel, at the end of the long red carpet leading from the doors to it, I realize that I had stood in exactly this same ten foot area at so many turnings of my life, all the graduations from church school classes, my confirmation, and now my wedding. It was later to become the very place in which hands were laid upon me at my ordination into ministry.

The going back into this sanctuary again every Sunday rearranged and refocused all of these memories, and more besides. I remembered where my grandfather had sat, and my grandmother. I remembered where my mother sat. Then I remembered their caskets being wheeled down the aisle. I remembered where I sat when the casket of my best friend in high school, who'd been killed in a car accident, was rolled down the aisle. I remember her mother's scream. I began, too, to remember moments in sermons from years ago. I remember one word once dwelt on, "Nevertheless," when Jesus takes upon him his life's mission, or the words from Isaiah, "Here I am, choose me." Or I remember the look of the preacher, where he stood. I once had sat at the organ, in high school, eventually playing for the services for three years. I remembered being back on the organ bench too. I even found a photograph in my mother's album of this, taken after church.

For all the years I had lived away from all of this ongoing church life, my mother kept it alive in her letters and phone calls to me. I knew of all the events, the church fairs, the Ladies Benevolent Society. I knew of all the tiffs. I knew of all the politics. I knew of how my mother felt everyday about something at church. But I remained a member in name only. My mother kept up my membership, every week placing an envelope for me in the collection plate. I now think her fifteen hundred gestures of offering, envelope into plate, surely called me back here as much as that found letter. What soul could withstand this kind of patience?

Place, this particular place, the old church place, began to matter to me over the next few years of my prodigal return. I now wonder if it sometimes matters too much. I begin to wonder whether it mattered too much to my family. Can a particular church place matter too much? What was and is this church place, this building of memory, this center of activity, for me, for them? Can the church place be a memory house, such a memory house, yet also then still be a "temple?" I wrestle with this question.

We, our family, never talked of spiritual things. We said grace at the evening meal. We rarely otherwise invoked the name of God or Jesus in ordinary conversation. These were profoundly private matters. Once I asked my mother as she sat beside me traveling home one day, "do you believe in resurrection?" She didn't really seem to know what to say, nor did she really even want to talk about it. I was becoming a "theological talker," I was becoming unafraid of speaking of spiritual matters, but my birth family was not. I never knew what she thought. My grandmother listened to Billy Graham on the television in the 50s and early 60s. Our church was not evangelical. How did she reconcile these things? I do not know. Only once my grandfather, in a hushed voice, as he sat on the porch, said to me, "Eileen, when I was confirmed, I had to stand up in front. I was asked, along with all the others, to say yes to the affirmation that the Lutheran church was the only true church. You know, I could not do it. And so I just pretended to say yes, but didn't." That is all I know of his theology.

Perhaps in some attempt to understand my birth family's unspoken, spiritual relationship to church (was it the building? the place? or was it really the community of believers?), I threw myself into church life with appetite. Perhaps if I acted as they acted I would come to know what they knew. First I sat on various committees, attempting to solve all the usual political problems of the moment. Then, exhausted, I turned to becoming an organist there again, so that I could help plan the liturgy. Finding this more satisfying than the committee work, I nevertheless needed to do something with the place of the church, with the building. I had, in some way I do not even yet understand, to come to grips with this particular church building, storehouse of all my early memories, physical temple for my birth house.

And so, fresh from my own house building, I began to throw myself into refurbishing the weary church building. Following in my grandfather's and mother's steps, they who had painted and scoured, with my builder's eye, I began to notice the mold on the outside. I began to see every paint chip, every black mark on the interior walls. I began to ask, when was the last time this was painted? It was clear that over twenty years had passed. No one else seemed to look at these walls. We didn't have the money to hire others.

First I tackled this solo. I bought the paint and I painted the pastor's study for our incoming pastor. It took hours, three times as many hours as I'd anticipated. How could I, who'd built houses, not know this? I'd fuss over the old fixed-paned windows. I knew the man who was going to sit in this study and liked him. And this helped me to take care for this. I needed to begin my temple renovation project with this personal connection, since I wasn't so used to painting for others I didn't know so well. This was more like painting one of the rooms in my house that I wouldn't spend much time in myself but that I wanted to make pleasant and lovely for another I cared about.

But after I finished this small room, I moved out into the adjacent choir room. It too was dismal. My eyes, seeing fresh paint, saw the dinginess everywhere now. The robes were off to be cleaned. So I began, again by myself, again with my own paint, to paint where the robes were going to be. I painted just part of the room—so that I'd be forced to go back to do the rest.

By then, word was getting out about my painting (I had cleared this first with the Trustees who were grateful someone would do this needed work). Someone else volunteered to help me. I began to realize that I should share my solo work. The lesson of our church community was beginning to work in me. The new minister spoke with me: others need to help. It's better for them, better for you. I agreed. Church was no place for a private reclamation project.

I then organized a larger painting project, inviting others to donate the paint, and trying to sign up a team of painters to tackle a large room. There were three "regulars," including me, and five or six others who came in here and there. One was an older woman, now dead, who needed to sit on a stool to paint a radiator. After this room, we tackled two more, though by then the team had petered out. By the time we painted the little chapel, though we'd still use others' donated paint, it was my brother and I who did most all the work, with help a couple days from the church secretary and two other members, one who painted a door, the other who spray painted the radiators.

All of this time pushing my rollers over the old walls and sanding the chipped places and carefully painting the window trim, all this time I was changing. I was changing partly in my relation to my own new house, three miles down the road, and I was changing in relation to this church building.

It felt different to be painting these windows. This wasn't my house. It's none of our house. I happened then to have a key, because I was the organist. Not everyone has a key. But that was an accident of time and my temporary position. The house seemed no more "mine," though, because I had a key. When I locked it up after leaving, I didn't lock all the others out. I never would hold the deed to this place. No one does. We're not going to be passing this house on to heirs. Nor is the paint something I bought, not for the later projects. Some of us together, the Trustees, approved the color. Twenty people, each, donated a gallon. I didn't waste any of it. Any drip on the floor—I couldn't say, I won't notice it. Someone else might. As I touched the window sashes, I'd think, who else painted this years ago, and years before that? What went on in this Fellowship Hall years ago? I knew myself then part of a procession. I was neither contractor nor architect nor dispenser of checks. Everyone was in this equally with me. This work was the only cooperative building work I'd known, the kind I was looking for in building my own houses but couldn't find.

This house, this house not of my own, I came to know, has different kinds of walls. When I look out at these freshly painted walls, I don't see myself mirrored in the same way I see myself inside my own house. I see only part of my work, alongside others whose claim is as full as my own, and as empty as my own. And I only spend a certain kind of time inside these walls. I have no private life here. The presencing at this wall is not like that at my own house's wall. And so my own body does not seem the same to me here. I don't know myself in the same way at all. And the others around me, whose memory was and will be in the church wall: they are not people I've hired or visiting friends. They are instead fellow walkers with me, uninvited by me.

Sometimes I also help "keep" house here in this church building. Even this kind of "house-keeping" is different. When I dust the altar, I do not know who has dusted it before me. I may perform the circuit of checking lights and door locks as I leave for the night, but another night someone else who is there will have to do these things. When I bake for a funeral, I set my plate of cookies down beside another's. And so its "keeping" does not enclose "me," does not give me the assurance that my own house-keeping does that I have secured the boundaries, kept the outside alien world at bay for another day. There are always wide-open doors here. This is, after all, in each of its rooms, and not only in the worship space, a sanctuary space, a refuge place for any who walk in here. There is no alien world here; the dichotomy of home world and alien world so alive in the private house has here been broken open.

I cannot see my own house three miles down the road as I stand at the church door or look out the windows. But it's as if I'm holding up a telescope. My own house, the second house I built, now seems so small, so far away. I do not feel myself the owner of it as I stand here. All of this church "house-building" and "house-keeping" has begun to change it for me, changes my private house. When I return home I feel the kind of small shock, the hesitating foot-fall one feels entering a new and strange house. I'm carrying around me the other built walls now, the other door latches, the other windows. I begin to understand, now as a grown-up, Eliot's comment anew: my own house is precarious yet I both can know and dwell within its precariousness because there is this other house not of my own down the road.

It is the *purpose* of the houses that is different. And I want the purpose of the church house to radiate into my own house. Spending time in the other house helps me spread it into my own. Our common purpose, in this other house, is strange for some people. We come together not just to be with friends and family and other people in the town. This is not a reunion or a party or a town meeting. We come, instead, to stand beside these people we might never otherwise stand beside. We together face a simple table, an altar table, a communion table. We come to witness and feed here. And we come to express that entirely odd, missing response in the rest of our lives: we come to offer thanks, to praise, to humble ourselves, to remember that all that we have is a gift and that we are far smaller than we think we are. In the liturgy of my Congregational tradition, the deacon passes around a plate of tiny morsels of bread. I feed at their hands, and the food is humble, more than enough, but humble.

But can one become too attached to a church house? Can private memory and too much building and repairing of it keep one from some other kind of spiritual knowing? I keep pondering this question. For me the memories are so thickly matted in this one church house. And it is so often memories of that childhood drive and Sunday dinners and whose coffin was where. It is not memories of what these others really were experiencing in church. I'm looking all the time at the shells of the past.

I recognize this attachment to this place when I try to imagine how I would feel if this particular physical church house burned. It could. The first did. Lightning sometimes strikes the bell in the steeple and burns a church. Sometimes vandals and racists burn churches. What if I couldn't stand by this office door, turn that door knob, and see myself at three years of age intermittently turn that knob to check to see if my mother were still standing there outside, waiting for me? What if I couldn't imagine her standing inside the church door beckoning me in, or see her hands deposit the weekly collection, her money on my behalf, in the place where she always sat? What if I couldn't look over in the corner of this fellowship hall and recall our bright banners and our tables and chairs set up nearly fifty years ago now for our annual "Vacation Bible School" classes? What if the pews that now house the sitting ghosts of my family were destroyed? What if I start going to another church building now?

Bachelard says that "a great many of our memories are housed." Our memories are "localized" in space (1958, 8). And, "a house constitutes a body of images that give mankind [sic] proofs or illusions of stability" (1958, 17). This church house stabilizes my memories of my own history here. Winston Churchill apparently remarked on the rebuilding of the House of Commons, "we shape our buildings, and afterwards our buildings shape us."[61] This is not only true in that architecture shapes our movements in a place, but also true in that our time moving in buildings creates memories that continue to shape us. Without the building, we risk losing that memory. Once I asked my students to close their eyes and think of someone they had lost. Then I had each talk about the memory (we were readings poems of loss). In every case each person was remembered *in a particular place.*

But these personal memories can crowd on me even as they comfort. And so wonder if that memory, the memory of my self, my biographical self in history, is what this other house is really supposed to be all about. Or is it? Should I be here to know myself, my mother, my past, my friends? I wrestle.

And what about the memory of gestures in a particular church house? Are these helpful? I know all the gestures peculiar to this place, where the usher stands to hand me a bulletin, the feel of the pew latch, this pew latch, in my hands. I know the height of this sanctuary, at whose ceiling I sometimes look during the sermon. The particular panes of glass of the window I sit there: they too have been witness to what I call holy stirrings in me. They, the details of this particular church house, are like a friend who takes my hand and asks me to sit and become quiet.

Eliade says that what I'm feeling, the impulse to mark a place where one has a holy experience, is common not only among those of us who prefer houses with sturdy foundations, but also among earlier peoples. Eliade says that when people passed a stone and felt something holy there, they would turn such stones into altars. Do I need to do this? Do we? Need to mark, reserve, some special places? But then what happens when they become the object of holy wars? What happens when I notice someone has chipped the wall I've just painted?

I grow into the place of the other two epigraphs. The floating ark, the living stones of believers as the only foundations of spiritual houses: these disturb my and our land, altar-making ways. I cannot see or touch the ark. I can touch a cornerstone made of granite in my church building, but I cannot touch the living stone of me. I am, in the company of others, building something else around me now, not a building at all. I need to build some boat for the water. I need to put the stone of my body alongside another's in an architecture that has no walls made of ordinary materials. This is the next house, the next house not of my own.

Notes

[1] *Drift Ice, 2008, 5.*

Chapter I, pp. 9-21
[2] 183.
[3] Building is not the only route to this kind of awareness. In his book, *If These Walls Had Ears: A Biography of a House,* James Morgan talks to people, opens books, looks at photos, and then writes the lives of the families who once lived in the house he'd bought. He imagines how they moved through rooms where he now lives. He positions himself as one in a line, and so takes his "measure" in his house.

Chapter III, pp. 36-64
[4] 73.
[5] Janice Goldfrank's is the first collection of women builder stories (*Women Builders and Designers: Making Ourselves at Home.*) More recently, in 2005, Judy Ostrow in *The House that Jill Built* interweaves her summary of several woman-built houses with a translation of some building terms.
[6] *Walden* (1854) is the Ur-text of the American male building memoir. Michael Pollan's 1997 *A Place of My Own* is our contemporary one. The other two contemporary full-length memoirs written by men who actually built their houses (there are other stories about other people building, the most well-known of which is Tracy Kidder's 1980 *House*) are Witold Rybczynski's *The Most Beautiful House in the World* (more about designing than building), and Hugh Howard's 2001 *House-Dreams* (2001). Michael Pollan in his more recent account of building traces his lineage to Thoreau, casting his humble writer's hut as a descendent of Thoreau's American version of the mythic hut and Adam's presumed though invisible hut in Eden. In this way Pollan situates his own desire to build his own writer's hut as historically (and, implicitly, masculine-ly) inevitable. Pollan is

more modern (and less reliant on a "frontier's-man" motif) than Thoreau. Pollan does not build alone, but with the help of an architect friend and an experienced carpenter working beside him. And his hut sits in full view of his family house. (Although Thoreau builds alone and in the woods, he is not the savage building from scratch in the wilderness, but he depends on his neighbors and his own access to tools, land and other resources.) Pollan is also more modern in claiming less about his house; he does not make Thoreau's salvific, proto-religious claims about it. Pollan's story begins and ends with the building itself and his telescopic lens focuses on the history of house parts. Pollan addresses people who read, people he assumes are curious about the history of building yet who know very little about such things as the history of windows. Pollan stays largely "in the house" in his book, while Thoreau goes "beyond the house" in his. Pollan's book emerges from, and does not supersede, a technological culture that has lost touch with the origins of tools and house parts and is curious about these. Thoreau's is seated in a nineteenth century culture which still sees building as a sacred act, a moral act, affecting the whole of a life and others' lives. The other two memoirs by male owner builders[6] are more narrowly focused than Thoreau's and Pollan's. Rybczynski, as an architect, ponders the course he took designing a boat house that eventually became a dwelling house. One of the problems he ponders is different from Thoreau's and Pollan's. He is concerned about how his house will fit with others' houses (for both Thoreau and Pollan the hut exists in some personal space, of solitude or family, not in a public landscape of other houses).

      Howard's building narrative, although it occasionally includes historical material, is the most specifically focused on the day-to-day building process. Although Howard, like Thoreau and Pollan, hasn't had much experience in the building trades, he, also like them, appears to undertake the project in stride, as if it is expected of him. He tells the story of how the dream of house building took root while he was in college. He spent two summers working in a furniture factory as an electrical assistant. It was a man's world. One day at lunch he overheard one co-worker ask another, "when you built your house…you did the plumbing, right?" Howard, looking at this man, suddenly gets the germ of his idea: "one guy could build a house for his wife and daughters" (37). Since

Howard has a wife and child and another on the way, it's a seemingly "natural" step for him as husband and father and he undertakes it without sharing any misgivings. (Even if he or the other male writers had any misgivings, other men asking questions such as "when you built your house…you did the plumbing, right?" would silence them! The "right" means, "you'd better had."

[7] In contrast, clearly some of the questions Goldfrank asked all of her interviewees were "how did you get started?" "Did your father help you?" "Did you have shop in school?" "What kinds of other skills did you have, sewing, cooking, that may have translated?" The narratives by the men only need to justify why house-building is a worthwhile activity or to explain how to build a house, *not* account for how *they* came by their presumption or skill to do these things. Goldfrank knows the questions every reader wants to ask a woman builder.

[8] See Rykwert's *On Adam's House in Paradise*.

[9] Casey (1993, 368, n. 107) says that for Emmanuel Levinas (*Totality and Infinity*) "home" includes "a factor of 'wandering.'"

[10] *The Four Quartets*. I.

Chapter V, pp. 94-128

[11] 1979, 231. By permission of Oxford University Press, Inc.

[12] 1979, 9. By permission of Oxford University Press, Inc.

[13] 42.

[14] 1997, 216-7; emphasis added.

[15] Lead pencils were unknown until 1565. Before that time, architects drew drafts first in crayon, then with a quill pen dipped in black ink made from oak apples. The paper was heavy, watermarked. Other tools included wooden rules, set squares, and a compass. (Rybczynski 2002, 39).

[16] Before people could read, there were no dimension lines on drawings. It would be up to the builder to decide exactly where the window would go. (Rybczynski 2002, 43).

[17] This reference to a "Madeleine" is from the most famous scene in Proust's *Swann's Way*. The taste of the cookie, a Madeleine, opens up a forgotten memory.

[18] Susan Stewart (1993, 62) locates these desires historically and socially, its engagement of the eye, its prohibitions on touching, its

expensive furniture too grand for the owner of the dollhouse to purchase, its frontal view, all modeling and motivating the desire for an upper-class life that was "perfectly complete and hermetic" in the newly emerging private house.

[19] See *Writing on Hands: Memory and Knowledge in Early Modern Europe*. Writing on hands began to disappear as printing became more widely available, ushering in a more shared sign system.

[20] 1979, 161. By permission of Oxford University Press, Inc.

[21] See his and others' *A Pattern Language*.

[22] Alexander does not, however, consider the historical nature of the body's experiences, as is true of many archetypal thinkers.

[23] See Merleau-Ponty (1968, 138) for an extended and profound discussion of the body, my body, others' bodies, and the witnessing consciousness. He argues here that we need to move out of a retreat into the mind and that we need to re-experience our "consciousness" the body not as "our own" consciousness, but as a shared one. This is the only way that we can not only inhabit our own bodies fully, but, as importantly, know that others have them as well, far beyond what is visible to us. Our shared consciousness of the body is what allows us to connect with each other as fully equally participants on the earth.

Chapter VI, pp. 129-165

[24] 108.

[25] 1992. From "Daisies" (39) and "Early Darkness" (45)

[26] Merleau-Ponty, quoted in Casey (1997, 234).

[27] Excerpt from pg. 85 of *W.B. Yeats: A Life. II. The Arch-Poet*, by Foster, R.F. (2003) by permission of Oxford University Press.

[28] See, for example, Denis Wood's *The Power of Maps* (1992).

[29] Rykwert (1976, 135) says that "the rite is 'truly' understood as long as it is practiced. And it was practiced as long as it was needed."

[30] See the opening section of *A Room of One's Own* (1929).

[31] *Middlemarch* (1965: 1871-2, 226).

[32] Schleuning (1997, 100) observes that "by the end of the nineteenth century, the American landscape was completely enclosed, owned...By the end of the twentieth century most of us did not even miss owning the land."

[33] Harbison's argument (from *Eccentric Spaces*) is summarized in Casey (1987, 365, n.66). The study of the Ha-Ha! is open to different

interpretations; Harbison suggests it is an English "joke on law and order,"that is the law of the enclosure acts, fiercely contested in British history. But what is the nature of this "joke"? Is it criticizing the acts, by reminding those who gaze across the landscape that British earth was once unenclosed, was once undotted by stone walls? Yet, at the same time, the fence does exist, suggesting that the very vista that once appeared held in common, was at the same time even then marked with invisible walls of class division.

[34] Ryden (1993, 26-30) says that from the earliest days of Christianity up to the sixteenth century priests led their parishioners on border walks as a way of educating the young about the boundaries of the parish. He goes on to talk about early surveys of land which used landmarks, "witness trees," and so the land had to be walked in order to be known. In these bodily experiences of the boundary, "subjective interpretation" was elevated over "objective geographical knowledge." The maps of the Shakers give us an impression of what it felt like to live in a place.

Chapter VIII, pp. 206-226

[35] 76.
[36] 143-4.
[37] 1953, 22-23.
[38] Poulet 1977, 12-13.
[39] Mairs 1989, 35.
[40] Ricoeur 1992, 138.
[41] One recent exception is Louise DeSalvo's recent book, *On Moving*.
[42] Dickinson, "I Years Had Been from Home."
[43] Wilbur
[44] Secrest, 1992, 224.
[45] Rykwert, 1976, 70.

Chapter IX, pp. 227-266

[46] 1971, 154.
[47] Rev. Dr. Duncan D. Newcomer, unpublished sermon.
[48] From "Mending Wall."
[49] The Jewish autumnal festival of Sukkot recreates for the participants the experience of partial shelter. It reminds Jews of the Israelites' exodus from Egypt; it reminds them of what it is like to live without a permanent home, being at the mercy of the weather.

Participants built (or buy) small buildings with semi-porous roofs so they can experience being only partially sheltered.

[50] *Moby Dick,* 1967, 56.

[51] Reckman says that now plumbers, electricians and carpenters do not work together to solve problems, partly because of the intervention of the architect who leaves them little to say about the design of their work (1979, 97).

[51] "A Refusal to Mourn the Death, by Fire, of a Child in London," 1957, 112.

Chapter X: pp. 267-293

[53] 103.

[54] W. B. Yeats, from "The Lake Isle of Innisfree" and "The Tower."

[55] Mugerauer 1995, 15.

[56] "Because I Could Not Stop For Death."

[57] The *Oxford English Dictionary* gives as one of the possible (though unlikely) meanings of the word "shelter" "interlocking shields."

[58] See Bruce Feiler's *Walking the Bible.* New York: Perennial, 2001.

[59] Quoted in Harold W. Turner, *From Temple to Meeting House: The Phenomenology and Theology of Places of Worship* (Mouton: The Hague, 1979), p. 207.

[60] Lathrop (1993, 38) says the Hebrews sanctified one day of rest as a time to remember God's mercy, a "day that witnesses both to the God beyond creation, to God's rest (Exod. 20:8-11), and to the community's rescue from slavery, to human rest beyond all authorities and powers (Deut. 5:12-15)."

[61] Quoted in Turner (1979, 3).

Bibliography

Alexander, Christopher, Sara Ishikawa, Murray
 Silverstein, et.al. *A Pattern Language*. New
 York: Oxford Univ. Press, 1977.
_____. *The Timeless Way of Building*.
 New York: Oxford Univ. Press, 1979.
Atkinson, Jennifer. *Drift Ice*. Wilkes-Barre: Etruscan Press, 2008.
Altman, Irwin and Carol. M. Werner. *Home
 Environments*. New York: Plenum, 1985.
Ardener, Shirley. *Women and Space: Ground Rules and
 Social Maps*. New York: St. Martin's Press,
 1981.
Aries, Philippe and Georges Duby, Gen. Eds. *A
 History of Private Life*. Volume V: Riddles of
 Identity in Modern Times. Cambridge: Belknap, Harvard
 Univ. Press, 1991.

Bachelard, Gaston. *The Poetics of Space*. Boston:
 Beacon, 1958.

Bemis, Albert Farwell. *The Evolving House, Vol II: The Economics of Shelter*. Cambridge, Mass.: The Technology Press MIT, 1934.

Benjamin, Walter. *The Arcades Project*. Trans. Howard Eiland and Kevin Mclaughlin. Cambridge, Mass.: Belknap, Harvard Univ. Press, 1999.

Benson, Tedd. *The Timber-Frame Home: Design-Construction-Finishing*. Newtown, Ct.: The Taunton Press, 1988.

Beston, Henry. *The Outermost House*. New York: Henry Holt, 1928.

Birch, Eugenie Ladner, Ed. *The Unsheltered Woman: Women and Housing in the 80's*. New Brunswick, N.J.: Rutgers Univ. Press, 1985.

Bloomer, Kent C. and Charles W. Moore. *Body, Memory, Architecture*. New Haven: Yale Univ. Press, 1977.

Bourdieu, Pierre. "The Berber House." In *Rules and Meanings: The Anthropology Of Everyday Knowledge*. Ed. Mary Douglas. New York: Penguin Books, 1973.

Bourdieu, Pierre and Alsayyad, eds. *Dwellings, Settlements and Tradition: Cross Cultural Perspectives*. Lanham: Univ. Press of America, 1989.

Buber, Martin. *I and Thou*. New York: Scribner, 1958.

Busch, Akiko. *Geography of Home: Writings on Where We Live*.

New York: Princeton Architectural Press, 1999.

Butler, Judith. *Bodies That Matter: On the Discursive Limits of 'Sex.'* New York: Routledge, 1993.

Cameron, Julia. *The Artist's Way: A Spiritual Path to Higher Creativity.* New York: Tarcher, Putnam, 1992.

Cannell, Michael. *I.M. Pei: Mandarin of Modernism.* New York: Carol Southern, 1995.

Casey, Edward S. *The Fate of Place: A Philosophical History.* Berkeley: Univ. of California Press, 1997.

_____. *Getting Back Into Place: Toward a Renewed Understanding of the Place-World.* Bloomington: Indiana Univ. Press, 1993.

_____. *Remembering: A Phenomenological Study.* Bloomington: Indiana Univ. Press, 1987.

Certeau, Michel de. *The Practice of Everyday Life.* Trans. Steve Rendall. Berkeley: Univ. of California Press, 1984.

Cisneros, Sandra. *The House on Mango Street.* New York: Vintage, 1984.

Colegate, Isabel. *A Pelican in the Wilderness: Hermits, Solitaries and Recluses.* Washington D.C.: Counterpoint, 2002.

Csikszentmihalyi, Mihaly & Eugene Rochberg-Halton. *The Meaning of Things: Domestic Symbols and the Self.* Cambridge: Cambridge Univ. Press, 1981.

Cunningham, Colin. *Stories of Witness: Church Architecture and Function.* U.K.: Sutton, 1999.

Daniel, Stephen H. "Reading Places: The Rhetorical Basis of Place" in *Commonplaces*: *Essays on the Nature of Place*, ed. David W. Black, Donald Kunze, John Pickles. Lanham: Univ. Press of America, 1989.

DeSalvo, Louise. *On Moving: A Writer's Meditation on New Houses, Old Haunts, and Finding Home Again.* New York: Bloomsbury, 2009.

Dickinson, Emily. The Poems of. Ed. R. W. Franklin. Cambridge: Belknap, Harvard Univ. Press, 1998.

Dooling, D.M., Ed. *A Way of Working: The Spiritual Dimension of Craft.* NewYork: Parabola, 1979.

Doolittle, Hilda (H.D.) *Trilogy*. New York: New Directions, 1998.

Dripps, R.D. *The First House: Myth, Paradigm, and the Task of Architecture.* Cambridge: MIT Press, 1997.

Dubus, Andre III. *The House of Sand and Fog.* New York: Norton, 1997.

Ehrenhaft, George. *The Builder's Secret: Learning the Art of Living Through the Craft of Building.* Rocklin, Calif.: Prima, 1999.

Eliade, Mircea. *The Myth of the Eternal Return*. Princeton: Princeton Univ. Press, 1971.

-_____. *The Sacred and the Profane, The Nature of Religion*. Trans. Willard R. Trask. San Diego: Harcourt, Brace and World, 1957.

Eliot, George. *Adam Bede*. London: Penguin Books, 1980 (1859).

_____. *Middlemarch*. London: Penguin Books, 1965 (1871-2).

_____. *Mill on the Floss*. London: Penguin Books, 1979 (1880).

Eliot, T.S. *The Complete Poems and Plays of*. New York: Harcourt, Brace and World, 1958.

Evans-Wentz, ed. *Tibet's Great Yogi Milarepa*. London: Oxford Univ. Press, 1928.

Foster, R.F. *W.B. Yeats: A Life. II. The Arch-Poet*. Oxford: Oxford Univ. Press, 2003.

Fox, Everett, trans. *The Five Books of Moses*. New York: Schocken, 1983.

Franklin, Jill. *The Gentleman's Country House and Its Plans 1835-1914*. London: Routledge & Kegan Paul, 1981.

Friedman, Alice T. *Women and the Making of the Modern House: A Social and Architectural History*. New York: Harry N. Abrams, 1998.

Frost, Robert. *The Poetry of*. New York: Henry Holt, 1969.

Foucault, Michel. *Discipline and Punish*. New York: Vintage, 1995.

_____."Of Other Spaces" *Diacritics*. Spring 1986. 22-27.

Gallagher, Winifred. *The Power of Place*. New York: Poseidon Press, 1993.

Garber, Marjorie. Sex and Real Estate. New York: Pantheon, 2000.

Gardiner, Stephen. *Evolution of the House: An Introduction*. New York: Macmillan, 1974.

Gardner, E.C. *The House that Jill Built*. Springfield, W.I.F. Adams, 1896.

Gluck, Louise. *The Wild Iris*. Hopewell, N.J.: Ecco, 1992.

Grindley, William C. "Owner-Builders: Survivors with a Future," in *Freedom to Build*. Ed. John F.C. Turner & Robert Fichter. New York: Macmillan, 1972.

Goldfrank, Janice. *Women Builders & Designers: Making Ourselves at Home*. Watsonville, CA: Papier-Mache, 1995.

Hale, Jonathan. *The Old Way of Seeing: How Architecture Lost Its Magic (and How To Get it Back)*. Boston: Houghton Mifflin, 1994.

Hayden, Dolores. *The Grand Domestic Revolution: A History of Feminist Designs for American Homes*, Neighborhoods and Cities. Cambridge, Mass: MIT Press, 1981.

──────────. *Redesigning the American Dream: The Future of Housing, Work, and Family Life*. New York: W.W. Norton, 1984.

Heidegger, Martin. "Building, Dwelling, Thinking." In *Poetry, Language, Thought*. New York: Harper & Row, 1971.

Herbert, George. *The Works of*. Oxford: Clarendon, 1941.

Higonnet, Margaret R. and Joan Templeton. *Reconfigured Spheres: Feminist Explorations of Literary Space*. Amherst: Univ. of Massachusetts Press, 1994.

Hillier, Bill and Julienne Hanson. *The Social Logic of Space*.
 Cambridge: Cambridge Univ. Press, 1984.

Hillman, James. *The Soul's Code*. New York: Random House, 1996.

Hiss, Tony. *The Experience of Place*. New York: Knopf, 1990.

Hopkins, Gerard Manley. Ed. Catherine Philips. Oxford: Oxford
 Univ. Press, 1986.

Howard, Hugh. *House-Dreams*. Chapel Hill, N.C.: Algonquin
 Books, 2001.

Hughes, Francesca, ed. *The Architect: Reconstructing Her
 Practice*. Cambridge: MIT Press, 1996.

Jackson, J.B. *The Necessity for Ruins*. Amherst, Mass.: Univ.
 of Mass. Press, 1980.

_____. *A Sense of Place, A Sense of Time*. New Haven:
 Yale Univ. Press,1944

Jacobson, Max, Murray Silverstein, Barbara Winslow. *The Good
 House: Contrast as a Design Tool*. Newtown, Ct.: The Taunton
 Press, 1990.

Jung, Carl. *Memories, Dreams, Reflections*. New York:
 Vintage, 1989.

Keim, Kevin P. *An Architectural Life: Memoirs and Memories of
 Charles W. Moore*. Boston: Little Brown, 1996.

Kidder, Tracy. *House*. Boston: Houghton Mifflin, 1985.

Kline, David. *Great Possessions: An Amish Farmer's Journal*.
 San Francisco: North Point, 1990.

Kushner, Lawrence. *God Was in This Place & I, I Did Not Know.* Woodstock, Vt.: Jewish Lights, 1994.

Lathrop, Gordon. *Holy Things: A Liturgical Theology.* Minneapolis: Fortress Press, 1998.

Lefebvre, Henri. *The Production of Space.* Oxford: Blackwell, 1974.

Lhualungpa, Lobsang P. *The Life of Milarepa.* New York: Dutton, 1977.

Mairs, Nancy. *Remembering the Bone House: An Erotics of Space and Place.* 1989; 1995. Reprinted by permission of Beacon Press, Boston.

Mansfield, Howard. *In the Memory House.* Golden, Co.: Fulcrum Publishers, 1993.

_____. *The Same Ax, Twice: Restoration and Renewal in a Throwaway Age.* Hanover: Univ. Press of New England, 2000.

Marcus, Clare Cooper. *House as a Mirror of Self.* Berkeley: Conari, 1995.

Massey, Doreen. *Space, Place and Gender.* St. Paul, Minn.: Univ. of Minnesota Press, 1994.

McDowell, Linda and Joanne P. Shays. *Space, Gender, Knowledge.* London: Arnold, 1997.

Melville, Herman. *Moby Dick.* New York: Norton, 1967.

Mendelson, Cheryl. *Home Comforts: The Art and Science of Keeping House.* New York: Scribner, 1999.

Merleau-Ponty. *The Visible and the Invisible.* Evanston, Ill.:

Northwestern Univ. Press, 1968.

Milosz, Czeslaw. "My River." *Architectural Digest*. May 1998, pp. 48-54.

Mitchell, John Hanson. *Trespassing: An Inquiry into the Private Ownership of Land.* Reading, Mass.: Perseus Press, 1998.

Moore, Charles W., Gerald Allen and Donlyn Lyndon. *The Place of Houses*. NewYork: Holt, Rinehart & Winston, 1974.

Morgan, James. *If These Walls Had Ears: The Biography of a House.* New York: Warner, 1996.

Mugerauer, Robert. *Interpretations on Behalf of Place.* Albany: SUNY Press, 1994.

_____. *Interpreting Environments: Tradition, Deconstruction, Hermeneutics.* Austin: Univ. of Texas Press, 1995.

New Oxford Annotated Bible (New Revised Standard Version). NewYork: Oxford Univ. Press, 1991.

Norberg-Schultz, Christian. *Genius Loci: Towards a Phenomenology of Architecture.* New York: Rizzoli, 1979.

Norris, Kathleen. *Acedia & Me.* New York: Riverhead, 2008.

O'Donohue, John. *Anam Cara: A Book of Celtic Wisdom.* New York: Harper Collins, 1997.

Ostrow, Judy. *the house that jill built: a woman's guide to home building.* Salt Lake City, Ut.: Gibbs, Smith, 2005.

Pascal, Blaise. *Pensees.* Trans. A. J. Krailsheimer. New York: Penguin, 1966. Revised edition, 1995. Copyright A.J.

Krailsheminer, 1966, 1995. Reproduced by permission of Penguin Books Ltd.

Perrin, Constance. *Everything in Its Place; Social Order and Land Use in America.* Princeton: Princeton Univ. Press, 1977.

Pollan, Michael. *A Place of My Own.* New York: Random House, 1997.

_____. *Second Nature.* New York: Delta, 1993.

Poulet, George. *Proustian Space.* Trans. Eliot Coleman. Baltimore: Johns Hopkins Univ. Press, 1977.

Proust, Marcel. *Swann's Way.* Trans. C.K. Scott Moncrieff. New York: Modern Library, 1928.

Reckman, Bob. "Carpentry: The Craft and the Trade." In *Case Studies in the Labor Process.* Ed. Andrew Zimbalist. New York: Monthly Review Press, 1979, pp. 73-102.

Rennie, Bryan S. *Reconstructing Eliade: Making Sense of Religion.* Albany: SUNY Press, 1996.

Ricoeur, Paul. *Oneself as Another.* Translated by Kathleen Blamey. Chicago: Univ. of Chicago Press, 1992. Paperback Edition 1994. Originally published *Soi-Meme Comme une Autre,* Editions du Seuil, March 1990.

Riley, Terence. *The Un-Private House.* New York: The Museum of Modern Art, 1999 (published on the occasion of the exhibit of the same name).

Rilke, Ranier Maria. *The Poetry of.* Trans. Edward Snow. New York: North Point, 2009.

Romines, Ann. *The Home Plot: Women, Writing & Domestic Ritual*. Amherst: Univ. of Mass. Press, 1992.

Ruskin, John. *Lectures on Architecture and Painting*. Vol. VIII. New York: Merrill and Baker, 1853.

Rybczynski, Witold. *The Most Beautiful House in the World*. NewYork: Vintage, 1989.

_____. *The Perfect House*. New York: Scribner, 2002.

Ryden, Kent C. *Mapping the Invisible Landscape: Folklore, Writing, & the Sense of Place*. Iowa City: Univ. of Iowa Press, 1993.

Rykwert, Joseph. *The Idea of a Town*. Cambridge, Mass.: MIT Press, 1976.

_____. *On Adam's House in Paradise: The Idea of the Primitive Hut in Architectural History*. Cambridge, Mass.: M.I.T. Press, 1981.

_____*The Seduction of Place: The City in the 21st Century*. New York: Pantheon, 2000.

Saile, David G. "The Ritual Establishment of Home." In *Home Environments*. New York: Plenum, 1985.

Salzman, L.F. *Building in England Down to 1540*. Clarendon: Oxford Univ. Press, 1952.

Schleuning, Neala. *To Have and To Hold: The Meaning of Ownership in the United States*. Westport, Conn.: Praeger, 1997.

Seamon, David and Robert Mugerauer, eds. *Dwelling, Place,*

   Environment. NewYork: Columbia Univ. Press, 1989.
Secrest, Meryle. *Frank Lloyd Wright*. New York: Knopf, 1992.
Snyder, Don J. *The Cliff Walk: A Job Lost and a Life Found*.
   Boston: Little Brown, 1997.
Snyder, Gary. "Axe Handles." *Axe Handles*. San Francisco: North Point Press, 1983.
Soja, Edward W. *Postmodern Geographies: The Reassertion of Space in Critical Social Theory*. London: Verso, 1989.
Spain, Daphne. *Gendered Spaces*. Chapel Hill, N.C.: Univ. of North Carolina Press, 1992.
Steinbock, Anthony J. *Home and Beyond: Generative Phenomenology after Husserl*. Evanston, Ill.: Northwestern Univ. Press, 1995.
Stevens, Wallace. *The Collected Poems of*. New York: Knopf, 1957.
Stewart, Susan. *On Longing*. Chapel Hill: Duke Univ. Press, 1993.
Stilgoe, John R. *Common Landscape of America 1580-1845*. New Haven, Conn.: Yale Univ. Press, 1982.
Thomas, Dylan. *Collected Poems*. New York: New Directions, 1957.
Thoreau, Henry David. *Walden*. New York: Modern Library, 1937.
Tillich, Paul. *The Courage to Be*. New Haven: Yale Univ. Press, 1952.
Tressell, Robert. *The Ragged-Trousered Philanthropists*. London: G. Richards, 1914.

Troutman, Anne. "Inside Fear: Secret Places and Hidden Spaces in Dwellings." In *Architecture of Fear*. Ed. Nan Ellin. New York: Princeton Architectural Press, 1997, pp. 143-157.

Tuan, Yi-Fu. *Space and Place*. Minneapolis: Univ. of Minnesota Press, 1977.

_____. *Topophilia*. Englewood Cliffs, N.J.: Prentice- Hall, 1974.

Upton, Dell. *Architecture in the United States*. New York: Oxford Univ. Press, 1998.

Valentine, Gill. "Making Space: Separatism and Difference." In *Thresholds In Feminist Geography: Difference, Methodology, Representation*. Ed. John Paul Jones III, Heidi J. Nast, and Susan M. Roberts. Lanham, Md.: Rowman & Littlefield, 1997, pp. 65-76.

Weisman, Leslie Kanes. *Discrimination by Design: A Feminist Critique of the Man-Made Environment*. Urbana: Univ. of Illinois Press, 1992.

White, E.B. "Removal," from *One Man's Meat*. Text copyright 1938 by E. B. White. Copyright renewed. Gardiner, Me.: Tilbury House Publishers, 1942.

Wilber, Ken. *No Boundary*. Boulder: Shambhala, 1981.

Wilbur, Richard. *New Poems and Translations*. New York: Harcourt Brace, 1971.

Williams, Raymond. *The Country and the City*. New York: Oxford Univ. Press, 1973.

Wood, Denis. *The Power of Maps*. New York: Guilford Press, 1992.

Woolf, Virginia. *Mrs. Dalloway*. New York: Harcourt Brace and World, 1925.

——————. *A Room of One's Own*. New York: Harcourt Brace and World, 1929.

——————. *To the Lighthouse*. New York: Harcourt Brace and World. 1927.

——————. *A Writer's Diary*. New York: Harcourt Brace Jovanovich, 1953.

Wright, Gwendolyn. *Building the Dream: A Social History of Housing in America.* New York: Pantheon, 1981.

Writing on Hands: Memory and Knowledge in Early Modern *Europe*. Ed. Claire Richter Sherman and Peiter M. Lukehart. Seattle: Univ. of Washington Press, 2000.

Yeats, W.B. *The Collected Poems of.* New York: Macmillan, 1953.

Building a House, Building a Book

With thanks

One builds not alone. To the so many who helped me build the houses I love I offer my gratitude beyond words: to our timber framers in Maryland: Timbersmiths of Charlottesville, Va. and to our timber framers in Connecticut: Hennin Post & Beam of Woolwich, Me.; to the carpenters, especially Rick Otka, an artist in wood, to Richard Anderson, master electrician (and my second cousin); to our plumber, Bernie Romanowski, and our duct man, Guy, of A&B Cooling and Heating, whose joints are all beautiful; to Roger Trabucchi who loved the trees he cut and saved the birds' nests; to Peter Germini, neighbor and friend, who let me ride on his dozer. There are countless others unnamed here but remembered.

Abundant thanks to The Shelter Institute of Woolwich, Me. for stoking my courage and increasing my knowledge to build houses and to its wonderful teachers, the Hennins.

And then there are all the other beloved builders of this book whose presence radiates through it: The Rev. Dr. Duncan D. Newcomer, for always inspiring me and helping me open to the true foundation; the many friends and colleagues who worked with us on our houses, especially Pat Story and Peter Brunette; those who read countless versions of this manuscript and urged me patiently along these ten years: Margaret Yocom, Deborah Kaplan, Devon Hodges, Susan Thompson, Christine Reilly, Harriet and Hans Bergmann, the Rev. Barbara Melosh, Margaret Mikesell, William Tabb, Jody Cale and Ann Knight. I am awed that Jennifer Atkinson and Eric Pankey drew inspiration from this book's birthing for poems. Thanks as well to George Mason University for giving me study leaves to work on this project.

And, of course, undergirding all is the one who never fails, day in and day out, to believe that I can do anything and to help me to do so, even if it sometimes involves him more than he might wish: John, beloved husband and wise friend, co-builder of the houses and co-builder of my life.

And ever and always: Thanks Be to God

www.ingramcontent.com/pod-product-compliance
Lightning Source LLC
Chambersburg PA
CBHW030305080526
44584CB00012B/445